WHO KILLED
KIT MARLOWE?

A CONTRACT TO MURDER IN
Elizabethan England

M.J. TROW
AND TALIESIN TROW

SUTTON PUBLISHING

First published in 2001 by
Sutton Publishing Limited · Phoenix Mill
Thrupp · Stroud · Gloucestershire · GL5 2BU

British Library Cataloguing in Publication Data
A catalogue record for this book is available from the British Library

ISBN 0 7509 2689 9

Typeset in 11/14.5pt Sabon.
Typesetting and origination by
Sutton Publishing Limited.
Printed in Great Britain by
J.H. Haynes & Co. Ltd, Sparkford, Somerset.

DATE DUE FOR RETURN

ALLERTON
COMMUNITY LIBRARY

Books may be returned by personal call, telephone or post

ALLERTON ROAD

L18 6HG

TEL. No. 0151 724 2937

Contents

List of Plates

Acknowledgements

We would like to thank everyone involved in the development of this book; Jaqueline Mitchell and her team at Sutton for their support and kindness; Andrew Lownie, for his skill and friendship as a literary agent; the proprietors of the pictures featured for permission to use their photographs; but most of all Carol Trow, wife and mother, who did more to create *Who Killed Kit Marlowe?* than anyone else.

INTRODUCTION

The Gloriana Myth

'Elizabethan England,' wrote J.B. Black forty years ago,

> was, in a very real sense, Elizabeth's England. She it was who
> nursed it into being, and by her wisdom made possible its
> amazing development . . . she inspired its patriotism, its
> pageantry, its heroism, stimulated its poetry and shaped its
> destiny.[1]

S.T. Bindoff was even more glowing. Quoting Elizabeth's last speech
to her parliament in November 1601, he added,

> It was in such golden phrases of affectionate humility that the last
> of the Tudors wrote her epitaph, and the epitaph of her line, that
> line of statesmen-monarchs than whom, indeed, no wiser or
> mightier ever adorned the English throne, and of whom she
> herself, if she yielded perhaps to her grandfather in wisdom and to
> her father in might, was in the fullness of her genius the superb
> and matchless flower.[2]

At very worst, she was a queen adored by her courtiers, ruling with
the assent of a compliant people.

In 1964, the Shakespeare Birthplace Trust set up an exhibition to
commemorate the 400th anniversary of the birth of the playwright
who has since become the Man of the Millennium. It followed his
life down, as it were, a road in Elizabethan England, winding along
the confines of the marquee built to house it, from the glove-maker's
son in Stratford to the position of pre-eminence he holds today.

If we could take such a road through Elizabethan England
beginning with the triumphal coronation on 15 January 1559, what
sights would we see? The queen herself was twenty-five. 'Her face,'

wrote an Italian visitor in the previous year, 'is comely rather than handsome, but she is tall and well-formed with a good skin, although swarthy; she has fine eyes and above all a beautiful hand.' But some noted with alarm that the coronation in Westminster Abbey was in English rather than the customary Latin and the Bishop of Carlisle officiated, the Archbishop of York having refused to take part.

By June, the first of many suitors pressing for her hand, Charles, Archduke of Austria, had already been turned down. Elizabeth was a handsome catch; eminently eligible as the ruler of a thriving and growing nation, she was wooed by the ambassadors of many of Europe's rulers, although she never met any of her contemporaries face to face, except Philip of Spain, her former brother-in-law.

She loved music, dancing and hunting and people saw in her the female embodiment of her father, the 'bluff king' who had broken with Rome and destroyed the monasteries, leaving England friendless on the edge of a hostile Europe. She rode well, but only over the south of England. She spoke Latin, Greek, French and Spanish and preferred watered English beer to imported wine. She adored flattery and the gallants of her Court – Leicester, Essex, Ralegh – fluttered around her like moths to a flame. She may have slept with any one of them, but she would not make any man her Lord, because that would mean giving up the throne of England too. And as the road of her reign lengthened, the line between heart-centred flirtation and brain-centred politics grew impossibly blurred. It was part of the Queen's great game.

She hated making decisions. She hated extremism and the *via media* called the Church of England which she created in 1559 is a testament to that. But she reckoned without the bitterness and fanaticism of the Catholics who would continue to pose a danger to her and her religion for the rest of her long journey down the road. And without the paranoia of the Puritans who crowded along the road towards its end.

While Scotland and Ireland erupted into rebellion, and Catholic hatred of the 'English Jezebel' focused on her cousin Mary, the Queen of Scots, Elizabeth danced with Leicester, marvelled at the fireworks reflected in the great artificial lake he built at Kenilworth and encouraged her privateers to attack Spanish silver convoys at sea.

There were rebellions in the north; plots behind closed doors; nobody's virtue was over-nice.

If we first took our road through Elizabeth's reign early in the morning, when the sun shone on Westminster Abbey as it did on all new and hopeful reigns, by midday the sky had darkened. The Pope excommunicated the Queen, giving good Catholics carte blanche to kill her. With no police force but the geriatric constables of the watch and no standing army but the tiny and ornate Household Guard, the Queen watched warily from the centre of the hive as her Council droned about her.

A network of spies kept her government informed of any movement overseas. They lurked at doorways, submitted reports. Where there was no evidence of sedition, they invented it and untold numbers were sent to face the hangman by way of the 'Duke of Exeter's daughter', the rack.

We are struck today by the incestuous nature of Elizabethan England: at Court; in the royal palaces of Whitehall, Nonsuch, Placentia; in the shadowy corners of the Privy Council chamber; everywhere in the corridors of power, everyone was related to everyone else. Families held sway, zealously protecting their possessions, flattering the Queen in order to gain more and doing everything in their considerable power to pass them on to their sons.

The mistress of ceremonial, Elizabeth's 'progresses' across the south became legendary. Poets and playwrights flocked to pay her homage. The nobility vied with each other in their patronage of theatrical companies. They clashed together in foolhardy lance-passes in the tilt, which had already claimed the life of the King of France and laid that country open to civil war as a result. They wrestled for her attention and sulked on their country estates when they were ignored.

'Are you then,' the poet Thomas Dekker might have stopped us on our road,

travelling to the temple of Eliza? Even to her temple are my feeble limbs travelling. Some call her Pandora, some Gloriana, some Cynthia, some Belphoebe, some Astraea – all by several name to express several loves. Yet all those names make but one celestial body, as all loves meet to create but one soul. I am one of her own country, and we adore her by the name of Eliza.

It is at the end of the road that this book pauses. It is mid-evening now, perhaps unseasonably cold for the end of May. Against the lapping waters of the mighty river, where the cormorants dip and the rigging creaks in its housing, can be heard a darker sound, a distant, tolling bell. There is plague in the city, creeping death. At the top of the tower of the church of St Nicholas in Deptford, the turrets of the Queen's palace of Placentia pierce the sky, with the dark woods of the gathering night to the south. The Queen is old. Her teeth are black, her chest scrawny and pale. One by one her favourites and her friends are dying around her. Her country is writhing under war and rising taxation. No one feels safe on the road anymore, with night coming and a wind ruffling the waters to the east.

It is about seven o'clock on the road. A Wednesday. There is a scream from a room overhead, from a house somewhere on Deptford Strand. Then an eerie silence.

A man is dead. His name, though we never knew him, was Kit Marlowe. . . .

ONE

A Death in Deptford

Kit Marlowe spent the day at the widow Eleanor Bull's house on Deptford Strand. He had arrived there at about ten in the morning. With him were Ingram Frizer, Nicholas Skeres and Robert Poley, all of whom gave their addresses as 'late of London'. They passed time together, perhaps smoking, perhaps playing backgammon. After lunch, they walked in the garden, perhaps one of those intricate knot gardens made of herbs which the Elizabethans loved.

What they talked about we do not know, but at about six, the four men went indoors again for supper. No one thought to mention what they ate; it was not relevant. And it must have been shortly after the meal that a quarrel broke out between Marlowe and Frizer, over who was to pay the bill for the day's hospitality. Marlowe was lying on a bed. Frizer had his back to him, sitting wedged at a table with Poley on one side and Skeres on the other. Frizer's dagger, as was the custom, was lying in its sheath in the small of his back. Given to sudden bursts of temper as Marlowe was, he grabbed it, slashing wildly at Frizer's head, gashing him twice before Frizer could move. Hemmed in as he was by his friends, Frizer grappled with Marlowe and in the scuffle drove his own blade into Marlowe's head, above the right eye.

Death was instantaneous.

Kit Marlowe was the greatest playwright of his age. His death at Deptford on 30 May 1593 was the greatest loss to literature that England has ever sustained. If it had not happened, there may never have been a William Shakespeare to become the Man of the Millennium. The version of the man's death you have just read is a modern re-telling of the official story, the inquest of Coroner William Danby before a sixteen-man jury held on 1 June. It has come down to us in the shorthand of history as a tavern brawl, a sordid clash over who paid the bill – 'le recknynge'.

Except that it did not happen that way. All of it was fiction, an elaborate fabrication to cover up the murder of Kit Marlowe. This book uncovers the reason why.

DEPTFORD, 30 MAY 2000

Deptford Strand lies on the river, to the south-west of the loop in the Thames known as the Isle of Dogs. There were windmills there once, where the new glass-fronted regeneration of the Docklands now stands, the great winking monolith of Canary Wharf dwarfing the curious, spiky, web-like Dome.

We walk along Deptford High Street, past African fabric shops and doner kebab houses, the new ethnic symbols of our late Elizabethan age. This was once Butt's Lane that ran through fields. Further towards the river, the older buildings are still there, derelict Victorian terraces with gaping, glassless windows along Greek Street; the Harp of Erin pub. We face the 'Private' gates of Conroy's Wharf where the royal docks stood in the days of bluff King Hal. Away to our right, along Evelyn Road, once stood the manor house of Sayes Court where the 1960s high-rise flats now cluster. Traditional 'Mash and Pie' shops proudly boasting their establishment in 1890 are a reminder of an older culture, but not old enough for us.

Watergate Street is cobbled, a narrow cul-de-sac that leads to the river. The water is brown and sluggish, but cormorants bob here, as they did long ago. Fix your eyes on the lapping waters and years slip away and time stands still. Walk along Borthwick Street and you are struck by the dereliction of the area – an abandoned Mini and a burnt out caravan are the debris of a society struggling to rediscover itself. Huge adventure playgrounds where the kids climb to find light among the high-rise buildings and plane trees provide oases of shade.

Everything is dwarfed by the great derricks that swing beyond Deptford substation, like giant descendants of their smaller forebears that built the ships of Henry VIII's navy. They are building Fairview's Millennium Quay, the last of the gentrification projects that have transformed the greatest docks in the world.

Deptford Green leads us to all that remains of Christopher Marlowe's Deptford – the church of St Nicholas where he is buried.

On either side of the gates the stone skulls known as Adam and Eve grin sightlessly at passers-by. They carried Marlowe's body here on the night of 30 May 1593 before they buried him somewhere in the north-east corner of the churchyard by the Queen's Gate where Elizabeth had come to give thanks for the victory over the Armada five years before.

There are large tombs in the churchyard, fine vaults of a bygone age, but these are Jacobean at best and none of them commemorates Kit Marlowe. His memorial is a modern plaque set into the wall with the usual and infuriatingly vague 'On a spot near this place . . .'.

The church is large and airy, almost square in shape, with wooden carvings by Grinling Gibbons, who worked in the dockyards in the days when the diarist John Evelyn lived at Sayes Court. The church is dedicated to the patron saint of sailors, but also, aptly in the case of Christopher Marlowe, of students and those in sudden danger. There was plenty of that in October 1940 when the incendiary bombs of Goering's Luftwaffe destroyed the interior. Two years later, they destroyed the church of St George the Martyr in Canterbury too. In both cases, only the tower of the church survived. One had seen the baptism of Christopher Marlowe; the other his funeral.

There is nothing of Marlowe in the body of the church. The reredos is by Gibbons and the oak furniture imported from elsewhere and of a later date. The tombs are seventeenth-century at the earliest; even the worn inscriptions on the stone near the altar are eighteenth-century, the relics of a huge rebuilding programme paid for largely by the Honourable East India Company long before the Luftwaffe's handiwork. The tower is fourteenth-century, but its stones are whitewashed, courtesy of the Reformation, and the royal arms nailed to it are of William and Mary – and a 1950s refurbishment at that. Everything is second hand, removed, copied. A modern lectern commemorates the aptly named Richard Wyche, the Lollard vicar of Deptford and friend of John Wycliffe, burned for his heresy on Tower Hill in 1439. A modern plaque reads 'To the immortal memory of Christopher Marlowe who met a tragic death near this spot on the 30th May 1593, this tablet is erected in 1957 by the Association of the Men of Kent and Kentishmen to replace an earlier memorial unveiled by Sir Frank Benson[1] on the 3rd June 1919 and destroyed by enemy action in 1940'. And below it is a quotation from Marlowe's *Faustus*, 'Cut is the branch that may have grown full straight'.

We climb the tower, a tight, dark spiral of Purbeck marble. There are initials of eighteenth-century bellringers carved into the stone and pigeons brood among the silent bells. Towards the top, where incendiary damage was done, the steps become cement and the interior brick. The beacon that guided ships around the sharp curve of the river has long gone. Below the flapping White Ensign of the Royal Navy (St Nicholas is the only church in the country to be allowed to fly this flag) the view is commanding.

To the north lies the busy, regenerated skyline of the Isle of Dogs, a monument to late Elizabethan money the second time around. To the south, the masts of Crystal Palace on Sydenham Hill catch the spring sunlight. To the west, the London Eye dwarfs any of the buildings that Marlowe would have known; and to the east, the gilded turrets of the Greenwich Observatory and Naval College stand on the site of Elizabeth's great palace of Placentia.

Below the tower to the west lies Deptford Strand itself, hemmed in by Borthwick Street nearest the river, the delightfully named Twinkle Park and bisected by Benbow Street, after the admiral of the same name. The Strand is one big housing estate owned by the Greater London Council and called the Charlotte Turner Gardens. To the east, perhaps in the north-east corner of the churchyard, lie the mortal remains of Kit Marlowe, poet, scholar, playwright, spy, Machiavellian, atheist, homosexual, over-reacher – see him as you will. Less than a century after his death, he was given a huge amount of company. The church's Plague Book of 1666 contains the names of nearly twelve hundred people from Deptford who lie buried in a plague pit on the same site.

Only Marlowe's works live on. And the unanswered questions.

DEPTFORD, 30 MAY 1593

Deptford Strand lay on the river to the south-west of the loop in the Thames and to the west of the Raven's Bourne, a sluggish tributary of the greatest artery in the country. In the fourteenth century there was still a deep ford which gave the village its name and, as

'Deepford', it is still carved on the tomb of the shipbuilder Jonas Shish in St Nicholas churchyard. By the age of Elizabeth a wooden bridge had replaced it to cope with the huge increase in traffic and trade.

As early as 1513, Deptford had been earmarked by Henry VIII to build his great shipyards. The Tudors were inveterate shipbuilders, with warships like the *Great Harry* and the *Mary Rose* riding the sea roads that guarded England. A ruined monastery near the church of St Nicholas was commandeered as a storehouse – the stowage – for the hemp, iron and timbers which were the raw materials of the Tudor navy.

Symonson's *A New Description of Kent* published in 1596 shows the spire of the church dwarfed by the royal estate beyond the Raven's Bourne at Greenwich, one of the many Tudor palaces that dotted the countryside south of the Thames. Bought by Henry VII, much expanded by Henry VIII, Greenwich – 'Placentia' – was one of the marvels of the age, eclipsed only by Nonsuch at Eltham. To the south of the Greenwich lands lay the bleak high ground of Black Heath where Wat Tyler and his peasants had gathered in the 'hurling time' to begin their march on London.[2] And further south still rolled the excellent hare-coursing country around Shooters' Hill, where, legend has it, Henry VIII and Anne Boleyn met the outlaw Robin Hood while hunting.

In the 1590s, the noise and bustle of the king's shipyards would have been incessant during the day. Much British timber was considered inferior and Russian hardwood was imported from the Hanseatic League all the way from the Baltic to supplement the solid oak of Sussex and Kent for the clinker-built pinnaces and the high-hulled caravels.

The parish records of St Nicholas tell us that nearly four thousand new settlers had arrived to join the jostling throng of shipwrights, carpenters, rope and sailmakers and the courtier hangers-on from Placentia.

The earliest detailed map of Deptford was drawn in 1653. Various landowners are mentioned as having held land 'since the rebellion' (the Civil War) and the diarist John Evelyn is cited as the owner of the manor house at Sayes Court. The basic geographical lay-out of the area is not likely to have changed since Marlowe's time.

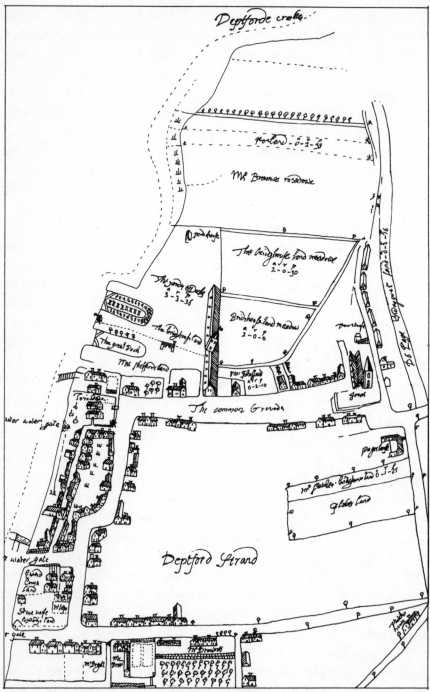

Map 1. The earliest known map of Deptford Strand, dated 1653. It is impossible now to pinpoint with accuracy the location of Eleanor Bull's house. (Redrafted from the original by the author)

To the west of the area trickled Deptford Creek, forming the boundary of parcels of land owned by the church and a Mr Browne, clearly the largest landowner in the parish. It was still, in the 1650s, meadowland and the roads across it designated 'lanes'. There were two 'great docks' as well as the king's yards with stone wharfs built between the lower, middle and upper water gates. To the east was the Tudor manor house owned by Sir Richard Browne in Elizabeth's time and to the south the church and the lands of the Master, Wardens and Assistants of the Guild Fraternity or Brotherhood of the Most Glorious and Undivided Trinity and of St Clement – the future pilots of Trinity House and already in the 1590s a long established mariners' guild.

Along the Thames waterfront rode the *Golden Hind*, the spirit of the age in which Francis Drake had rounded the world. He had knelt on the tarred planking of his own ship to receive the Queen's knighthood at Deptford in 1581. The Devon sailor owned land in the area and two of his descendants became vicars of St Nicholas in the eighteenth and ninteenth centuries. Lord Howard of Effingham, one of the greatest sailors of his age and a national hero in the year of the Armada (1588) owned a large house on Deptford Green and regularly attended services in St Nicholas Church.

Somewhere in the centre of this burgeoning, bustling community with its cosmopolitan shifting population and its cross-section of society stood a rectangle of land bordered by trees and called Deptford Strand. And it was here, in the house of a widow, Eleanor Bull, that the poet and playwright Christopher Marlowe died early on a summer's evening, Wednesday 30 May, in the thirty-fifth year of the reign of the queen he served and the 1,593rd of the Lord in whom Christopher Marlowe did not believe.

The mythology of the death of Christopher Marlowe continues to dog us despite eighty years of research and scholarship. We must peel away the legends that have grown up over the centuries. In their otherwise excellent screenplay of *Shakespeare in Love*, writers Marc Norman and Tom Stoppard perpetuate the notion of the infamous tavern brawl. Shakespeare (Joseph Fiennes) falls in love with Viola de Lesseps (Gwyneth Paltrow) and pretends to be Christopher Marlowe to avoid the wrath of Viola's fiancé, the psychotic Lord

Wessex (Colin Firth). When he hears of the real Marlowe's death, Shakespeare is naturally distraught, believing Wessex is the killer and that the fault is his.

'It's true, Will,' says the actor Ned Alleyn (Ben Affleck), 'it was a tavern brawl . . . Marlowe attacked and got his own knife in the eye. A quarrel about the bill . . .'.

Christopher Marlowe's stature today is greater than ever and Norman and Stoppard in their screenplay put these words into Shakespeare's mouth. 'Marlowe's touch was in my *Titus Andronicus* and my *Henry VI* was a house built on his foundations . . . I would exchange all my plays for all of his that will never come.'

There are those who contend today that Marlowe, had he lived, would have been far greater than Shakespeare. There are those who contend that he *was* Shakespeare, faking his own death at Deptford and churning out masterpiece after masterpiece for the oddly uninspiring Mr Shaxper from Stratford on the Avon.

We have to go back to the seventeenth century for the first fictionalized accounts of Marlowe's death.[3] In 1618, the rabid Puritan Edmund Rudierde published *The Thunderbolt of God's Wrath against Hard-Hearted and Stiffe-Necked Sinners*. In Chapter 22 he wrote,

> We read of one Marlin, a Cambridge Scholler, who was a Poet, and a filthy Play-maker, this wretch accounted that meeke servant of God Moses to be but a Conjurer, and our sweete Saviour but a seducer and a deceiver of the people. But harken yee braine-sicke and prophane Poets and Players that bewitch idle eares with foolish vanities; what fell upon this prophane wretch, having a quarrell against one whom he met in a streete in London and would have stabd him: But the partie perceiving his villainy prevented him with catching his hand, and turning his owne dagger into his braines, and so blaspheming and cursing, he yielded up his stinking breath: marke this yee Players, that live by making fooles laugh at sinne and wickednesse.

Aside from Rudierde's paranoia on the evils of actors and playwrights (both of them Hell's agents to a dyed-in-the-wool

Puritan) the notion of an open air killing – 'in a street in London' is peculiar and almost certainly a misreading of another source.

Eighteen years earlier, William Vaughan had produced a slightly more accurate version of events in *The Golden Grove*:

> Not inferior to these was one Christopher Marlow by profession a playmaker, who, as it is reported, about 7 yeares a-goe wrote a booke against the Trinitie; but see the effect of God's justice; it so hapned, that at Detford, a little village about three miles distant from London, as he meant to stab with his ponyard [dagger] one named Ingram, that had invited him thither to a feast, and was then playing at tables [probably backgammon] he quickly perceyving it, so avoyded the thrust, that withall drawing out his dagger for his defence, hee stabd this Marlow into the eye, in such sort, that his braines coming out at the daggers point, hee shortlie after dyed. Thus did God, the true executioner of divine justice, worke the ende of impious Atheists.

Two years before that and only five years after Marlowe's death, Frances Meres, a Cambridge-educated contemporary, added details of his own in *Palladis Tamia* – 'As the poet Lycophon was shot to death by a certain rival of his; so Christopher Marlow was stabd to death by a bawdy Serving man, a rival of his in his lewde love.' It was this version which was expanded in 1691 by Anthony à Wood in *Athenae Oxoniensis*:

> For it so fell out that he being deeply in love with a certain Woman, had for his Rival a bawdy serving-man, one rather fit to be a Pimp, than an ingenuous Amoretto as Marlo conceived himself to be. Whereupon Marlo taking it to be a high affront, rush'd in upon, to stab him, with his dagger: But the serving-man being very quick, so avoided the stroke, that withal catching hold of Marlo's wrist, he stab'd his own dagger into his own head, in such sort, that notwithstanding all the means of surgery that could be wrought, he shortly after died of his Wound. . . .

The origin of all these versions seems to be Thomas Beard, another Puritan and the tutor of Oliver Cromwell, writing *The Theatre of God's Judgements* in 1597:

Not inferior to any of the former [other targets of God's vengeance] in Atheisme & impiety, and equall to all in maner of punishment was one of our own nation, of fresh and late memory, called Marlin, by profession a scholler, brought up from his youth in the University of Cambridge, but by practise a playmaker, and a Poet of scurrilitie, who by giving too large a swinge to his owne wit, and suffering his lust to have the full raines, fell (not without just desert) to that outrage and extremitie, that hee denied God and his sonne Christ, and not only in word blasphemed the trinitie, but also (as it is credibly reported) wrote books against it, affirming our Saviour to be but a deceiver, and Moses to be but a conjurer and seducer of the people, and the holy Bible to be but vaine and idle stories, and all religion but a device of pollicie. But see what a hooke the Lord put in the nosthrils of this barking dogge: It so fell out, that in London streets as he purposed to stab one whom hee ought [owed] a grudge unto with his dagger, the other party perceiving so avoided the stroke, that withall catching hold of his wrest, he stabbed his owne dagger into his owne head, in such sort, that notwithstanding all the means of surgerie that could be wrought, hee shortly after died thereof. The manner of his death being so terrible (for hee even cursed and blasphemed to his last gaspe, and togither with his breath an oth flew out of his mouth) that it was not only a manifest sign of Gods judgement, but also an horrible and fearefull terrour to all that beheld him. But herein did the justice of God most notably appeare, in that hee compelled his owne hand which had written those blasphemies to be the instrument to punish him, and that in his braine, which had devised the same.

What can we learn of Marlowe's death from the bigoted, abridged, lifted and paraphrased versions above? Only Vaughan cites Deptford as the murder scene – Rudierde happily copies Beard in placing the action in the open air – 'London street' becomes 'a street in London'. The possibility here is that Beard, who very probably had the opportunity to talk to those involved, placed widow Bull's house in London Street, listed in the Subsidy Rolls[4] for East Greenwich and only a few hundred yards west of the Raven's Bourne, close enough, albeit in a different parish, to Deptford Strand.

Marlowe quarrelled with a man named Ingram, described as 'a bawdy serving-man' which is Elizabethan for a pimp. By introducing a 'certain Woman' into the picture, the crime becomes particularly low in early seventeenth-century eyes and is both a typical Puritan example of contempt for sex and women in general and also leads us frustratingly in the wrong direction.

It is unclear whose knife was used in the attack; was it Marlowe's own, as Rudierde and à Wood contend, or Ingram's, as Vaughan claims? Beard is ambiguous on this point.

Did Marlowe die instantly? Rudierde has him blaspheming and cursing, as does Beard. Vaughan says he 'shortly after dyed' and à Wood implies at least that there was some medical attempt to save his life – 'notwithstanding all the means of surgery that could be wrought'.

In the 1820s the antiquarian James Broughton unearthed crucial details from the parish records of St Nicholas, Deptford. In the *Gentleman's Magazine* for January 1830, Broughton published the information that Christopher Marlowe was 'slaine by Ffrancis Archer' and another name had entered the litany of errors, embellishments and downright fiction. The mistake seems to have been that of the Reverend D. Jones, Minister of St Nicholas, in a careless transposition of the Elizabethan handwriting from his parish registers. The entry actually reads 'Christopher Marlowe slain by Ffrancis Frizer sepultus [buried] 1. of June Anno Dom. 1593.' The entry is typical of the Elizabethan habit of mixing English with Latin, but the misreading of 'F' for 'A' in Frizer seems odd after getting it right on the previous line in 'Ffrancis'. The incorrect Christian name remained a subject of controversy until Dr J. Leslie Hotson arrived on the scene in the 1920s.

Research into the death of Marlowe is a time-chart of historical study in itself. Beard, Meres and Rudierde felt free to use the killing as an example of God's wrath against atheists. For them, it was a morality tale, a caution against flying in the face of the true faith. Broughton, two centuries later, has no polemical axe to grind, but has the antiquarian's obsession with the artefacts of the past, poring over the dusty archives of parish churches and asking himself the wrong questions. The renewed interest in Elizabethan dramatists in the nineteenth century (after Colley Cibber, Nahum Tate and David Garrick had tinkered to give Shakespeare's tragedies happy endings!)

led both British and French writers to speculate on the Puritan half-truths. The poet Watts-Dunton described Marlowe's killer as a villain. The Dido brothers, Hugo and Mézières, call him a 'valet' and 'un homme en livrée'. Charles Kingsley, Christian socialist, author and hypocrite, described him as a footman and Arthur Bayldon put him in the kitchens as a scullion.

'Undoubtedly,' wrote J. le Gay Brereton, 'he brushed from Marlowe's hose the mire of the London kennels and sponged from his doublet the stains of grease and sack.'

Another writer, Pinkerton, elaborated on the theme of the lady over whom Marlowe quarrelled with his rival, but he and the others who did so were all circumscribed by the obscenity laws and censorship of their century. The Didos call her 'une fille de basse condition' (a prostitute) and the murder site was 'the kind of place where they sell bad beer'[5] (a brothel).

The Harvard scholar Leslie Hotson was looking for something else entirely in the Public Record Office in 1925. As an expert in literary convention, he knew that the first Elizabethans often referred to people by their Christian names. So the unusual first name of 'Ingram' mentioned by Vaughan in 1600 as Marlowe's killer leapt out at him from the Calendar of Close Rolls.[6] The entry, however, referred to nothing more sinister than a property deal. In *The Death of Christopher Marlowe* Hotson cannot hide his excitement on the research trail, nor the sense of despair at meeting brick walls. The *Inquisitions Post Mortem* told him precisely nothing. Neither did the records of the Court of Queen's Bench.[7] And the Rolls of Assize,[8] for all their relevance to Kent in the South-Eastern Circuit had no mention of either Marlowe or Ingram. Hotson believed he might have missed something vital in the original documents within the infuriating curls and loops of the Tudor clerks.

In a flash of either brilliance or sheer exasperation, Hotson checked the Patent Rolls[9] for 35 Elizabeth which related to pardons granted by the Queen in 1593. He found it:

Regina xxviij de Junij concessit Ingramo ffrisar perdonam de se defendendo –
   The Queen, on the 28th day of June granted a pardon to Ingram ffrisar in self defence.

This sent Hotson back to the *Chancery Inquistions Post Mortem* he had already checked and at last the motley selection, covering some four centuries, yielded pure gold. The sequence of documents that Hotson found runs as follows: first comes the writ *a certiorari* (from a high court to a lower court):

> Elizabeth, by the grace of God of England, France & Ireland, Queen, Defender of the Faith etc. To our well-beloved William Danby, Gentleman, Coroner of our household, greeting. Wishing for certain causes to be certified upon an indictment made in your presence concerning the death of Christopher Morley, upon view of the body of the same Christopher, at Detforde Strande in our County of Kent within the verge lying dead and slain, whence a certain Ingram ffrysar, late of London, Gentleman, is indicted (as by the record thence remaining with you it fully appears) slew the aforesaid Christopher in self-defence & not feloniously or of malice aforethought, so that in no other wise could he avoid his own death, or not; we command you to send the tenor of the indictment aforesaid with everything touching it and whatsoever names the parties aforesaid in that indictment are known by, to us in our Chancery under your seal distinctly & openly without delay & with this writ. Witness myself at Westminster on the 15th day of June in the year of our reign the thirty fifth.[10]

It is signed simply 'Powle'.[11]

Sir William Danby, the Queen's coroner, complied with the order, this time with one or two English phrases creeping into the legal Latin. It is the official version of Christopher Marlowe's death:

> Inquisition indented taken at Detford Strand in the aforesaid County of Kent within the verge on the first day of June in the year of the reign of Elizabeth by the grace of God of England, France & Ireland, Queen, defender of the faith &c thirty fifth, in the presence of William Danby, Gentleman, Coroner of the household of our said lady the Queen, upon view of the body of Christopher Morley, there lying dead & slain, upon oath of Nicholas Draper, Gentleman, Wolstan Randall, gentleman, William Curry, Adrian Walker, John Barber, Robert Baldwyn,

Giles ffeld, George Halfepenny, Henry Awger, James Batt, Henry Bendyn, Thomas Batt senior, John Baldwyn, Alexander Burrage, Edmund Goodcheepe & Henry Dabyns, Who say [upon] their oath that when a certain Ingram ffrysar, late of London, Gentleman, and the aforesaid Christopher Morley and one Nicholas Skeres, late of London, Gentleman, and Robert Poley of London aforesaid, Gentleman, on the thirtieth day of May in the thirty fifth year above named, at Detford Strand aforesaid in the said County of Kent within the verge, about the tenth hour before noon of the same day, met together in a room in the house of a certain Eleanor Bull, widow; & there passed the time together & dined & after dinner were in quiet sort together there & walked in the garden belonging to the said house until the sixth hour after noon of the same day & then returned from the said garden to the room aforesaid & there together and in company supped; & after supper the said Ingram & Christopher Morley were in speech & uttered one to the other divers malicious words for the reason that they could not be at one nor agree about the payment of the sum of pence, that is le recknynge,[12] there; & the said Christopher Morley then lying upon a bed in the room where they supped & moved with anger against the said Ingram ffrysar upon the words as aforesaid spoken between them, And the said Ingram then & there sitting in the room aforesaid with his back towards the bed where the said Christopher Morley was then lying, sitting near the bed, that is, nere the bed, & with the front part of his body towards the table & the aforesaid Nicholas Skeres & Robert Poley sitting on either side of the said Ingram in such a manner that the same Ingram ffrysar in no wise could take flight; it so befell that the said Christopher Morley on a sudden & of his malice towards the same Ingram aforethought, then & there maliciously drew the dagger of the said Ingram which was at his back, and with the same dagger the said Christopher Morley then & there maliciously gave the aforesaid Ingram two wounds on his head of the length of two inches & the depth of a quarter of an inch; whereupon the said Ingram, in fear of being slain, & sitting in the manner aforesaid between the said Nicholas Skeres & Robert Poley so that he could not in any wise get away, in his own defence & for the saving of his life, then & there struggled with the said Christopher Morley to get back from him his dagger aforesaid; in which affray the same Ingram could not get away from the said Christopher Morley; and so it befell that in that affray that the said Ingram in defence of his life, with the dagger aforesaid of the value of 12*d.* gave the said Christopher then & there a mortal wound over his right eye of the depth of two inches & the width of one inch; of which mortal wound the aforesaid Christopher Morley then & there instantly died. And so the Jurors aforesaid say upon their oath that the said Ingram killed & slew Christopher Morley aforesaid on the thirtieth day of May in the thirty fifth year named above at Detford Strand aforesaid within the verge in the room aforesaid within the verge in the manner and form aforesaid in the defence and saving of his own life, against the peace of our said lady the Queen, her now crown and dignity; And further the said Jurors say upon their oath that the said Ingram after slaying aforesaid perpetrated & done by him in the manner & form aforesaid neither fled nor withdrew himself; But what goods or chattels, lands or tenements the said Ingram had at the time of the slaying aforesaid, done & perpetrated by him in the manner & form aforesaid, the said Jurors are totally ignorant. In witness of which the said Coroner as well as the Jurors aforesaid to this Inquisition have interchangeably set their seals.

Given the day & year named above etc.

By William Danby,
Coroner.

The turgid legalistic prose, laced so heavily with bureaucratic jargon and dripping with 'aforesaids' nonetheless makes it clear what happened. It was a cut and dried case of self-defence and the final document which Hotson discovered in the Chancery records repeats the details of the killing and ends:

And so that the said Ingram killed & slew Christopher Morley aforesaid at Detford Strande aforesaid in our said County of Kent within the verge in the room aforesaid within the verge in the manner & form aforesaid in the defence and saving of his own life aginst our peace, our crown & dignity. As more fully appears by the tenor of the record of Inquisition aforesaid which we caused to come before us in our Chancery by virtue of our writ We therefore moved by piety have pardoned the same Ingram ffrisar the breach of our peace which pertains to us against the said Ingram for the death above mentioned & grant to him our firm peace Provided nevertheless that the right remain in our Court if anyone should wish to complain of him concerning the death above mentioned in the testimony &c Witness the Queen at Kewe on the 28th day of June.

Commentators and theorists ever since Hotson have found Coroner Danby's version of the events at Deptford Strand a little difficult to swallow. It rests entirely on the word of three men and perhaps one woman. There is no record of the specific questions asked of them or of the answers they gave. Above all, because of the lack of forensic knowledge at the time, the dead man could tell no tales. Today, we would know exactly how Christopher Marlowe died, precisely where and when from the nature of his wounds and the condition of his body and the murder scene. We would even know what delicacies the widow Bull fed him for his last meal.

We wish to take up the challenge that the Queen left open in her pardon and to complain of Ingram Frizer concerning the death above mentioned, although at 407 years distance in time, it may be a little late. Ingram Frizer, Nicholas Skeres, Robert Poley, Eleanor Bull; these are the names that lurk like spiders in the web that sucked in the fly that was Christopher Marlowe. It was a web of intrigue and subterfuge, a web of darkness and murder. And other spiders lived in its myriad strands. We shall meet them all in this book.

TWO

Merlin's Race

. . . mad and scoffing poets, that have propheticall spirits as bred of Merlin's race.

Robert Greene, *Epistle to Perimedes* (1588)

There is an old adage in police circles: if you want to know how a man died, look at how he lived.

Christopher Marlowe, known to his friends and perhaps his family as Kit, was born in the parish of St George the Martyr in the city of Canterbury, Kent, on 6 February 1564. The parish records mark his christening:

> The 26th day of ffebruary was Christened
> Christopher the sonne of John Marlow.

Christopher – the carrier of Christ – was a slightly unusual name in the 1560s and its irony cannot have been lost on the intellectual world that the future poet came to know; the atheist bearing the name of the son of God.

Canterbury lies on the banks of the Stour,[1] meandering today a little sluggishly between the half-timbered houses that were new in Marlowe's day. The Romans called it Durovernum; the Saxons, Cantwaraburh (the fortress of the men of Kent) and as such it was the capital of one of the seven Saxon kingdoms. The Vikings sacked the town repeatedly, attracted by the great cathedral founded by Augustine in 597. It survived to be enlarged by Archbishop Odo in 950 and rebuilt by the Normans Lanfranc and Anselm from 1070. Fires and rebuilding continued throughout the Middle Ages.

It was another murder, that of Thomas Becket in 1170, that turned Canterbury Cathedral into the first of the English shrines. The prelate had suddenly found religion after a highly secular life at Court and clashed continually with his king, Henry II, over the issue of criminous clerks and the degree of obedience that he should show to the pope. The matter was resolved on the night of 29 December 1170 by four knights, Reginald fitz Urse, Hugh de Morville, William de Tracy and Richard le Breton. Clattering through the cloisters and into the chapel of St Benedict, one of them launched the attack on the praying Archbishop and he died with his brains spilled on the altar steps. Miracles were attributed to the dead man within weeks and on 21 February 1173 he was canonized as St Thomas of Canterbury.

It was the elaborate shrine erected over Becket's tomb that gave Canterbury its pre-eminence, only a little diminished by the time Christopher Marlowe was born. Pilgrims travelled the civilized world in the Middle Ages, out of piety or wanderlust or both and Canterbury was reckoned on a par with the shrines of St James at Compostela or Jerusalem itself. It is no accident that almost the first work of fiction written in English, Chaucer's *The Canterbury Tales*, should centre on a visit to the place.

In its heyday, the shrine was a fabulously gilded casket, studded with pearls, rubies, diamonds and sapphires, some, as the humanist Erasmus marvelled, 'larger than a goose's egg'. Pilgrims crawled on their hands and knees on the cold, worn stones to the tinkling of Canterbury bells, the choking smell of incense and the Gregorian bass echoing and re-echoing through the vaulted chambers. Then came the Reformation.

This book does not have the scope to chronicle in detail Henry VIII's quarrel with Rome, although the rift's bearing on the murder of Christopher Marlowe is important. The English, as opposed to the European, Reformation always had a political, dynastic and in a way parochial element to it. In what was very much a man's world, the girl (Mary) who stood as Henry's heir would not do as ruler of a growing, powerful and disputatious realm. Hence the famous request in 1529 to the pope for a divorce, leading to an equally famous refusal. In desperation, the good Catholic king broke the centuries' old bonds with Rome, established himself as head of the Church in England and stage-managed the divorce he sought from Catherine of Aragon.

Under excommunication as he was and, with the birth of Elizabeth in 1533, still without the heir he longed for, Henry went the whole hog and destroyed the monasteries. The aim was twofold. First he could eliminate the centres of papal support and second he could obtain the vast resources of the Church for his own treasury.

As the most sumptuous cathedral in the country, Canterbury was an obvious target. Between 1537 and 1538, when Marlowe's grandfather, also Christopher, was still alive and a tanner in the city, over four hundred sacred items were pillaged by order of Thomas Cromwell and the King's Commissioners. Legend says it took more than thirty carts to remove it all. Perhaps Canterbury came in for special treatment because of the symbolic image of the murdered saint – a churchman who had dared defy a king. The immaculate shrine was destroyed and a way of life came to an end.

Since the twelfth century an endless throng of pilgrims, themselves drawn from all ranks of society, had made their journey along the Pilgrim's Way once the spring rains were over. They were rich pickings for craftsmen, victuallers and innkeepers all over northern Kent. Canterbury also lay on the main road from Dover, the largest port for travellers from Europe. Merchants passed this way with silks and spices, battered troops returning from foreign wars, eager recruits marching off to others. Courtiers on palfreys and sailors on foot mingled with the priests who came and went, and Canterbury had become a large and cosmopolitan city.

William Urry, the City Archivist in the 1960s, has done more than anyone to chart the life of Marlowe in the city common to them both. Lancastrians and Yorkshiremen lived amicably enough side by side there. Marlowe's father's friend was Thomas Plessington, a baker from Cheshire; the future poet's brother-in-law came from Preston in Lancashire. There were Scotsmen living in Canterbury, lured down from their harsh wilderness by the promise of a softer life; Irishmen from the desperate peat bogs of the west; Welshmen seeking their fortunes – the family names have survived – Davy, Vaughan, Williams, Evans.

The Marlowes had settled in Canterbury by 1414 when the name first appears in the city records. Variant spellings of the family name abound – Marlow, Marlo, Marloe, Marley, Morley, Marlye, Morle, Marlin, Marlen, Marlynge and Merlin – all are recorded. The poet's only known signature, even allowing for the idiosyncrasies of Elizabethan quill work, is clearly Marley.

Merlin's race underwent various changes of occupation. They were fullers (thickening and shrinking woollen cloth); vintners (involved in the importation of wine along the Dover road); rope makers and tanners (dyeing and finishing cowhides for the leather trades). In the fifteenth century the tanneries, with their appalling stench, were strung along the city walls, facing away from the town. The poet's grandfather followed this trade and in his will left two houses to his unborn child, 'to the child that she [his wife, Joan] goyth with all if hitt be a man child.'[2] The son John, born about 1540, became a shoemaker. This is not much of a departure from type – tanners and cobblers shared the same guild as leatherworkers in Canterbury as in most other towns. Marlowe senior served his apprenticeship, traditionally for seven years, under Gerard Richardson.

On 22 May 1561, now a master in his own right, he married Katherine Arthur, whose family came from Dover. In the social and economic melting pot of the sixteenth century, families and even individuals rose and fell according to the vagaries of fortune, the harvest or the ways of the Lord, depending on how they viewed the world. It was once believed that Katherine's father was a priest in Elizabeth's new and struggling Anglican Church. William Urry established that he was a general dealer and A.D. Wraight, probably today's expert on Marlowe's life, says he was of yeoman stock. Katherine's brother Thomas was a bailiff of the Archbishop's secular court, a post which placed the Arthur family on a higher social footing and may well explain how John and Katherine first met.

The couple were married in the church of St George the Martyr near to the south-eastern gate of the city. The church with its square tower was a stone's throw from the gate of 1470 (now demolished) with its drum towers and portcullis. These powerful defences (an exact copy of which still stand at Westgate) loomed large over the Marlowes in Christopher's boyhood. 'Two lofty Turrets that command the Towne' which he refers to in his play *The Jew of Malta* almost certainly bear witness to this. The tower of St George's, with its odd Victorian clock, stands incongruously today on the pavement. The church took a direct hit during a bombing raid on 1 June 1942 and the nave was demolished in 1954.

The Marlowes moved often within the medieval walls of the city, usually because John Marlowe seemed to have a habit of quarrelling with his neighbours. There were also times when he did not pay his rent or his rates. William Urry paints a picture of the man as a 'busy, active, pugnacious fellow, clearly very fond of the limelight, prone to go to law at the slightest excuse, ready to perform public business [he became churchwarden] and probably rather neglectful of his business'. Urry has found the Marlowes living in North Lane, which ran north-west from Westgate. *Christopher Marlowe's Canterbury*, the current town trail of the poet, lists their residence at the corner of St George's Lane near the church. Charles Norman, writing in 1948, says that tradition dictates that Christopher was born in a house on the corner of St George's Street and St George's Lane.

The willingness to rush to law, the respectable status of churchwarden coupled with the non-payment of debts are typical of the complexity and paradox of the age. The Shakespeare family, whose son William was born miles to the north-west in Stratford two months after Kit Marlowe, presents a very similar history.

The Marlowes' first child was Mary and although the parish records of St George are unclear, it is likely that she was born in the first year of their marriage, christened on 21 May 1562. Christopher followed in February 1564, Margaret in May 1565, Thomas in October 1568 and John in August 1569. The list is a copy and may be inaccurate.

We can know nothing about the circumstances of Marlowe's birth. By 1559 all churches and their congregations were nominally Anglican by virtue of Elizabeth's creation of the Church of England in that year, but the melting-pot of the Reformation had created a fluid situation in which nominal Anglicans were actually closet Catholics. Whether this applied to the Marlowes we do not know. Childbirth was another matter. It happened at home, probably with Katherine sitting in a specially adapted chair and with the attendance of a local female who doubled as a midwife and who swore not to exchange the baby for a changeling. Katherine, in what was still an age of signs and portents, may have worn coral around her neck to protect the baby 'from fascination and bewitching'.[3] John would have been kept well away from the last stages of confinement, checking that the bell-ringers of St George rang their chimes to frighten away evil spirits. He hammered his shoe-soles and pattens in the open-fronted workshop of the room that faced the street and loosened all the knots in the house as was the custom at the time of a birth. Did he gaze up at the stars on the previous night? Check the almanac for signs in the heavens? Superstition had not been left behind by the new queen and her *via media*. Little Kit would have been dressed in his sister's clothes and if the boy was born downstairs, John would have carried him upstairs as a sign of good luck.

It was common, in an age of chronic infant mortality, to baptize a child within a day or two of its birth. We cannot know why the Marlowes waited. Was the baby or mother ill? All the more reason to hurry, to 'church' the child by bringing priests to the house. On the day itself, little Kit would have been dressed in his Chrism clothes, the symbolic garb of a new Christian. Perhaps John had a 'Rocking Cake' baked and friends gave the baby Apostle spoons and yet more coral. He was named for his grandfather – 'God send thee sound rest, my little boykin.'

We know nothing, either, about relationships within the family. A.L. Rowse, the doyen of Tudor experts forty years ago, refers to one of Marlowe's sisters, Ann (not specifically listed in the parish records) as 'blasphemous', because she was punished for it. Blasphemy in the sixteenth century was a crime against man because it was a crime against God. When the boy was about a year old, his father emerges as something of a pious busybody. In a libel suit, he swore an oath 'that divers tymes most sclanderouslie affirmed . . . that godwiff Chapman did owe unto hym the same Laurence [a mutual neighbour] two shillings . . .'. He also reported hearing the derogatory remark that Applegate, a local tailor, had 'hadd his pleasure of godlyve Chapman's daughter'.

Did the pious churchwarden and his wife really give birth to a brood of heretics and freethinkers? It is unlikely, but perhaps it was not only the future poet's Cambridge education which fitted him for the fatal outlook he had as a man. It is tempting too to try to fit the boy into that classic pattern promoting homosexuality – a female culture in which Katherine and her daughters dominated and John was merely the figurehead and breadwinner. We simply do not, after four hundred years, have the information.

Babies slept in wooden cradles and older children shared beds whatever their ages and sex. Little Kit may have learned to walk around his father's workshop with 'hanging sleeves' (reins) and wooden cages trundling on wooden wheels. His toys would have been rattles and teething rings of horn and wood, gravitating to drums and popguns. It is possible he played with 'Bartholomew babies', his sisters' dolls. He would have been as familiar as we are with Tom Thumb, Little Jack Horner and Old Mother Hubbard.

Most parents, especially fathers, in Elizabethan times, were strict. It was not until 1577 that Hugh Rhodes wrote his *Boke of Nurture or Schole of Good Manners* but he was merely embodying the standard behaviour of his day – '. . . nor let your children go whither they will, but know where they go . . . and when you hear them swear or curse, lie or fight, thou shalt sharply reprove them.'

As the eldest son, however, it is certain that Kit would have learned, from a very early age, the cobbler's trade. This was standard practice in all walks of life; for sons to follow their fathers. There was even believed to be biblical precedent for it in Christ the carpenter from Nazareth working at Joseph's lathe. It took an exceptional child – a Shakespeare or a Marlowe – to break the mould; and what worked that exception was education.

Literacy is a difficult skill to measure historically. The ownership of books was not necessarily a sign of a bibliophile – nabobs of the seventeenth century and the nouveau riche of any modern period buy them by the yard. When John Marlowe died in 1605, no book, not even a manuscript of one of his famous son's plays, nor, perhaps tellingly, a Bible, is mentioned in his will. Conversely, John Gresshop, Master of the King's School, Canterbury, who died in February 1579, left whole pages of books, together with their individual values. Virtually all of them were written in Latin or Greek, the languages of the scholar.

We do not know if John or Katherine Marlowe could read[4] or whether either of them had any burning zeal for education. What is likely, however, is that the shoemaker came into contact with all strata of society including the great and good of Canterbury, both by being a churchwarden and as a craftsman. The sixteenth century was the age of the patron. Skill, ability, brilliance even, counted for little without the support of some guiding spirit, someone with sufficient birth and the right connections to open doors. In the case of young Marlowe, that patron was Sir Roger Manwood, a fearsome Justice of the Peace who earned the name 'scourge of the night-prowler'. He lived in the village of Hackington 2 miles from the city's West Gate and his sword and funerary helmet are still displayed in the city museum. His tomb in the village church of St Stephen shows him in the cap, ruff and fur-lined robes of a Baron of the Exchequer with the gilt collar of SSs and sealed knots around his shoulders. We know that the knight took an interest in young Marlowe as a teenager, but this protection may have been established earlier.

There were three schools in Canterbury in the 1560s, two in Marlowe's own parish of St George and a third in St Peter's Street that was also the Hospital of St Thomas the Martyr. This was the largest of them and had been founded by Matthew Parker, Archbishop of Canterbury, in 1569 for twenty poor boys. No rolls have survived from any of these schools, but Parker's foundation seems the most likely. Kit was five when the school was opened (most boys began their formal education at seven) and with the vagaries of the local economy following the collapse of the pilgrimage business, he certainly qualified as a poor boy.

Here he would have learned to read and write, with a horn book dangling from his neck (paper was still far too expensive for mere school use) not only in his native tongue, for which there were yet no rules of spelling, grammar or punctuation, but also in Latin, the language of the law and the Church. The possession of these skills already marked Marlowe out as a cut above his parents and placed him on the first rung of the rickety ladder of success. The discipline in Tudor schools was severe by modern standards, although Roger Ascham, the tutor to Princess Elizabeth, wrote in 1570 that 'children are sooner allured by love than driven by beating to attain good learning'.

Marlowe was probably still at Parker's school when the Queen visited in September 1573. 'To see a fine lady upon a white horse' was an ambition in a nursery rhyme still taught to children in the twentieth century. Elizabeth was the last of the peripatetic monarchs, travelling with bells and music, pomp and splendour, so that her subjects would marvel and whisper and be overawed. No doubt the twenty scholars of St Thomas's were given the day off to cheer their queen as she rode under her gilded canopy to Parker's palace. The Archbishop was delighted with it all and wrote to Archbishop Grindal of York days later to tell him how well the visit had gone.

The Queen, of course, was no stranger to Canterbury. In 1568 she had granted the use of part of the cathedral's crypt to the Huguenots, as their own private chapel; it had been the chantry of the Black Prince.[5] The Inquisition and the zeal of the Jesuits in particular had forced many Huguenots out of their native France and the Spanish Netherlands. Many sought refuge in the more tolerant Protestant states of northern Europe, including England. London was a natural target, but so too was Canterbury. The houses of the weavers still stand in their half-timbered magnificence along the banks of the Stour. The original eighteen families were growing rapidly during Marlowe's boyhood – perhaps he learned his French from them. It was time for this casual education to be given a more direct focus and that focus was the King's School.

There had been a school at Canterbury since the founding of the cathedral by Augustine. The Reformation, however, had dislocated the educational, as well as the religious, political and economic life of the country. Henry VIII gave financial compensation to the displaced Catholic monks of Canterbury in the 1530s, but what they were allowed to teach and how they were allowed to teach it changed forever.

The Tudors were generous school benefactors and Henry's charter of 1541 paid for a master, an usher (deputy) and fifty scholars. They entered at the age of nine and left at fifteen, an important part of their role to sing treble in the cathedral choir. The scholars were defined in the statutes of 1541 as 'poor boys, both destitute of the help of friends, and endowed with minds apt for learning . . . and shall be sustained out of the funds of our church'.

We do not know exactly when Marlowe joined the school. The only reference to him, as 'Christopher Marley', is at Lady Day (then 14 January) 1579 when he was nearly fifteen. Because of his age, the assumption has been made that he was a commoner (paying fees) before that date. John Marlowe seems to have been in funds in the mid-1570s, employing a maid and two apprentices; if this is so, then perhaps the Marlowes could afford the school's fees. By this time,

John was acting as bondsman for couples seeking marriage licences; this would have been an additional source of income. As a King's scholar, Kit received a stipend of £1 8s 4d a year, as well as two and a half yards of cloth for a new academic gown each Christmas and 'commons' (food). The total value was perhaps £4 a year.

The boy's route each morning would have taken him along St George's Street, past the yard of the huge Bull Inn that ran from Buttermarket to the High Street. For much of the year he would be up before dawn, perhaps leaping the puddles and dung around the Bullstake. He would have run (or like Shakespeare's more famous schoolboy 'with his satchel/And shining morning face, creeping like a snail') along the narrow length of Sun Street, with its over-arching medieval buildings and its odd sliding wooden shutters, their runners still visible today. To his right would have been the heraldic magnificence of the Christchurch Gate, its stone traceries and painted shields bright with the colours of the cathedral and the Queen. He would have turned along Palace Street and right into the Mint Yard.

As the cathedral bells chimed the hour, the usher, Robert Rose, took his junior scholars through the Prior Sellingegate and the low arch of Dark Entry to the cloisters and the cathedral itself. There were prayers and a psalm sung by the choristers, Marlowe among them. Musicality was not only part of school life, but a necessary qualification for the scholarship which Marlowe won to Cambridge. His brother Thomas also sang with the cathedral choir in his turn. Both boys, the younger Marlowe certainly, would have sung the *Sacred Songs* of Thomas Tallis and his pupil William Byrd, published in 1575; so impressed was the Queen with their music that they were granted a twenty-one year monopoly to print all the church music in the country. The oldest buildings in the school, with its Norman-arched staircase, Strangers Hall and Almonry Chapel, were all part of the medieval monastery, abandoned by the monks in Kit's grandfather's time.

The King's School laid down what was expected of its scholars. The rigid medieval timetable of the Trivium (grammar, logic and rhetoric) and the Quadrivium (arithmetic, music, geometry and astronomy) was giving way, slowly, to a new learning. Latin prose and poetry were the order of the day, 'practised in poetic tales, the familiar letters of learned men, and other literature of that sort'.[6] This was followed in the Fifth Form by 'translating the most Chaste Poets and the best Historians'. Perhaps it was their very chastity that drove Marlowe to translate the raunchier Ovid later in life! In the Sixth Form, debate was expected, preparing the future free thinker, no doubt, for his clashes with orthodoxy as an adult – 'Horace, Cicero and other authors of that class' were the daily diet. Intellectual competition was fierce and encouraged by both headmasters of Marlowe's time, John Gresshop and Nicholas Goldsborough, who personally examined the boys every week.

The long school day ended at 5 p.m. and a closing service was held before the day's lessons were recounted by way of homework until 7.

Marlowe's love of theatre may well have been sparked by the plays performed in the cathedral by the school each Christmas. These were 'Tragedies, Comedyes and interludes' but always in Latin or Greek. There is no direct evidence from the 1570s that they were performed, although the vogue for child actors and children's companies was catching on in London in this decade. The impact of this form of drama on Marlowe may be less than some commentators imagine. After all, the future 'Muses' darling' was to create a new form of theatre and the revolutionary rhythm of iambic pentameter – what Ben Jonson was to call 'Marlowe's mighty line' – and there is no evidence that he ever set foot on stage as an actor.

Marlowe was a day boy, rubbing shoulders with sons of the gentry, and such distinctions still mattered in his time. William Urry lists eighty scholars contemporary with Marlowe, but the list for 1578–9 has only fifty-six names, itself a sign that the school was already growing beyond its 1541 scope. It is impossible now to know who were Marlowe's friends, finding the mercurial Kit a fascinating companion, and who were his enemies, scornful perhaps of the cobbler's son from the parish of St George. Marlowe himself is listed at number 50 at Ladyday, Midsummer and Michaelmas and William Urry has winkled out the names that had other links with the future poet. Henry Bromerick was a scholar in 1582 and followed Marlowe to Cambridge; Ralph Groves came from Henley-on-Thames and probably knew Marlowe's future brother-in-law John Crawford; John Reynard who joined the school in 1582 became sizar (poor scholar) of Clare College, Cambridge in 1591; Matthew Parker, the grandson of the Archbishop, matriculated fellow-commoner of Marlowe's future college of Corpus Christi and received over eleven hundred books from his grandfather's library. Mungay (Christian name unknown) and John Parrett both had shoes made for them by John Marlowe. Most interesting of all, in the light of Marlowe's murder and the reason for it, is Thomas Colwell, who became the first married Bishop of Salisbury and a friend of the enigmatic Walter Ralegh.

The next – and in many ways the most important phase of Marlowe's career, one that led indirectly to his death – was his winning of the Parker scholarship. Matthew Parker senior was Master of Corpus Christi College, Cambridge between 1544 and 1553. In his will, dated 5 April 1575, he added three new scholarships worth £3 6s 8d a year each, one of which was to be given to a scholar of the King's School who was also Canterbury born and bred. There were certain requirements:

> All which schollers shall and must at the time of their election be so entered into the skill of song as that they shall at first sight solf and sing plaine song. And that they shalbe of the best and aptest schollers well instructed in their grammer and if it may be such as can make a verse.

It was Parker's son John who singled out Marlowe for the award.

While Marlowe was spending his long days on the worn, polished oak of the benches at the King's School, declaiming with the best of them in Latin and Greek, possibly still working on rare holy days for his shoemaker father or, according to Canterbury folklore, sweating as a pot-boy in the Star Inn along St Dunstan's Street beyond the West Gate, the forces that would shape his end were already in being.

Of Ingram Frizer, who, according to the official account of Coroner Danby, was so outrageously attacked by Marlowe in Widow Bull's house on 30 May 1593, we know nothing, except that he was living in Basingstoke in the autumn of 1589, where he bought the Angel Inn for £120.

Nicholas Skeres, present at Marlowe's death, is better chronicled. He was born in London in March 1563, making him a year older than Marlowe. His father was a member of the guild of Merchant Taylors, a rich livery company, and the Skeres family, Nicholas, Audrey, Jerome and Nicholas junior, lived in the parish of Allhallows-the-Little, along the Ropery that ran parallel to the Thames between the wharfs of Dowgate and Ebbgate. The family originally came from Yorkshire and owned land there as well as in London and Surrey. The death of the paterfamilias in a Tudor household was a serious blow and when his father died in 1566 the boy perhaps had no strong hand to guide him. By the mid 1570s, as Marlowe probably entered the King's School, Skeres was already in debt and had fallen into the clutches of the money lenders Richard Parradine and John Wolfall, the latter a skinner from Silver Street in the city. The life of petty crime and con-artistry known to the Elizabethan underworld as 'coney-catching' or 'cosenage' had an appeal to a shiftless young man who doubtless had a glib tongue and winning ways.

Robert Poley, the third in the Deptford triumvirate of 1593, was probably born in the mid-1550s. The first record of him is as a sizar of Clare College, Cambridge in 1568 (preceding John Reynard from the King's School, Canterbury). The poverty associated with sizars (they carried out menial tasks for richer students to earn their keep, the Tudor version of working their way through college) never quite left Poley. And such men, greedy, ambitious, lean and hungry, were often dangerous. Frizer, Skeres and Poley, although none of them yet knew it, were waiting in the wings.

On the national stage, the years of Marlowe's childhood were those described by historian J.B. Black as the years of crisis. The Queen had been on the throne for six years, assailed from all sides by the cares of state.

First there was the marriage question. Elizabeth herself had become queen on the death of her elder sister, Mary, who had suffered a long history of amenorrhoea (absence of periods, caused by any number of conditions) and heart disease. The official diagnosis was dropsy, her lungs filling with fluid as she lay, abandoned and bitter, in her chambers at St James's Palace. Before her, Elizabeth's younger brother, Edward, had reigned for six years, dying of tuberculosis at the age of fifteen. Elizabeth had, as she herself famously said, 'the body of a weak and feeble woman', a fact made obvious to all when she caught and nearly died from smallpox in October 1562. The likelihood of a woman coping as queen in her own right was slim. Before Mary (whose five-year reign was wracked with its re-conversion to Catholicism and some three hundred public burnings) the last queen of England[7] had been the dubious Matilda, whom some had backed in a reckless civil war against the rightful king, Stephen, in the twelfth century. It was a man's world, hence Henry VIII's obsession with his 'great matter' (divorcing Catherine of Aragon) and his risking Hell and damnation to produce a son.

For Elizabeth to marry was essential or the Tudor dynasty would die with her. The 1560s and '70s saw a variety of suitors come and go. Closest to her heart was Robert Dudley, the Master of Horse created by her Earl of Leicester. When the fever of smallpox gripped her at her palace of Hampton Court, she insisted that he be declared protector of the realm in the event of her death. Their affair, which was undoubtedly sexual, was the talk of the Court. They danced the volta together, the rhythm and closeness of which were thought shocking to decency, especially between a queen and her subject. The death of Dudley's wife, Amy Robsart, after falling from 'a pair of stairs' led to speculation and rumour. That, coupled with Dudley's arrogance as obvious royal favourite, combined to bring Elizabeth to her senses and she dropped him, despite the fortune he spent entertaining her in sumptuous style to the tune of an estimated £3,000 a day at his castle at Kenilworth.

After Leicester, the suitors were diplomatic projects and that meant the spectre of foreign domination. In Elizabeth's age, with parliament a cypher and democracy non-existent, this was more likely. The first offer came from the ascetic Catholic fanatic, Philip II of Spain, Elizabeth's former brother-in-law, who had spent a miserable fourteen months in England as Mary's husband before returning to his curious monastic palace of the Escorial. The offer carried too many strings, not least of which was that Elizabeth should return to the bosom of the Catholic Church, and she politely, persistently, refused. It would take twenty years for Philip's dealings with Elizabeth to change from marriage proposal to war.

Hot on the heels of Spain was Prince Erik of Sweden, although to be fair the man had proposed to Elizabeth when she was a princess. Despite the ardent love-letters he sent her, the sticking place was that neither monarch was prepared to leave his or her country, so the ardour cooled. Elizabeth never took Sweden's claim all that seriously but, as was her way, she kept Erik dangling for as long as politics deemed it expedient.

Erik in fact was regarded as a genuine threat by the Holy Roman Emperor, Ferdinand I, who offered, via the usual ambassadorial channels, either of his sons, the Archdukes Ferdinand and Charles. 'For many thought,' wrote Count von Helfenstein in the spring of 1560, 'that one of them would soon become consort of the Queen, and rule her and England.'8 Elizabeth kept Archduke Charles guessing until the summer of 1570, by which time he was actively pursuing a Bavarian princess.

In 1571, France entered the game. When the Queen was thirty-eight years old and dangerously near to the menopause, Catherine de' Medici put forward her nineteen-year-old son Henri, Duke of Anjou, as a possible suitor. There were strong political reasons in both English and French camps for this alliance to be made to work and even Leicester, whatever his personal feelings, saw it as the least of several possible evils. Feelers were put out in Paris under the watchful eye of the English ambassador – a man who would become central to the Marlowe case, Sir Francis Walsingham. In the event, time and politics moved on and the following year, Anjou's brother François, Duke of Alençon, twenty years the Queen's junior, was put forward by his redoubtable mother. Elizabeth kept this project going for six years, by which time she was forty-five. Things looked good. Elizabeth took to Jean de Simier, Alençon's ambassador and referred to the duke as her 'frog'. 'I have very good hope,' wrote Simier in the April of 1579, 'but will wait to say more til the curtain is drawn, the candle out, and Monsieur [Alençon] in bed.'9 He was right to be cautious; it was another example of Elizabeth playing the matrimonial game for political reasons, and the political moment was not right.

The other great problem confronting Elizabeth was that of religion and this, unlike the marriage issue, was to involve Christopher Marlowe directly. Elizabeth had set up the Church of

England in 1559 as a *via media*, a compromise between Catholics and Protestants. Like all compromises, it offered an often difficult tightrope for good men to walk and was bitterly attacked by the extremists on both sides.

The Catholic assault on the church settlement was both the older and the more obvious. Decisions taken by Elizabeth in convocation with her bishops cut no ice with men whose families had been diehard adherents of Rome for centuries. It may be that most ordinary people were ready to accept whatever state religion was thrown at them, but this did not apply to the fanatics. Elizabeth had been careful to minimize persecution, as this lent her and Protestantism an aura of tolerance and even popularity. It was Rome itself that cranked the bigotry up several notches on 25 February 1570 when Pope Pius V published his famous bull of excommunication. In Catholic eyes, Elizabeth was the daughter of the king's whore, Anne Boleyn, and therefore illegitimate. She had no right to rule England, still less to make arbitrary pronouncements on spiritual matters such as the government of the Church. Her claim to be 'governor' of the Church of England fooled no one; she ran it and was running it to Hell. The bull was an open incitement to rebellion. Good Catholics must obey Rome. That was unequivocal and there was no room for the fence-sitting in which too many English Catholics had indulged for the last eleven years. The 'Jezebel of England' must be resisted and the true path followed. Perhaps the bull was supposed to be timed as a rallying cry for the rebellion of the North, but given the communication problems of the age, the result was a failure.

Briefly told, the north was discontented. Fuelled by their continued support for Elizabeth's rival Mary, Queen of Scots, great Catholic lords like the Earls of Westmorland and Northumberland (not to mention the Spanish ambassador) threatened a rising which threw the Queen and her Protestant Privy Councillors into a state of high alert. Thomas Howard, the Duke of Norfolk (whose family had never left the 'old religion') was quick to distance himself from the half-baked scheme to murder most of the government and to place the imprisoned Queen of Scots on the throne of England. Even so, he went to the Tower and other Catholic lords, like Arundel and Pembroke, were placed under house arrest. An army was sent north under Lord Hunsdon, the Queen's cousin, who sacked village after village with alarming zeal. By the late winter of 1570 (when Pius published his bull) as many as 750 had been executed, 'the bodies to remain till they fall to pieces where they hang',[10] no doubt to encourage the others. Two hundred landowners had lost their estates and Norfolk was stripped of the highest order of chivalry in the land, the Garter.

The failure of the northern rebellion and Elizabeth's reaction to it proved two things. First, Catholicism and treason were becoming synonymous and second, the Queen pulled no punches unleashing the full terror of the state. On 8 July, when the Catholic John Felton fixed the Pope's bull to the gate of the Bishop of London's palace, he was arrested, tortured and executed. In the following year, Elizabeth passed an Act of Parliament (13 Eliz.cap.1) which made it a treasonable offence to refer to the Queen as a heretic, usurper, schismatic, tyrant or infidel. Later legislation would pass the death sentence on anyone implying that Elizabeth would even have a successor, much less guessing who it might be. The paraphernalia of the Church of Rome, such as rosaries and the Agnus Dei, symbols increasingly associated with idolatry and the Antichrist, were banned from importation. What was needed, if the Catholics were to regain lost ground, was a full blown Jesuit mission on Counter-Reformation lines; and that was provided in the summer before Christopher Marlowe went up to Cambridge.

The newer – and more insidious – threat to the stability of Elizabeth's fledgling Church was the rise of Puritanism. As early as December 1565, a hard core group centred on St John's College Cambridge, criticized the Queen for moving too slowly against popery. The monster of protest brought into being by the monk Martin Luther fifty years earlier had grown a hundred heads by the time the papacy launched a Counter-Reformation against it. In the German states in the 1520s and 1530s, it had led to open warfare between the two sides and physical attacks on clergy and their churches. In Elizabeth's England, the adherents of the new fundamentalism followed the ascetic principles laid down by the Frenchman Jean Calvin in Geneva; Christ, not Elizabeth was the governor of the Church. By the following year, the new fanaticism showed itself in a distinctly unholy row over church vestments.

Criticism of the playing of organs in church services, kneeling at communion and the sign of the cross during baptism assumed second place to the fury evoked by the wearing of the surplice – 'the livery of Antichrist'. In vain did the scholarly Matthew Parker, chosen by Elizabeth as her Archbishop of Canterbury, try to control the priesthood in his *Book of Advertisements* in 1566. Many clergy ignored it, including his own bishops, and some went so far as to undermine the essentially hierarchical nature of the Elizabethan Church and State by asserting that 'all ministers must be equal'.

From Cambridge came a Puritan leader whom J.B. Black describes as 'the most dangerous man in the church'.[11] His name was Thomas Cartwright, Fellow of Trinity College and a professor of divinity. As Cartwright used the evidence of the Bible to argue that much church practice and belief was simply an accretion of medieval ritual, he was deprived of his living, first as professor, then as Fellow and, finally, by 1574, was driven to flee to Europe for his safety. The Puritans were making their mark, however. In 1571 and 1572, two *Admonitions* were submitted to parliament. The character of English Puritanism is highly complicated, but the broad change happening in this period was from Calvinism, with its depressing predestination, to Presbyterianism with its egalitarianism and opposition to bishops. By involving parliament, the Puritans were not only by-passing the Queen and her Privy Councillors, they were issuing a challenge to the Commons, itself becoming increasingly Puritan in its outlook and increasingly vocal as a group. Unknowingly, they were lighting the slow fuse that would lead to the Civil War and the execution of a king.

On 17 May 1575, while Christopher Marlowe was probably a commoner at the King's School, Matthew Parker died. He had effectively been a pawn in Elizabeth's game (as were many others among her subjects), given the impossible task of implementing the church settlement, often without her active support and equally often with opposition from influential courtiers like Robert Dudley. Parker's replacement was Edmund Grindal, the former Archbishop of York, who quickly fell foul of the Queen over the 'prophesyings', a series of meetings of clergy which were turning more and more into forums for discussion and criticism. Elizabeth ordered them stopped and when Grindal refused, he was effectively dismissed. For the last six years of his life, his powers as the Primate of All England were severely curtailed.

The on-going struggle between the rival denominations produced a chaotic number of shades of grey. If we take the Marlowes' church of St George's in Canterbury as an example, we have no idea what actual liturgical practices were followed when Christopher was baptized and John became churchwarden. Was the prayerbook followed or did the congregation sing psalms? Where was the communion table – 'altarwise a yard distant from the wall', or elsewhere? Did the priest wear his surplice at Kit's christening? Did he use leavened or unleavened bread for communion? It was to settle these issues that Archbishop Parker wrote his *Advertisements*; but even under his nose, the priest of St George's may have defied him.

Throughout the years of crisis, the sword of Damocles over Elizabeth's head took the form of her cousin, Mary Stuart, Queen of Scots. It is beyond the scope of this book to chronicle the Amazonian battle between these two, but inasmuch as Mary became the totem for Catholic hopes and directly or indirectly the hub of several plots, her life did indeed touch Kit Marlowe's. The daughter of James V of Scotland by his second wife, she was born at Linlithgow in 1542. At a week old, she was Queen of Scotland and at the age of six was packed off to France in a marriage of convenience to the Dauphin, eldest son of the formidable Catherine de' Medici. In the space of two years, she was Queen of France and then widow of Francis II, returning to Scotland in 1561 to find her Catholic religion under mounting attack from John Knox[12] and the Presbyterians.

As with Elizabeth, there was a flurry of suitors for her hand. In the event, Mary married her cousin, Henry, Lord Darnley. Political intrigue and backstairs double-dealing saw an increasingly alienated Darnley involved in the murder of Mary's Italian secretary, David Rizzio, at Holyrood Palace in Edinburgh in 1566. Darnley himself was blown up in a house in Kirk o'Field on Sunday 9 February 1567; with or without his wife's connivance is uncertain. When Mary took the fatal step of marrying James Hepburn, the Protestant Earl of Bothwell, who probably organized Darnley's murder and had certainly been her lover, the nobility of the Lowlands rose against her. Crossing to England after a series of reversals, Mary effectively became Elizabeth's prisoner for the last twenty years of her life and the focus for any discontented or deranged Catholic throughout the entire period.

Much of the work of Lord Burghley, Elizabeth's greatest Secretary of State, and that of Francis Walsingham, her spymaster, revolved around the carefully guarded movements of the Scottish queen; they noted to whom she wrote and at whom she smiled. Their world, of intrigue, suspicion and forked-tongues, was one that Kit Marlowe would come to know soon enough.

On the international stage, Europe was convulsed with the struggles of the Counter-Reformation and the birth-pangs of nationhood. In 1545 the Council of Trent had spearheaded a fighting comeback by the Catholic Church, reeling as it had been under the attacks of Luther, Zwingli, Melanchthon, Calvin and many more. The *Index Prohibitorum* was a list of banned books which good Catholics should not read; Henry VIII himself had been named *Fidei Defensor* (Defender of the Faith) for destroying Luther's tracts. The Society of Jesus, founded by the Spanish ex-soldier Ignatius Loyola, in 1540, was an attempt to provide sound and simple rules by which good Catholics should live. Out of this order came the Jesuits, a fanatical band of missionary priests prepared to give their lives for Rome. Many of them would have to. The most odious product of the Counter-Reformation was the Holy Inquisition with its rack, its thumb-screws and its 'Spanish Horse'.[13] There is no doubt that thousands perished in the middle to late years of the sixteenth century as the Roman Church clawed back some of the land lost to Protestantism.

Because the Pope was an Italian prince[14] and because the Queen of England was also head of her Church, religion and politics went hand in hand. Philip II of Spain and Catherine de' Medici of France were powerful, shrewd and ambitious rulers of their respective countries; they were also good Catholics. And across the Channel from them both lay the Protestant whore, an excommunicant whose lands could, at least in theory, be wrested from her by diplomacy or war.

The years of crisis in which Christopher Marlowe grew up left their mark on England. The government, already rattled and without recourse to an organized police force or a standing army, was driven to paranoia by plots, real and imaginary. Bigotry and superstition went hand in hand too, along with religion and politics. How much of this affected the scholar of the King's School with his Latin and his Greek, his grey fustian robes and his singing of the works of the Catholic recusant William Byrd, we cannot know.

At Cambridge, all that would change.

THREE

Bene't's College

... by profession, a scholler ...
Thomas Beard, *Theatre of God's Judgement* (1597)

We do not know exactly how Christopher Marlowe got to Cambridge or how long the journey from Canterbury took. He left early in December 1580, probably crossing the Thames by ferry at Greenwich before finding the road north to Cambridge.

It was an age of maps. The cartographer Christopher Saxton, himself probably Cambridge educated, was commissioned by the Queen to carry out, under the patronage of Thomas Seckford, Master of the Queen's Requests, a survey of every county of England. By 1579, after four years' work, he had completed the monumental task with extraordinary accuracy. Had young Marlowe seen such an atlas, the first of its kind produced? Or did he merely trust to luck, rustic signposts and asking directions? In his portmanteau, he carried letters from Canterbury announcing him as Archbishop Parker Scholar, making for Corpus Christi.

Oppidum Cantabrigia, the town of Cambridge, carefully engraved by Richard Lyne in 1574, straddled the Cam on its way to Huntingdon and the Fens. From the south, Marlowe would have walked along Trumpington Street and into the High Ward (today's King's Parade). There was no city wall like the one circling Canterbury and no barbican gates. Cambridge was small and lacked the status of Marlowe's birthplace. Its castle, on high ground to the north, was already a ruin in 1580. Cambridge had probably been a Roman settlement, although no record survives of its name. Its oldest churches are pre-Conquest and it earned a royal charter in the twelfth century. The river brought wool from Norwich, wood and charcoal from the forests of the Midlands and seacoal from the north. In 1581 the university of Cambridge numbered an estimated

1,862 students and according to a contemporary report to parliament 'an hundred preachers at least, very worthy men'.[1]

The college of Corpus Christi, the body of Christ, lay between the churches of St Botolph and St Benedict (Bene't). Lyne's map shows walled gardens behind the college still labelled in 1574 Augustine Friars. The feast of Corpus Christi had been instituted by the Church in 1264 in honour of the Holy Eucharist, when Pope Urban IV decreed that the festival be kept on the Thursday after Trinity Sunday. By the fourteenth century, when the Cambridge college was founded, the feast was observed throughout western Europe. It was marked with pageants and miracle or mystery plays of the guilds and this gives the clue to the founding of the college.

Unique among 'Oxbridge' colleges, Corpus Christi was the creation of two town guilds, that of St Mary and Corpus Christi. St Mary's was the older organization, established between 1278 and 1285. It amalgamated with Corpus Christi in the late 1340s and planned a college of priests whose primary function would be to pray for members of the guilds. If cynics today dismiss this as buying a place in Heaven, it was considered an important element in Catholic medieval life; this world was simply a brief and relatively miserable precursor to something wonderful and perpetual in the next.

The official founding date for the college was 1352 when the building began on what today is called Old Court. The entrance was a low archway from Bene't Street leading into the quadrangle which housed Fellows and students, who shared rooms rather in the manner of guildsmen and their apprentices.

Slowly the college began to build its reputation and its wealth. Plate, money, land and houses were bequeathed to the place, including the drinking horn and the Swan Mazer, still used at college dinners. Medieval universities were often lawless institutions and the cause of frequent rifts between 'town and gown' which Bene't's College may in part have been established to heal. All students (the term in Marlowe's day was 'scholar') had to be in holy orders. Their entire curriculum was canon law and theology. They ate communally, to the rhythm of Bible readings in Greek or Latin. There were penalties (the Statutes from 1356 have survived) for crimes such as sacrilege, perjury, theft, adultery and murder.

The college that Christopher Marlowe joined in the winter of 1580–81 had undergone something of a renaissance after a century of neglect. The Duchess of Norfolk and her sister, Eleanor Botelar, endowed the place – the buttresses in Old Court are a reminder of their cash input. New rooms and galleries were built by Dr Cosyn, Master until 1515, who also provided books and desks at a cost of £170. All windows, previously shuttered, were now glazed, and attic rooms with gables and roofs were built around Old Court. Much of the grandeur of Bene't's is attributable to Matthew Parker, who had provided Marlowe's place there. He was Master for nine years (1544–53) and under him the Master's Lodge was extended into a long gallery with a covered walkway below it.

Parker joined the college in 1521 and was a Fellow (lecturer) six years later. In 1533 he was invited to London to become chaplain to the queen, Anne Boleyn, which threw him into the centre of Reformation politics. It was Anne who gave birth to Elizabeth, the future mistress in a political sense of both Parker and Marlowe, and the arrival of another daughter merely estranged the increasingly desperate Henry VIII from her. Seeking solace with Jane Seymour, he eventually accused Anne of adultery, treason and even incest and she was executed, at her own request with a sword, on 19 May 1536. It speaks volumes for Parker's political acumen that he survived the fall of his mistress to become Master of Bene't's College. His acceptance of the new Protestantism quickly manifested itself and he became the first married Master of what had, of course, been a Catholic institution, marrying the Lodge's hostess, Margaret Hailstone, in 1547. When Elizabeth was queen and Margaret the wife of the Archbishop of Canterbury, the last Tudor's bigotry was exposed in her attitude towards married priests – 'Madam I may not call you: and Mistress I am ashamed to call you: so I know not what to call you: but yet I do thank you.' There were many who received such scant courtesy from Her Majesty.

In the year of Marlowe's birth, Bene't's had thirty-two scholars; by Parker's death eleven years later, there were more than ninety. Space was at a premium; the 'Christopher', a house outside Old Court, and the unfinished bakehouse were both renovated as accommodation for pensioners (undergraduates). Three years before Marlowe arrived, Sir Nicholas Bacon, an old Bene't man and Keeper of the Great Seal, endowed a chapel to replace an older one adjoining St Bene't's church. The great and the good of Elizabethan England contributed to its building; Francis Drake, soon to begin his epic voyage of global circumnavigation, sent cash; the Earl of Bedford had 146 tons of stone carted from Thorney Abbey on his estates; the Queen herself sent thirty loads of timber for scaffolding and the roof. But it was years before the full debt was paid.

The regimen followed by Marlowe at Cambridge was probably more strict than in Canterbury. Most scholars entered the various colleges at the age of fourteen and some as young as ten so that in one sense Cambridge colleges were merely schools, not unlike the King's School that Marlowe had just left. Dr Robert Norgate was Master when Marlowe arrived and under him regulations were tough.

The scholars' day began at four in the morning, when the Siberian winds for which Cambridge is legendary would have been at their most biting.[2] We do not know precisely where in the college Marlowe lived, although the external appearance of all the upper rooms of Old Court remains unchanged since his day. In 1898, the official history of Corpus Christi said that Marlowe 'kept in the ground floor room on the right-hand side of the old court staircase . . . this room had long been used as "the store house" but it had lately been fitted up as a chamber where three of the Parker scholars might live'.[3] Wherever he lodged, the place had no heat and the furniture was probably a wooden box bed, a table and a chair.[4] By definition, the room's only artificial light came from candles. Typical of an institution created for the clergy and in which its scholars still read for the Church, the first hour of the day was spent in the new chapel. Breakfast, probably of bread or oatmeal, followed at six. The morning was then given over to study and even in casual conversation scholars could talk to each other only in Latin or Greek. The gamut of study at Cambridge was the traditional medieval diet in which Latin and Greek dominated, but with a peppering of mathematics, philosophy, divinity, logic and Hebrew. J.H. Ingram, writing in 1904 of Marlowe's time includes details of the mid-day meal – 'a penny piece of beef among four, having a pottage made of the broth of the same beef, with salt and oatmeal'.

The afternoon was spent in 'discoursi', as the fashionable Italians called it, philosophical arguments and debates. Marlowe was building on the tradition he had already learned at the King's School, and it was this ability to shoot his mouth off that would lead to his death. After that, in the Cambridge day, came private study in his room or perhaps even Parker's admirable library. To avoid the freezing cold of Cambridge streets at bed time, scholars were – 'fayne to walk or runne up and down halfe an hour, to gette a heate on their feete'.[5] There were distinct rules too about appearance; Archbishop Parker himself had laid them down. Dress was a long woollen gown of black or brown, a colour which no doubt appealed to the growing number of sombre Puritans at the university. For Parker scholars, laundry and haircuts were free, but the regulation haircut insisted on polling, knotting or rounding.

Each scholar received a weekly allowance of one shilling to supplement the meagre diet at the Buttery, where a wider variety of more exciting fare was on offer. Richer students could of course spend more there, but in the college's hierarchy this meant the Fellow-commoners who were sons of gentry. The pensioners, usually schoolmasters' boys and, by Marlowe's day, sons of the Anglican priesthood too, were by definition poorer. It was only his holding of a Parker scholarship that placed Marlowe here – 'Secundus Convictus' – rather than among the third group, the sizars, who were effectively servants to the rest. It was Kit Marlowe's sudden change in spending habits that gives us a clue to the new direction his life had taken by 1585.

The structure of Bene't's in 1580 reflects the vertical nature of Elizabethan society. Below the Master were thirteen Fellows, twenty scholars, four Bible-clerks and fifty-four students in the modern undergraduate sense. Records have survived from Marlowe's time at Cambridge and give us a glimpse of the pecking order among the faculties too. The *Nomina Professorum et Auditorum* (Names of Professors and Auditors) of the university is dated 29 October 1581. First come the Regius and Lady Margaret Professors of Theology, Whitaker and Baro; then Lyler, Professor of Hebrew; Bing, Professor of Law and Medicine; philosophy and mathematics bring up the rear. Marlowe's name appears in the Corpus Christi list as 'Merling', reading dialectic (logic) under Professor Johns. By this time, Marlowe was in his second year, the first having been devoted to rhetoric.

Until he obtained his Bachelor of Arts degree, Marlowe would have been under strict college discipline. That meant a curfew. No one could leave college without a chaperone and the gate was locked at nine o'clock between Michaelmas (autumn) and Easter; ten o'clock for the rest of the year. Floggings were carried out on scholars who transgressed, in front of the whole college 'to encourage the others', every Thursday at seven in the evening. Other punishments included fines, imprisonment or expulsion. When Dr Norgate was libelled by a student, the lad was forced to make a public apology and spend a night in the stocks before being sent down.

The ever-critical Queen was not overly impressed by Cambridge on her only visit there, in the year of Marlowe's birth. Despite the usual adulatory addresses in Latin and Greek (to which she replied in those languages) and numerous presents including a pair of locally made gloves, she found the students' habits and hoods were torn and too much soiled[6] and in the services she attended 'their voices were small and not audible'.[7]

The fact of university life, of course, is that there was a great deal more to it than the narrow curriculum and the winning of a degree. During the holidays, from June to October, students were encouraged to help with the harvest and by statute had to spend four days in local parishes repairing the roads. This brought them into contact with the town and often caused problems. The traditional student pastimes of archery, tennis and bowls were considered dull, probably because the university authorities tolerated them. Football was altogether more fun.[8] Although allowed in college quadrangles, it was banned with townspeople because of the trouble it caused – there was a celebrated battle between scholars and a team from the local village of Chesterton late in the Queen's reign. The same village laid on bear-baiting in 1581 and was far enough out for the university proctors to have no jurisdiction there. Despite an outright ban on swimming, the Cam must have had its appeal for the more adventurous undergraduates.

Wealth created its own problems. The Fellow-commoners were the sons of the seriously rich, young men whose status was already superior to some of their fellows and even the Masters. Such students used their cash to outdo each other in dress, flagrantly flouting college rules. Their one aim seemed to be to 'ruffle and roist it out, exceeding in apparel'. Their numbers were increasing in the 1580s and it may be from them that Kit Marlowe learned his fencing skills. The Stourbridge Fair, held in the fields between the Cam and the Stour from St Bartholomew's Day to St Michael's Day each September, was the source of most trouble. The fair had its own courthouse dealing with debt, assault and double-dealing and there seems to have been plenty of that; the town provided the stalls, but the university the weights and measures. Punch-ups were frequent.

Who were Marlowe's contemporaries at Cambridge? One, who became his friend, was Thomas Nashe, from Lowestoft. Younger than Marlowe by three years, he was a scholar of St John's and although this was a centre of rabid Puritanism at the time, Nashe seems not to have been an extremist. Physically small, notoriously pugnacious and boyish, he is typical of the set, including Marlowe, who would become known in London as 'the university wits' and it may have rankled with lesser men, like William Shakespeare, that they were not among them. Nashe may have begun his first work *The Anatomie of Absurdity* while still at Cambridge. He was resident there between 1582 and 1586, taking his BA degree then.

Robert Greene was a very different kettle of fish. He would defame both Marlowe and Shakespeare later in lines delivered when he was already dying. A woodcut shows him scratching away with his pen, sitting already wrapped in his woollen shroud, a bitter and resentful man. Like Nashe, he was a scholar at St John's, returning there in 1580 after a dissolute life in Europe. 'I light among wags as lewd as myself, with whom I consumed the flower of my youth.'[9] Probably a manic depressive, he turned from a friend to become one of Marlowe's bitterest enemies. He was enormously proud of the MA degrees he took from both Oxford and Cambridge by 1584.

Another enemy was Dr Gabriel Harvey, the arrogant Fellow of Pembroke Hall who seemed to resent scholars generally. To his far more sensitive friend, the poet Edmund Spenser, he wrote in the year before Marlowe went up to Cambridge,

> You cannot step into a scholar's study but (ten to one) you shall
> likely find open either Bodin or Leroy's Exposition upon
> Aristotle's Politics or some other like French or Italian political

discourses. And I warrant you some good fellows amongst us begin now to be pretty well acquainted with a certain parlous book called, as I remember me, Il Principe di Nicolo Machiavelli and I can peradventure name you an odd crew or two that are as cunning in his Discorsi . . .

Harvey was a prig and no doubt Marlowe would have been one of the 'odd crew' he was referring to by the summer of 1581. Harvey and his brother Richard were well known in Cambridge and Thomas Nashe later remembered Marlowe's complaint about him – 'Kit Marloe was wont to say he was an ass, and fit to preach only of the Iron Age.'[10] Both Harveys enjoyed the cut and thrust of literary debate and were litigious. Gabriel would later try to sue Robert Greene for libel, but death caught the prose writer first. He had been tutor to Edmund Spenser at Pembroke Hall and basked in the poet's reflected glory for the rest of his life. He was a pedant and it was probably this that made him loathe Marlowe – 'all fire and air' as he was. The Harveys' background was as humble as Marlowe's; the sons of ropemakers from Saffron Walden, Gabriel's brothers, in strange quirks revolving around the fate of Kit Marlowe, went into tantalizing career areas. John became an astronomer and Richard rector of Chislehurst, Kent, where Marlowe was to spend the last days of his life.

It was at Cambridge that the scholar became the poet and the free thinker; the one passion leading to immortality, the other, paradoxically, to his death. William Urry provided, for the quatro-centenary exhibition of Marlowe's birth, a collection of books he might have read as part of his 'official' study. The New Testament of 1544, *The Apology* of J. Bale (1541) and his *Arts of the English Votaries* (1550), Tyndale's English Bible of 1551, and the Book of Common Prayer (1552). Although Urry does not list it, Fox's *Book of Martyrs*, the second most popular book after the Bible in the country, was also likely to have been on the scholar's reading list.

He also read Aristotle and Ramus,[11] very much in vogue among serious scholars in the Cambridge of the 1580s, but what marked him out as a rebel (who probably became something of a legend among other undergraduates) were his translations of Ovid and Lucan.[12] The particular poems he worked on, and which fascinated

him, were Ovid's *Amores* (Elegies) and Lucan's *Pharsalia*. One spoke
of love, the other of war – titanic themes which were to mark
Marlowe's early plays that took London by storm in the years
ahead.

In Ovid's *Elegy V* of the *Amores*, Marlowe translated (not always
very accurately) the seduction of Corinna:

> Stark naked as she stood before mine eye,
> Not one wen [mole] on her body could I spy.
> What arms and shoulders did I touch and see,
> How apt her breasts were to be press'd by me!
> How smooth a belly under her waist saw I!
> How large a leg and what a lusty thigh!
> To leave the rest, all like'd me passing well;
> I cling'd her naked body, down she fell;
> Judge you the rest; being tir'd she bade me kiss;
> Jove send me more such afternoons as this.'

How much of this is Marlowe and how much Ovid is impossible to
say. His 'judge you the rest' is the sixteenth-century equivalent of the
row of coy dots that Victorian writers were forced to employ
to avoid offending the sensibilities of their readers. But the humour
of the last line gives the lie to those literary critics who can find
no humour in Marlowe's writing at all. We have to remember,
however, that Elizabethan attitudes are different from our own. 'The
past,' wrote L.P. Hartley in *The Go-Between*, 'is a foreign country.
They do things differently there.' Marlowe was nineteen or twenty
when he worked on the *Amores*, but he was working secretly by
candlelight in a college which was exclusively male and which fitted
young men for a career in the Church. It had only been a generation
since that Church allowed its priests to marry for the first time and
thus implicitly sanctioned the heterosexual relationship among its
scions that that implied. Tame stuff as it seems today, the *Amores*
would have been regarded as soft porn at best – it is highly likely
that Marlowe's translations were passed around the student
population in Cambridge, with knowing winks and sniggers.

Certainly, after Marlowe's death the *Amores* were publicly burned
on the instructions of both the Archbishop of Canterbury, the

sanctimonious John Whitgift, and the Bishop of London. It would be 250 years before the German poet Heinrich Heine said, 'wherever books are burned, men also, in the end, are burned'. The Tudors were quite happy to do both. The illicit nature of the *Amores* meant that publication was difficult. After June 1566 censorship was virulent in England. It was in that month that the Stationers' Company obtained a monopoly of publishing for Elizabeth. The Stationers were both publishers and printers, their name deriving from the stalls or stations set up in cathedral precincts from which they sold their wares. St Paul's in London quickly became an unofficial headquarters and book titles, like plays, had to be registered there in advance of publication. This was a sensible attempt to control copyright and plagiarism, but a more pernicious angle was that the Bishop of London ruled (often quite arbitrarily) on a book's legality. Anything deemed unsuitable (clearly the *Amores*) was burned in the kitchens of Stationers' Hall.

The answer, rather like pornographic videos today, was to manufacture elsewhere and smuggle the finished article back into the country. The title page of one edition – *All Ovid's Elegies* – is cryptically inscribed 'By C.M., Epigrams by F.D.' and was printed at Middlebourgh, the prosperous cloth centre in Walcheren, 4 miles from Vlissingen (Flushing), a place which was to feature prominently in Marlowe's life. Apart from the obvious first glimpse of Marlowe's genius as a poet, his work on the *Amores* tells us something else; it gives us a fleeting picture of the young man behind the flimsy facts we have here. Had Marlowe been caught in possession of Ovid, still less producing English translations, he would have been flogged and sent down. Like his later heroes Tamburlaine, Faustus and Edward II, Marlowe is a tragic hero in the Shakespearean sense – a man of greatness whose own weakness will one day bring him down. There are signs of this already in the Matthew Parker scholar at Bene't's College.

The work on Lucan was less contentious, as is evidenced by its production in London in 1600 – 'Lucan's First Booke, translated line for line by Chr. Marlow at London, printed by P. Short and are to be sold by Walter Burre at the Signe of the Flower de Luce in Paul's Churchyard.' Not even the Bishop of London could quarrel with the recounting of a Roman civil war between the colossi Pompey and

Julius Caesar. The lines, however, were lifted time and time again by William Shakespeare in the years ahead:

> Strange sights appear'd, the angry threat'ning gods
> Filled both the earth and seas with prodigies;
> Great store of strange and unknown stars were seen
> Wandering about the North, and rings of fire
> Fly in the air, and dreadful bearded stars,
> And comets that presage the fall of kingdoms.

There can be little doubt that Marlowe began his writing while still at Cambridge and that classical influences like Ovid had much to do with that. But darker works played on his mind and the reading of them and the living of them, as if he were an actor playing out a part and increasingly obsessed by it, were to bring Kit Marlowe to Deptford in the May of 1593. First came Machiavelli's *The Prince* and *Discourses* which Gabriel Harvey found so offensive among the secret books of certain students.

There was no English edition of any of the man's works, but clearly Marlowe read them in the original Italian/Latin and they became the inspiration for the play *The Jew of Malta*. It has even been claimed that Marlowe was nicknamed 'Machiavel' by his contemporaries. Today, based essentially as it is on the realpolitik of the early sixteenth century and especially on the ruthless statecraft of Cesare Borgia, *The Prince* seems no more than a realistic manual for rulers of the time. Moralists in vast numbers and clergy in particular (beginning with Cardinal Reginald Pole in England) denounced Machiavelli not only as a cynic but as the very incarnation of evil. He was quite simply the Devil himself and the epithet 'Old Nick'[13] was applied to him and anyone who read him.

Another influence was even more pernicious. The Dominican friar Giordano Bruno championed Copernicus, with his heretical views of the Heavens. Drummed out of his order for his unorthodoxy, Bruno travelled widely, arguably abandoning Christianity itself in 1576. He was in England between 1583 and 1585, while Marlowe was still in Cambridge, and was excommunicated by German Lutherans in 1587. He left in his wake in England a variety of tracts – *The Expulsion of the Triumphant Beast* (*Spaccio della Bestia*

Trionfante); *The Heroic Frenzies* (*De Gli Eroici Fuori*) and *The Ash Wednesday Supper* (*Cena de le Ceneri*). Most Englishmen were contemptuous of 'that Italian didapper with a name longer than his body'[14] but his influence on Marlowe and on Marlowe's plays was immense. Since Bruno lectured at Oxford in 1583 and London the following year, it is conceivable that Marlowe heard him speak and may even have talked to him. Such men were considered mad, bad and dangerous to know.

The hothouse climate of Cambridge in Marlowe's day encouraged increasing freedom of thought and the out of joint times created their own anxieties. The feast of Corpus Christi had been one of the great highlights of the Cambridge year, with its obvious overlay of mystic tradition.

In the microcosmic world of Bene't's and its feast the tragedy of the Reformation was played out on a small scale. The Protestant Commissioners of Edward VI abolished the feast in 1549; it was reintroduced in 1553 under Mary and abolished for ever under Elizabeth. Only the violent demonstrations by the people of the town forced the college authorities to revive it, but it was now a Name Day Feast and the deep, joyful religious significance was lost.

The impact of Martin Luther's apparently suicidal stand against the corruption of the Catholic Church was quickly felt in Cambridge as it was elsewhere in decaying Christendom. The Master of Bene't's, Dr Nobys, remained a staunch Catholic, spending three years on a pilgrimage to Rome which had the blessing of the Bishop of Ely. His retirement in 1523 led to a relaxation of the old religion and something of an opening of the floodgates. Fervent Protestantism was beginning to replace fervent Catholicism and the mood was changing. William Sowode, Master in 1523–4 'a great favourer and fatherer of the truth in the dark days of King Henry VIII', was followed by Edward Fowke, a keen 'Gospeller', and Richard Taverner, who translated the Bible into English in 1539. More ominously, and a reminder of the obsessions and bigotry of the times, Thomas Dusgate was burnt for his faith in Exeter in 1531 and George Wishart at St Andrews in 1545. To claim that Bene't's was a centre of heresy would be to overstate the case, but the shock waves of the Reformation made the college and the university an exciting, even dangerous place to be in Marlowe's day.

Matthew Parker, for all his toleration and his valiant attempts to bury the religious hatchet when Archbishop of Canterbury, was nevertheless a staunch Protestant. His two successors, Lawrence Moptyd (1553–7) and Dr Porie (1557–69) were probably just as staunch, but they were also shrewd politicians and flexible enough to allow the jettisoning of the two Fellows who refused to sign 'Popish Articles' in Mary's reign. Under Porie matters seem to have worsened. A bitter hostility arose between moderate Anglicans, rabid Puritans and even a few covert Catholics. One of these was the President of the College, who fled to Douai to escape the flak.

Porie's successor as Master was the bigoted Thomas Aldrich, a radical Puritan who denounced the assailed Archbishop of Canterbury, his former patron Matthew Parker, as 'Pope of Lambeth and Benet College'. Aldrich jumped before he was pushed by the college authorities, and was replaced by the relatively benign Dr Norgate, Master in Marlowe's time.

If the Masters of colleges fought each other and their Fellows over doctrine and the whole claptrap of Indulgences, surplices and the allegiance (or lack of it) owed to the Bishop of Rome, the students were worse. To add to the normal loutish behaviour of the older scholars (and Marlowe probably belonged to this group, although there is no record of any punishment against him) in firing crossbows, guns and stonebows in the streets, excessive drinking and 'taking tobacco' in the taverns, they kept horses and greyhounds, hunted and coursed. And was it merely student high jinks when a group of scholars followed the Queen after her visit in 1564 as far as Hinchinbrooke, parodying the mass with a dog with the Eucharist wafer in its mouth and a 'Bishop' carrying and eating a lamb as he walked? Elizabeth was furious at the scorn with which religion was treated.

Did Kit Marlowe already show a similar contempt?

What of the three men with Marlowe when he died? Of Ingram Frizer, the rest is still silence. We have no record of him until four years after Marlowe obtained his BA degree, when he was living in Basingstoke, buying and selling property.

The increasingly shifty Nicholas Skeres is known to have been living in Furnival's Inn along High Holborn in the early 1580s.

Furnival's was one of the Inns of Chancery. There was no university in London, but the growth of humanist education earlier in the sixteenth century had elevated the status of the non-classical professions, and this included the law. The Inns of Chancery were considered inferior to those of Court – Lincoln's Inn, Gray's, the Inner and Middle Temples and Elizabeth's reign saw their heyday. Each Inn housed up to a thousand students, described by the contemporary chronicler John Stow in 1598 as 'a whole university . . . of students, practisers and pleaders, and judges of the laws of this realm'.[15] The law was seen in those days as a good training for a life of public service in any capacity and the Tudor age was a litigious one (witness John Marlowe's readiness to go to court to defend his rights in Canterbury). Yet its 'practisers' were often shady men, who knew how to use the law and bend it for their own ends.

In January 1582, records show that Nicholas Skeres was involved with the poet, Matthew Roydon, a legal student from Thavies' Inn up the road in Holborn. Roydon signed a bond to a local goldsmith for £40 and Skeres and his brother Jerome were co-signatories. In the year of Marlowe's death, Skeres appeared before the Court of Star Chamber on charges of money lending, and this was clearly a life-long habit of his. Another of Skeres's contacts in the early 1580s was George Chapman, the university wit (from Oxford) born near Hitchin, Hertfordshire. Both Roydon and Chapman were to become close friends of Marlowe when the free-thinking scholar came to London. Skeres was part of the web already.

We first heard of Robert Poley as a sizar of Clare College, Cambridge in 1568, but by the early 1580s he had moved south to London and was considerably richer. The source of his new-found wealth is unknown, but it is likely that it was the same as Marlowe's after 1585. He spent £40 refurbishing his lodgings and owned a chest of £110 of 'good gold'.[16] He married, probably in 1582 'one Watson's daughter' and the ceremony, carried out in a tailor's house in Bow Lane, indicates that he was a Catholic. A daughter was born to the pair in August 1583 and she was christened Anne at St Helen's Church, Bishopsgate. Poley's situation is typical of Catholics in Elizabeth's England. Increasingly a minority, they could not practise their faith openly – hence the clandestine marriage, not in a church, but in the house of a seditious tailor named Wood, who was engaged in the dissemination of illegal, underground tracts imported from the Continent.

By 1583, Poley was a 'close prisoner' in the Marshalsea. The prison south of the Thames in overcrowded Southwark ranked second only to the Tower as a place with a vicious reputation, and for that reason was twice attacked in the notorious risings of the later Middle Ages – Wat Tyler's in 1381 and Jack Cade's in 1450. There had been a riot and mass escape as recently as 1504 and the jerry-built premises were difficult to make secure. We do not know precisely why Poley was imprisoned here, but it may be that it was linked to the religious terrors of the time and the fact that he was committed by Elizabeth's great spymaster, Francis Walsingham.

By the mid-sixteenth century, the Marshalsea was increasingly used as a debtor's prison, but it had other connotations too. It was here that anyone guilty of royal contempt was placed, the Earl Marshal after whom the prison was named being a great officer in the ceremonial of the Court. It was also linked with religious prisoners. The deepest dungeon was known as 'Bonner's Coal Hole' after the last Catholic Bishop of London, Edmund Bonner, who had himself narrowly escaped a dunking in molten lead from the Pope when he had tried to arrange Henry VIII's divorce after Thomas Wolsey's failure to do so.[17] Bonner fell foul of Elizabeth in May 1559 when he refused to take the oath of supremacy. He died in his own 'Coal Hole' ten years later.

In 1585 Robert Poley wrote a letter to Robert Dudley, Earl of Leicester and formerly the Queen's favourite, referring to 'three years past determination to do her Majesty and the State some special service'.[18] It is possible that Walsingham, whose job it was to secure that State against any likely attack, put Poley in prison as a plant. His Catholicism would make him useful as an informer prior to his release on 10 May 1584. While in prison, Poley took up with Joan Yeomans, the wife of a London cutler,[19] who may have been some sort of accomplice in the informing business. Poley bought his way out of trouble with Joan's husband by presenting him with a silver bowl of double gilt.

In the summer before Kit Marlowe went up to Cambridge, the Pope launched a crusade against England. It came in the form of two

Jesuit priests, Edmund Campion and Robert Parsons.[20] Educated at Christ's Hospital and St John's College, Oxford, Campion was forty in the summer of 1580 and despite being ordained an Anglican deacon eleven years earlier, went to Dublin to re-establish a university there. In his heart he probably never abandoned Catholicism and fled, under mounting scrutiny from the authorities, to the English College at Douai. He was in Bohemia when he became a member of the Society of Jesus in 1573. He was still Professor of Rhetoric at the university of Prague when the summons came through from Gregory XIII and he sailed for England. His saintliness and popularity kept him one step ahead of trouble throughout that summer and there were, no doubt, Catholic families prepared to hide him from Elizabeth's inquisitorial officers.

Parsons hailed from Nether Stowey in Somerset and was six years Campion's junior. A Fellow of Balliol College, Oxford, he fell foul of the increasingly Puritan elements in the university and was forced to retire in 1574. His actual conversion to Catholicism followed and he joined the Jesuits in 1575, taking holy orders three years later. His organizational skills were phenomenal and it was he rather than the other-worldly Campion who played Hell with the government's attempts to catch the pair.

Arriving in disguise at Dover, the two spilt up, each of them originally backed by a small team. Campion rode through Berkshire and Oxfordshire, then turned north to Lancashire and Yorkshire, soon the most wanted man in England with a price on his head. Parsons reached the Midlands before swinging west to Worcester and Gloucester. Both men celebrated mass and communion behind locked doors at dead of night. Their followers were a persecuted minority and they were forced to adopt the behaviour of conspirators. A Justice of the Peace from Lancashire wrote 'this brood [Jesuit missionaries] will never be rooted out; it is impossible . . . to extirpate the papistical faith out of the land.'[21]

Even so, Elizabeth's spies were everywhere and of the thirteen missionaries, only the ever-resourceful Parsons escaped to the Continent. Campion, always touchingly naïve, could see no link between the attempted restoration of the old faith and aggressive European politics – 'We are dead men to the world; we travelled only for souls; we touched neither state nor policy: we had no such commission.'

They caught Campion in the July of 1581 and he was racked three times before they hanged him. He gave nothing away and impressed the Privy Council with his learning and gentleness. Because his joints were dislocated, his trial had had to be postponed. When it took place, at Westminster Hall, he was too weak to raise his hand to plead and two companions had to do it for him. The Council said 'it was a pity he was a Papist'.[22]

The effects of the Jesuit mission on England were twofold. First, there was an upsurge of Catholicism throughout the 1580s which is difficult, because of the enforced secrecy of Catholics, to measure. This was exacerbated by the politics of the decade which saw the execution of Mary, Queen of Scots and the unleashing of two Armadas by Spain. Second, the government's hysterical response to Campion's and Parson's campaign saw harsh laws imposed. Recusants (who refused to attend Anglican services) had previously paid a fine of one shilling for every Sunday missed; now it was a massive £20 a month. Saying the words of the Catholic mass cost 200 marks[23] and a year in jail. Persistent offenders lost two thirds of their property. Uttering slander against the Queen – 'that guilty woman of England' as the Pope's secretary called her – cost a man £200, the humiliation of the pillory and the loss of both his ears. For a second offence he was hanged. In July 1583 three men were hanged at Bury St Edmunds for writing grafitti on the royal arms in the local church implying that Elizabeth was a Jezebel (prostitute). Anyone publishing a seditious book or even speculating on who would succeed the Queen was likely to be executed. Anyone converting another to Catholicism would die, along with their acolytes.

It is clear from this legislation that the government believed that Catholicism and treachery went hand in hand. To follow Rome was to be a traitor, and treason was a capital crime. Historians today remark on the lack of persecution – just over two hundred executions for religious reasons during Elizabeth's reign. But that was not how Catholics saw it, and papal propaganda portrayed England as Hell on earth. J.B. Black gets the balance right and paints a picture of the sixteenth century all too familiar to historians and observers of the twentieth: 'Juries were biased, judges were convinced that every priest was a traitor and convictions were often obtained on evidence supplied by men of worthless character – renegades, spies and informers – who throve on their nefarious trade.'[24]

In 1583 Philip Stubbes underscored the rabidity of the age in *The Anatomie of Abuses*. It was a second edition, proving the popularity of his views, and in it he denounced football as a 'bloody and murdering practice rather than a fellowly sport'. He blamed it for an increase in 'malice, rancour, hatred and envy'. Bowling alleys, to which even national heroes like Francis Drake were addicted, were a waste of 'wit, time and money'. The phallic symbol of the Maypole, still in Marlowe's day to be found on village greens the length and breadth of the country, was 'a stinking idol' that led to 'whoredom and uncleanness'.

In the winter of the year in which Christopher Marlowe obtained his degree, there was another plot against the Queen. Francis Throckmorton was the nephew of one of Elizabeth's most distinguished ambassadors who had sided with the French Huguenots in their stand against the virulent Catholicism of Catherine de' Medici. 'Infamous pamphlets' were found in his London home and he was tortured on the rack twice. At last he cracked and admitted that he was agent for the still-imprisoned Queen of Scots. 'Now,' he said, 'I have disclosed the secrets of her who was the dearest thing to me in the world.'[25] Throckmorton told the authorities that four invasions had been planned, under the auspices of the Spanish ambassador, Bernardino de Mendoza. The idea was to whip English and Scots Catholics to fever pitch, rescue Mary and place her on the throne. Mendoza left England in disgrace and Throckmorton was hanged at Tyburn, then still a weathered oak on open heathland where Marble Arch now stands.

This was the world, of bigotry, hysteria and paranoia into which Kit Marlowe was about to make his debut.

Christopher Marlowe obtained his Bachelor of Arts degree on Palm Sunday 1584.

Christopher Marlin petitions that the twelve completed terms in which he has followed the ordinary lectures (even if not wholly according to the forms of the statute) together with all the opponencies, responsions and other exercises required by royal statute, may suffice for him to take the examination.[26]

The university Grace Book, which still survives, lists him as 'Dominus Marlyn', second in a body of twelve from Corpus Christi and 199th out of a total of 231. To qualify, Marlowe must have spent four years at Bene't's, continuous residence being essential.

The preliminary stage of what today would be a purely written examination was an oral disputation – 'responsio' – in the public schools against three students from other colleges. These debates took place in Latin and Marlowe had effectively to see off his opponents' arguments in front of a 'Moderator' who was already a Master of Arts. There is a certain grim poetic prescience in all this – Marlowe defending himself against three 'enemies', exactly as he would try to do at Eleanor Bull's house in Deptford nine years later.

Marlowe's written papers would have been taken in three days of the week before Ash Wednesday and he then proceeded to the oral questioning from Aristotle's *Prior Analytics* and similar vivas over a two day period.

Oddly, Corpus Christi's Buttery books have the letter D (Dominus) written alongside Marlowe's name the previous year. Perhaps his age (he was twenty by now) and his haughty manner caused this error. And it may be that the swagger and confidence emanated from someone else whom Marlowe had met – the spymaster, Francis Walsingham.

FOUR

Good Service . . . & . . . Faithfull Dealinge

. . . in all his accions he had behaved him selfe orderlie and discreetlie whereby he had done her Majesty good service . . .
Privy Council minutes, 29 June 1587

Ian Fleming has a great deal to answer for. Mention the word 'spy' today and the image that leaps to mind is of the anti-hero James Bond; cool, suave, shaken but never stirred. John le Carré, a far more realistic writer, has introduced us to George Smiley, a quiet, rather average-looking gentleman. Le Carré's spy stories were born of the same Cold War paranoia that inspired Fleming, but they spawned grubby men in raincoats coming in from the cold.

Recently, Tudor historians like David Starkey and literary experts like Curtis Breight have drawn strongly on the analogy of the post-1945 Cold War to explain the *raison d'être* of the Elizabethan government's methods. Allowing for the obvious changes in technology, the basics of surveillance, intelligence gathering, assassination, even recruitment are astonishingly similar and if the analogy makes sense to readers floundering in the alien world of Elizabethan England, then so be it.

Historians have moved away recently from the notion that Elizabeth's state was weak, with no police force other than the creaking Constables of the Watch provided by towns and no army other than a decorative force of Yeoman Warders. Even so, the traditional means of raising men, the feudal levies, had largely collapsed by the late sixteenth century. When, in desperation, Charles I needed troops in 1642 to bring his rebellious parliament to heel, he had to rely on the ancient Commissions of Array and technically was not that successful.

In the face of aggressive European politics, the English State was vulnerable. In the first decade of her reign Elizabeth had been pronounced illegitimate by the Pope, who virtually declared open season on the 'English Jezebel'. We have seen already that the plots against Elizabeth and the extremity of religious views, Catholic and Puritan, were real and dangerous. There was a need for the Queen and the stability of the realm to be protected and whereas this was the task of Secretary of State Cecil and the Queen's Privy Council, increasingly from the 1570s that work devolved into the hands of one man, Francis Walsingham.

Garrett Mattingly, the American scholar who so impressed European historians in the 1960s, is disparaging of Walsingham's secret service. In *The Defeat of the Spanish Armada* he wrote:

> . . . Sir Francis Walsingham built up for [the Queen's] protection what some historians have described as 'an omnipresent network of spies'; this impressive system of counter-espionage in England dwindles on inspection to a few underpaid agents of varying ability whose effects were supplemented by casual informers and correlated by a single clerk who also handled much of Walsingham's ordinary correspondence – a system hardly larger or more efficient, except for the intelligence of its direction and the zeal of its volunteer aids, than that which every first-rate ambassador was expected to maintain for his own information, one which the governments of Florence or Venice would have smiled at as inadequate for the police of a single city.[1]

Mattingly is wrong. His caveats say it all. Even he cannot but be impressed by the cold cunning and ruthlessness of Walsingham himself; neither can he hide the fact that a crusading cause (be it against Catholicism or Spain) produced men who got results.

Mr Secretary Walsingham was born about 1530, at Chislehurst in Kent, and was educated at King's College, Cambridge. In terms of geography, at least, his background is similar to Marlowe's. He was a student at Gray's Inn in 1552 and travelled extensively on the Continent during Mary's reign, perhaps because his austere Protestantism jarred with the ethos of enforced Catholicism. It was here that he acquired a flair for languages which would make him indispensable to the Queen's government and he returned home to

England on the accession of Elizabeth, six years before Marlowe was born.

Ambitious and zealous to serve, Walsingham's way to the top was via William Cecil, appointed Secretary of State in the year of the accession. The Cecils were Northamptonshire gentry who had been elevated by Henry VIII. By 1552, William had inherited his father's estates and was already an experienced politician, having served as *Custos Brevia* in the last year of Henry's reign, Master of Requests under Edward VI and Secretary to Protector Somerset by 1548.[2] He was Secretary of State by 1550 and knighted the following year. Cecil's unquestioning loyalty to Elizabeth (like Walsingham's) is what has remained as our image of him, but under Mary, Cecil openly espoused her Catholicism while corresponding with the Protestant Princess Elizabeth. He had also put his name to a document that nominated Lady Jane Grey as Edward's successor; yet despite this duplicity he was able to win the confidence of both 'Bloody' Mary and her sister. Above all what remains as Cecil's legacy, is what counts most in a great statesman – his ability to survive.

In hitching his wagon to this particular star, Walsingham made a shrewd decision and made himself indispensable to both Cecil and the Queen in the part he played in exposing the Ridolfi Plot. Roberto di Ridolfi was a Florentine adventurer who settled in London and schemed with the Catholic Thomas Howard, Duke of Norfolk, to place Mary, Queen of Scots on the English throne. Walsingham's methods were Machiavellian in the extreme. He encouraged his agents to befriend the plotters, stringing them along, giving them hope – and just enough rope to hang themselves. The enigmatic Robert Cecil, son of Sir William and a man central to Marlowe's death, would use exactly the same methods in monitoring and exposing Robert Catesby's Gunpowder Plot in 1605.

By 1572, Walsingham was English ambassador in Paris, conducting the on-off 'courtship' of the Queen and 'Monsieur', the Duke of Anjou. While there he witnessed the massacre of St Bartholomew's Eve, which coloured his life for ever. Kit Marlowe was still at one of the schools in Canterbury when Parisian bigotry, fanned by the Duc de Guise, spilled over into appalling violence in the streets of the French capital.[3] Accounts of the incident vary, but the gist is that hundreds of Huguenots had gathered in the city on 19 August to cheer the wedding of the Protestant Henri of Navarre to Margaret de' Medici, daughter of France's redoubtable Regent. Some of the atrocities carried out by rabid Catholics under her orders were reported by Juan de Olaegui, secretary to the Spanish ambassador:

> On Sunday, Saint Bartholomew's Day [24 August] at three o'clock in the morning, the alarm was rung; all the Parisians began killing the Huguenots of the town, breaking down the doors of the houses in which they lived and pillaging what they found within.
>
> [The Duc de] Guise, Anevale and Angoulême went to the Admiral's house . . . they went up to his room and in the bed where he was lying, the Duc de Guise shot him in the head with a pistol; then they took him and threw him naked out of the window into the courtyard . . .
>
> The massacre lasted until the morning of Thursday 25th August . . .[4]

Perhaps as many as 40,000 Protestants died in those bloody forty-eight hours and Walsingham, in an age before ambassadorial privilege, must have feared for his life. It gave him a lasting contempt for Catholics.

In 1573 Walsingham returned to England to be made Secretary of State, a prominent member of the Privy Council and a force in the corridors of power. The portrait of Walsingham painted some twelve years later (the year in which he almost certainly employed Christopher Marlowe) by Johann de Critz the Elder, shows a careful, determined man whose eyes are as blank as he wants them to be. He wears a simple skull cap of black and the only signs of vanity are his magnificent lace ruff and the medallion with the Queen's portrait dangling on his doublet. The chronicler William Camden called him 'the most subtle searcher of hidden secrets' and Elizabeth, mindful of his earlier swarthiness missing in the greying portrait of 1585, referred to him as her 'Moor'. He was of the pro-war party, in marked contrast to Cecil, who urged caution. Catholic Spain was the enemy and this became more obvious as the 1570s unfolded. Walsingham's daughter Frances was married to Sir Philip Sidney, the courtier poet and soldier who was the nephew of

Elizabeth's favourite, Leicester. Men like Walsingham were used to death and however honourable and patriotic their motives, they played the Machiavellian game of realpolitik to the hilt.

What kind of secret service did the spymaster operate? Not for nothing is he referred to as its father. He largely financed it himself and worried about lack of money for the rest of his life, dying in debt in 1590. Typical of the parsimonious Elizabeth, she expected total loyalty and unremitting hard work from all her subjects, but was rarely willing to pay for it. Such payments as she did make are discreetly chronicled under vague Privy Seal amounts for unspecified purposes; in 1582 it was £750; three years later, when Marlowe was recruited, it was nearly £2,000. Over and above that Walsingham was expected to dig into his own purse.

It was a less sophisticated world. News and intelligence gathering was slow, clumsy and unreliable. It was reported, sometimes in cryptic cypher, by men who were merely observers of affairs in key places. In Calais, the last gasp of the English occupation of France, the agent was Thomas Jeffries. In Venice, whose espionage network so impressed Garrett Mattingly, it was Stephen Paule. The extent of these observers was considerable. Thirteen towns in Catholic France had them. There were seven in the Low Countries, watching the desperate struggle of the Dutch against their Spanish overlords; five English agents operated out of Spain, although their position became less tenable as the 1580s wore on and Philip's patience with his former sister-in-law ran out. Nine lived in German towns where Catholic and Protestant eyed each other across the great divide that Martin Luther had created. There were five in Italy, the country regarded by English intellectuals as the cradle of civilization in Marlowe's day, three in the United Provinces which would emerge as Holland in the next century and even three in the distant, but powerful, Ottoman Empire. The work of these men was vital, passing information to travellers on the high seas and the roads of Europe, but they were in no sense covert. It is highly likely that sometimes they were fed information by the governments in whose countries they operated.

Working as Walsingham's shadow in the troubled decade in which Marlowe obtained his Cambridge degree was Thomas Phelippes, described by Mary, Queen of Scots, whose downfall he engineered, as 'a man of low stature, slender every way, dark, yellow-haired on the head, clear yellow-bearded, erred in the face with small pocks'.[5] Like Walsingham, he spent time in Paris, probably around 1580, where he seems to have been trailing Thomas Morgan, the exiled Welshman who was working there on behalf of the Queen of Scots. Morgan was shrewd enough to know that Phelippes, like most men of his or any other age, had his price. In October 1585 he wrote, '. . . try him long and in small matters before you use him, being a severe Huguenot [Protestant] and all for that state, yet glorious and greedy of honour and profit . . .'.

Phelippes' real strength, however, lay as Walsingham's code-breaker and in this context he was aided by Arthur Gregory who had a knack for 'forcing the seal of a letter, yet so invisibly that it still appeareth a virgin to the exactest beholder'. Twenty years before Francis Bacon's famous five element code based on aaaaa, aaaab, etc., agents were sending encrypted letters to each other, reporting the size and whereabouts of armies and navies and in particular, in England, the machinations of the Queen of Scots and those around her. The 'Bible' of 'secret writing' was *De Furtivus Literarum Notis* by Giovanni della Porta. Agents used invisible inks made from milk, urine, onion and lemon juice and if all this seems amateurish and rather juvenile today, it was simply the state of technology that precluded anything more sophisticated. The magus John Dee dabbled in cyphers, mostly to keep his demonic magic books a secret from the uninitiated. Elizabethan cyphers were largely of two types – transposition, with letters shuffled to make anagrams; or substitution, where numbers replaced letters entirely. In some cases, classical or astrological names were substituted for key players. Alan Haynes[6] cites a code in use in 1590 in which the Duke of Parma was Aries, Prince Maurice of Nassau, Gemini, and so on. Earlier in the 1580s, a numerical substitution passed between Robert Bowes, ambassador in Scotland, and Walsingham. In this, Scotland was 70; James VI, 91; Elizabeth 32; Mary Queen of Scots, 23. In keeping with the nature of espionage, new systems had continually to be found as old ones were cracked.

Below Phelippes were more shadowy men, whose roles are uncertain. William Waad and Robert Beale were Clerks of the (Privy) Council, but their jobs were far more important than mere secretaries. Waad, whom Walter Ralegh described when the former was Lieutenant of the Tower of London as 'that beast', grabbed incriminating papers that led directly to the execution of Mary, Queen of Scots and was directed to bring Morgan back from France in March 1585. Historian Alan Haynes believes it was specifically Waad who recruited Marlowe. Beale, out of Walsingham's service by 1592 but still bound to him as his brother-in-law, left advice on shaky agents – 'Take heed they deal not double with you, and abuse you with toys and matters of their own invention. And for dealing with such as the laws of the realm esteemeth traitors . . . beware.' Beale too had worked with Walsingham in Paris and appears to have handled easier cyphers which Phelippes may have considered beneath him. Francis Milles emerges as a key figure in the exposure of the Babington Plot in 1586. We know virtually nothing about him and in that sense he is far more modern (and successful) a spymaster than most of his contemporaries. Nicholas Faunt was altogether more relevant to Marlowe in that he was a Corpus Christi man. Described by Walsingham as 'very honest and discrete', he was already working for him by the time Marlowe went up to Cambridge. In later years Faunt wrote a treatise on the post of Chief Secretary and seems to have been more Cecil's man than Walsingham's, Faunt having reservations about the increasing size of the spymaster's bureaucracy. Like most of Walsingham's key men, Faunt had served his apprenticeship in Paris where he had met Anthony Bacon among the ambassador's entourage. The men remained friends for years, despite Faunt moving on on the Queen's business to Germany and then Padua. He was back in England, on Walsingham's orders, by 1584.

Beneath these men were spies on two levels. First, in terms of their value to the State and the payment they commanded, were the Projectors, *agents provocateurs* whose job it was to infiltrate conspiracies, pose as rabid Catholics or Puritans and manufacture plots out of thin air. William Cecil's son Robert, who succeeded him as Chief Secretary, used the same tactic against the gunpowder plotters in 1605. These men, it is true, have a swagger about them that lends some credence to the spy fiction literature of our own time; one example must suffice.

Anthony Standen was a Catholic from Surrey.[7] His family were recusants, risking the increasing paranoia of the Tudor State by taking a stand against the new religion. He had served the Queen of Scots before the murder of Lord Darnley in 1567 when he thought it safer to stay in France where he had been sent on a mission to King Charles IX. A will-o'-the-wisp to rank with the great agents in history, he maintained regular contact with the imprisoned Mary while shifting his allegiance to Walsingham. Working from Florence, ostensibly on her behalf in 1582–5, he was providing the spymaster with intelligence that Walsingham was quite prepared to use, despite the fact that he never fully trusted him.

Standen's speciality was buying diplomats like Giovanni Figliazzi, Florentine ambassador to the Spanish Court. Another conquest was the brother of a servant of the Marquis of Santa Cruz, Spain's Grand Admiral. These contacts cost Walsingham a staggering 300 crowns, a trifling sum as it turned out when the servant passed details of the Armada to Standen, giving England vital time to prepare. By 1588, again in Florence, he received a pardon from the Queen for his former Catholicism and a pension of £100 a year. Changing masters was Standen's métier too, but perhaps he was not so wise when he opted for the Earl of Essex in the 1590s.

Below the Projectors who made things happen were several layers of Intelligencers, the men who provided the raw material on which Walsingham and Phelippes could work. There were various levels of these – Edmund Yorke smuggled information out of France in a blood-stone which, when softened with water, yielded up its secrets; Nicholas Berden traded information for the release of Catholics; Robert Poley we have met already.

It is difficult to categorize the sort of men who became involved in espionage. Nicholas Berden wrote, two years after Marlowe obtained his degree, 'Though I am a spy, which is a profession odious though necessary, I prosecute the same not for gain, but for the safety of my native country.' It was taken for granted by true-blue Englishmen, Anglicans to a man, that no one in the service of the Queen could be anything other than a patriot. But Berden was a hypocrite at best. He made large profits from his dealings and even the tiniest scrap of information came with a price tag. Typically, the Elizabethan agent was of middle to low status, perhaps a gentleman, but more likely a man without means desperate to acquire some.

The lower ranks of Intelligencer would fit this bill. They were servants listening at keyholes, wandering around houses after dark. The Jesuit mission of 1580 that led to Edmund Campion's death must have been monitored in this way; so was every detail of the plot by Guido Fawkes to eviscerate James I and his government with gunpowder. Beyond this broad, all-embracing term 'servant', which has always covered a multitude of sins, the actual Elizabethan spy came in all shapes and sizes.

One of those shapes and one of those sizes was that of Christopher Marlowe.

On 19 June 1587, a letter was sent by Elizabeth's Privy Council to the University of Cambridge:

> Whereas it was reported that Christopher Morley was determined to have gone beyond the seas to Reames and there to remaine, Their lordships thought good to vertefie that he had no such intent, but that in all his accions he had behaved his selfe orderlie and discreetly wherebie he had done her Majestie good service & deserved to be rewarded for his faithfull dealinge: Their lordships request was that the rumor thereof should be allaied by all possible meanes, and that he should be furthered in the degree he was to take this next Commencement: Because it was not her majesties pleasure that anie one emploied as he had been in matters touching the benefit of his Countrie should be defamed by those that are ignorant in th' offices he went about.

It was signed by the Lord Archbishop, John Whitgift (who had replaced the disgraced Grindal in 1583); the Lord Chancellor, Christopher Hatton; the Lord Treasurer, Lord Burghley (formerly Sir William Cecil); the Lord Chamberlain, Lord Hunsdon; and Mr Comptroller, Sir James Crofts. Two of these men would have a direct hand in Marlowe's death seven years later. Walsingham's name is notable by its absence, although he had by now replaced Cecil as the Queen's Principal Secretary.

As we have seen, continuous residence was a prerequisite for all Cambridge scholars attaining their degrees. No doubt the Bene't college authorities were still making the assumption that Marlowe intended a career in the Church. The fact is that if we study his movements between Easter 1584, when he obtained his first degree, and June 1587, when the Privy Council intervened on his behalf, Marlowe's absences are both prolonged and striking. Where was he?

In the three terms at Bene't's between 1580 and 1581, 'Marlin' received his allowance as a Parker scholar of twelve or thirteen shillings. In the four terms (the complete university year – and Marlowe's second) the same figures applied. In the third term of 1582–3 there is a drop to six shillings, indicating only six weeks' attendance out of a possible thirteen. In the first term of 1584–5, he only received three shillings; in the second seven, the third, four and in the fifth, five. Infuriatingly, the records are missing for 1585–6, but his last two terms in 1586–7 again show a shortfall – nine shillings for the first term, five shillings and sixpence for the second. Marlowe's first drop in attendance (1582–3) could be explained by illness, but the sums for the fifth year, 1584–5, after he had obtained his degree, clearly reflect a permanent change. If Marlowe was not in Cambridge, where *was* he? And if he was there, but merely did not bother to collect his shilling a week, why didn't he?

The only definite date we have to place Marlowe anywhere in the years between his Bachelor's and Master of Arts degrees is one Sunday in November 1585. That day he was at home in Canterbury,[8] or more specifically in the house of the widow Katherine Benchkyn in Stow Street. Marlowe's signature appears as a witness to Benchkyn's will, still preserved in the Canterbury archives, along with other witnesses including Jhan Marley (presumably the scholar's father), Thomas Arthur (his uncle) and John Moore (a shoemaker who married Marlowe's sister, Jane). The illiterate Katherine made her mark on the will and Marlowe's presence was vital, in that she needed someone like him to tell her what the will contained. The records show that he read it 'plainely and distinktly'.

For the rest, we have only the veiled references from the Privy Council, but they are enough. Oddly, Charles Nicholl has misread them. He says that a careful reading of the Privy Council's letter to Cambridge implies that it was merely rumour that Marlowe had 'gone beyond the sea to Reames', whereas in fact the emphasis is on the next phrase 'and there to remain'. The earlier part of the sentence 'was determined' either shows Marlowe's keenness to be of service or is merely Elizabethan speak for 'was ordered'. There is little doubt that he went to Rheims and perhaps elsewhere on Walsingham's business and that this explains at least sixteen months' absence from Cambridge in the period 1580 to 1587, excluding a year (1585–6) for which there are no records. What took the young Dominus Merlin 'beyond the seas'?

Rheims lies between the Rivers Aisne and Marne in the rich, wine-growing area of Champagne. Six kings of France were crowned there and as such, Rheims assumed huge political and symbolic importance, greater than that of Paris, as the centre of French royal power. But it was not the city, nor the superb architecture of the cathedral, that Marlowe had gone to see. He had gone to the English college.

The English Reformation from Henry VIII's time had seen a steady exodus of Catholics from the country. Just as Huguenots and Flemings crossed to the Protestant tolerance of England, so discontented Catholics made the opposite journey to France. The English college was founded at Douai, to the north-west of Rheims, by the exiled William Allen in 1568. Allen came of an old Catholic family in Rossall, Lancashire, and was educated at Oriel College, Oxford, before becoming principal at St Mary's Hall in the reign of Mary. He refused to take the oath of supremacy demanded by Elizabeth in 1561 and went to Flanders. Never strong, he was home the following year with a wasting sickness but was back in the Low Countries by 1565. Receiving holy orders in Mechlin, he set up Douai first as a refuge for other exiled English Catholics and then as a seminary for Jesuit missionary work. The mission was nothing less than the reconquest of England for the old religion.

The college took boys and young men aged between fourteen and twenty-five (which means that Marlowe met this criterion) and of respectable family (this was shakier, but his Cambridge degree would probably have sufficed). On joining, a scholar took the following oath – 'I swear to Almighty God that I am ready and shall always be ready to receive holy orders, in His own good time, and I shall return to England for the salvation of souls, whenever it shall seem good to the superior of this college to order me to do so.'[9]

J.B. Black paints a grim picture of this seminary, the walls of its monastic cells hung with pictures of torture and excruciating death.

Douai's acolytes were to be soldiers of Christ, fighting to the death to lift the taint of apostatism from their former land. The fact that the Privy Council makes mention of Rheims (the English college had moved there in 1578) bears witness to their paranoia. The trickle of zealous Catholics fleeing increasing Puritanism had become a flood by then and the government was anxious to stop it.

Allen himself professed to having no political axe to grind, but both Pope Pius V and Philip of Spain were patrons of the college and the exile went on to found similar seminaries in Rome in 1579 (with Owen Lewis) and Valladolid in Spain ten years later. By 1582, Allen's position had definitely acquired a political dimension and he worked with the Guise faction in France, the Pope and Mary, Queen of Scots against Elizabeth. Even before the launch of Campion's and Parsons' crusade by Gregory XIII, there were, by Walsingham's reckoning, at least a hundred seminary priests operating covertly in England.

Life in Rheims was as tough as it had been at Douai, with fasting for two days a week. The Jesuits Edmund Campion and Cuthbert Mayne emanated from here, as, more crucially in the story of Marlowe's death, did the poet Thomas Watson, with whom Marlowe was to share rooms in Norton Folgate. The English universities, despite their increasingly Puritan tendencies, proved a fertile breeding ground for students flocking to the seminary,[10] and Walsingham was already watching with interest from 1571. We know that he sent agents to Douai with the intention of disrupting their programmes, sowing discord and possibly even 'turning' the less ardent Catholics there. Alan Haynes lists Gilbert and William Giffard, Edward Grateley and Solomon Aldred among their number.

If Marlowe was with these men in the mid to late 1580s, it would explain the grasp of military knowledge he was to show later in his play *Tamburlaine*; one of the priests sent from Rheims was John Savage, who had fought for Spain in the Low Countries between 1581 and 1583. He left the English college in August 1585, by which time Marlowe might have got there; in the fourth term of that year Marlowe was only present in Cambridge for five out of the fourteen weeks.

Alan Haynes believes that Marlowe's first assignment, however, was not to Rheims but to Paris. He would be, in Haynes's phrase, 'an unfamiliar face to the myriad watchers on the roads'. His Latin was first rate so that he could attend mass with impunity, read writs from Popes and cardinals, blend in. Assuming that Marlowe had learned reasonable French from the Huguenots in his native Canterbury (it was certainly not taught in the King's School) he would have coped easily in Charles XII's France. A stay in the French capital would explain the knowledge the future playwright displayed when he wrote his drama *The Massacre at Paris*. Haynes surmises that Marlowe's work, spanning 1585 to 1586, would be to monitor the movements of the notorious Stafford and Lyly.

Sir Edward Stafford became English ambassador in Paris in 1583. Described as wayward by various commentators, Stafford was Burghley's man and a compulsive gambler. He greatly extended his scope of operations and placed intelligencers in various key households in Paris, probably selling Elizabeth's secrets to feed his habit. Walsingham first sent Walter Williams to check on Stafford but after the ambassador got him drunk, Williams seems to have confessed all and the ruse failed. Perhaps Marlowe was a safer bet.

Closer to the Cambridge scholar-turned-intelligencer was Stafford's secretary William Lyly, whose younger brother had been at school in Canterbury with Marlowe. Lyly was summoned back to England by the Privy Council in the autumn of 1585 on suspicion of overly close contact with Catholic exiles in Paris like the Welshman Thomas Morgan. Lyly managed to wriggle out of their lordships' interrogations and Walsingham let him go back to Paris in January 1586. He and Stafford were marked men, however, and Alan Haynes believes that it was Marlowe's brief to monitor the espionage hot-bed that was Paris. If this is correct and the Privy Council's reference to 'good service and faithful dealing' reflects this, then Marlowe was considerably higher up the intelligence ladder than is commonly thought. He was no mere letter-carrier, but a man who could be trusted to use wit and charm in the service of his country, pumping more gullible souls for information which could be vital to the safety of the realm.

If Haynes's assumption is right, it might seem an unlikely and anticlimactic move to send Marlowe from Paris to Rheims, but there may have been leads to follow and good reasons now lost to time. Walter Walsh, as early as 1903, wrote – 'The seminary Colleges did not improve as the years went on. They became more and more political foes of the Queen and her Government and had to be treated accordingly.'[11]

One possible reason for Marlowe's being sent to Rheims by Walsingham was to root out a Catholic agent working inside Cambridge University. In his first year at Bene't's, when the Jesuit mission was still in existence, Robert Parsons wrote to the Jesuit general Claudius Acquaviva at his headquarters in Rome:

> . . . I have at length insinuated a certain priest into the very university, under the guise of a scholar or a gentleman commoner and have procured him help not far from the town. Within a few months he has sent over to Rheims seven very fit [appropriate] youths.[12]

There were a number of local recusant families who might have helped the agent, but his identity remains unknown. Was he still in Cambridge four years later when Marlowe was recruited to the secret service? And was Marlowe's task to pretend an adherence to Catholicism in order to infiltrate Rheims?

Rheims was aware of the covert operations in its midst – 'They resolved to begin another way of persecution, which was to put sedition among themselves, by sending over spies and traitors to kindle and foster the same.'[13] How successful Marlowe was in this context is impossible to know. He was certainly used abroad again, for example in Vlissingen (Flushing) in 1592, so it is unlikely that his cover was blown. On the other hand, from what we know about Marlowe's personality, which was to emerge via his writing as much as in his behaviour, he was volatile, outspoken, high profile. Such men do not make good spies, even in the days of less-than-good Queen Bess.

Charles Nicholl does not accept that Marlowe went to Rheims at all and because of that he paints himself into a corner. He has to find reasons for Marlowe's non-attendance in Cambridge in 1585–7 and floats the idea that he may have been engaged as a snoop for Walsingham in one or more of the great Catholic family houses, like that of the Earl of Northumberland at Petworth. It is true that he knew the 'wizard Earl' in the 1590s, but there is no evidence to make the link as early as this.

Two problems remain about Marlowe's entry into Walsingham's service. The first is how his recruitment came about and who was responsible. We have seen already that the English universities were targets of both Catholic and Puritan dogma and infiltration. The average age of entry to Oxford and Cambridge, fourteen, meant that students were amenable to indoctrination. Moreover, there was an arrogance about some of these young men, whose fathers may have secretly followed the old religion and whose grandfathers certainly did. Many of them were clever, all of them were literate; some, like Marlowe, were brilliant. Such men could be highly dangerous and may have presented a positive threat to the stability of the State unless they were channelled, controlled, perhaps even bought by the great officers of that State. It was here that Walsingham came in. He had no direct links with Cambridge, but that was not necessary; indirect links he had in plenty.

Alan Haynes believes (and does not cite his reasons) that it was William Waad who recruited Marlowe. Since Waad was Clerk to the Privy Council and later Lieutenant of the Tower and seems to have had no Cambridge connection, again this is unlikely. Most commentators plump for Thomas Walsingham as the most likely patron to introduce the future playwright into the shadowy world of espionage.

Thomas Walsingham was second cousin to the Queen's spymaster. A year older than Marlowe, Thomas followed his elder brother Guldeford into their cousin's secret service as early as 1580 when he was only seventeen. He seems to have been a courier between London and the ambassador in Paris, Sir Henry Cobham. Nothing important would have been entrusted to a lad of that age; Marlowe was twenty-one before he was recruited. Walsingham was in France until 1584 and he undoubtedly gained the trust of those around him. He monitored the activities of James Beaton, the former Catholic Archbishop of Glasgow, then working, along with many other plotters, on behalf of the Queen of Scots. Cobham was obliged to remind Elizabeth's penny-pinching government to pay the man for his services early that year.

By the time Marlowe was recruited, Walsingham was back home in London. It may be that this indicates elevation in the secret service, but it may just be the acquisition of property that gave him a new found status. Either way, it places him nowhere near Cambridge in 1585, the year in which it is likely that Marlowe became a spy for Her Majesty.

A more realistic bet would be Nicholas Faunt, known to be in Francis Walsingham's service by 1590. He was an ex-scholar of Bene't's College and although he had gone down by the time Marlowe joined, may well have maintained links with his alma mater, looking out on Walsingham's behalf for likely lads: such a one was Christopher Marlowe.

The other imponderable about the poet/spy is the famous portrait – or rather portraits, because there are two. The frontispiece to *The Works of Christopher Marlowe* edited by Lt Colonel Francis Cunningham in 1889 shows a portrait of a good-looking young man with van Dyck beard and upward swept moustaches, a thatch of hair combed backwards and the obligatory earring of the Elizabethan rake. The Victorians, like us, wanted to *see* their heroes and villains. In the absence of an authentic likeness, they simply invented a face. Whole generations of Victorians grew up blissfully believing that they knew exactly what Harthacanute and Edmund Ironside looked like because an engraver had been commissioned to fill a page. Then came 1953.

In that year the Master's Lodge at Corpus Christi was being refurbished for the arrival of the new Master, Sir George Thomson. An undergraduate, passing debris piled in a corner, noticed a battered painting projecting from the rubble. It measured 24 inches by 18 and was painted on wood, rather than the more obvious canvas. Intrigued by the broken portrait of what appeared to be a young man in Elizabethan costume, the student took it to Dr J.P.T. Bury, the college librarian. A Mr Edward Leigh photographed the portrait in the state in which it had been found and it was sent to the National Portrait Gallery, whose experts were able to confirm it as an authentic Elizabethan portrait. It was subsequently restored by a Mr Valence of the London art restorer W. Holder and Sons of Brook Street, who transformed the painting into living colour.

It is likely that the portrait came from a panelled wall or possibly fireplace, hence the painting directly on wood. The fact that it was found in Corpus Christi indicates an association with that college and we know that Bene't's had such a collection of portraits, as evidenced by an 1884 catalogue of the Fitzwilliam Museum in Cambridge. The portrait shows a man with arms folded, wearing a padded, slashed doublet of the type fashionable in the 1580s and a lawn web collar. Valence's restoration has provided flying chestnut hair, brown eyes, a black doublet with orange slashes and ornate studded gilt buttons down the chest and along both sleeves. What has convinced most people that this is Marlowe (the first to propound the idea was the American researcher Calvin Hoffman in 1955) is the date painted in the portrait's top left hand corner – '*Anno Dmi* [in the Year of Our Lord] 1585, *Aetatis* [lit. summers] *suae* 21' – his age twenty-one. At any time between February and December of 1585, this would fit Marlowe. The other inscription, below the date and again in Latin, is altogether more cryptic – *Quod me Nutrit me Destruit* – 'that which feeds me destroys me'. If this is Marlowe, the phrase is extraordinarily prophetic. Evidence indicates that what fed him by 1585 was his pay in Walsingham's service; indirectly it killed him too.

Given a portrait – more importantly, given a face – we cannot help speculating. Charles Nicholl gets the impression that the sitter was tall (or is it merely that the proportions of the head and shoulders are wrong?), that the casual pose, with arms folded, is theatrical. And what, Nicholl wonders, is Marlowe hiding, both in the left hand hidden beneath his right arm and in the enigmatic half smile? When the hero of Josephine Tey's brilliant detective novel *The Daughter of Time* begins his convalescence in hospital, he is haunted by an unknown face on a postcard:

A judge? A soldier? A prince? Someone used to great responsibility and responsible in his authority. Someone too conscientious. A worrier; perhaps a perfectionist. A man at ease in a large design, but anxious over details. A candidate for a gastric ulcer. Someone, too, who had suffered ill health as a child. He has that incommunicable, that indescribable look that childhood suffering leaves behind it; less positive than the look on the cripple's face, but as inescapable. . . . The slight fullness of the lower eyelid, like a child that has slept too heavily; the texture of the skin; the old-man look in a young face.

Josephine Tey is describing Richard III, whom Marlowe's contemporary Shakespeare credits with eleven murders. But Tey is cheating. Whereas her hero does not know the name until he turns the postcard, his creator does – and she is reading all the signs into Richard's face that fit what we know about him. So does Nicholl. Marlowe is hiding something because Marlowe was a spy; Marlowe's folded arms are theatrical because Marlowe was a budding playwright; Marlowe's lips are pink and his hair rather feminine because Marlowe was homosexual. To be fair to Nicholl, he is describing the reproductions of the Corpus Christi portrait which vary enormously in colour tone. Even so, when facing the portrait itself in Marlowe's old college, he finds the face pale and chalky, the outlook unhealthy and bookish because he knows that Marlowe was a scholar and increasingly, a maverick, whose ideas were becoming less healthy by the day.

Can we stand back from what we know and evaluate the portrait from another angle? First, a comparison of the alleged Marlowe depiction with others of the time. De Critz's painting of Francis Walsingham, from about the same year, shows the spymaster to the waist. His arms are by his side and he wears the short haircut and elegant moustaches expected of a middle-aged man. The symbolism (and the Elizabethan age was heavy on symbolism) is shown by the medallion of the Queen he is wearing; he is her servant and carries her portrait adoringly. Walter Ralegh, painted by 'H' in the year of the Armada, is also depicted to the waist. His earring, his expensive, flashy clothes, the pearl-encrusted cape almost concealing his sword-hilt, speak volumes for Elizabeth's soldier/poet/explorer who may already have entered Marlowe's circle of acquaintances by 1585. And William Cecil, made Lord Burghley by the Queen in 1571, has his right hand on a book and inks to emphasize his statesmanship; his left hovers near his sword-hilt as a man who will use violence if he has to. The eyes are grey and cold.

Of twenty-five famous portraits of Elizabethan men who were Marlowe's contemporaries, his is the only one with his arms folded. Animal behaviourist Dr Desmond Morris has identified seven different positions of arm folding.[14] It is a position we adopt without consciously copying others. Marlowe's is position four, the chest/chest clasp. Morris says that this is an example of auto-contact behaviour. The sitter in the Corpus Christi portrait is hugging himself subconsciously for comfort; he is also providing a barrier across his chest. Given that the pose may have been suggested by the painter and that neither he nor Marlowe would have the faintest notion of body language, we are really no further forward. Insist that the sitter is Marlowe, already in 1585 a covert agent, translator of disreputable Latin verse, perhaps attender of atheist lectures, and it all falls into place; here is a man with something to hide and he does not yet, at twenty-one, have the suavity and experience of Burghley or Walsingham to conceal the fact.

What can we learn from the face? Morris cannot help here, because the Corpus Christi face is placid, almost expressionless. The Chinese, however believe that facial characteristics provide patterns and these patterns tell us a great deal about personality.[15] The forehead is wide, believed by the Elizabethans as much as the Chinese to indicate cleverness, and the high hairline merely accentuates this. Again, it does not help. The sitter has 'ideal' eyebrows – 'shiny, thick and rather lighter than the hair on the head'. The eyes, for most people the most riveting feature of any face, fit the Chinese description of 'cow', with large areas of white to either side of the iris. Such a man is thought to be innovative, although the ideas may be risky and he is stubborn, frank and forthright, his direct manner sometimes likely to offend. The fleshy nose with its round tip is associated with a disinterest in money, although if this portrait is Marlowe, he was spending it like water in 1585–6. The groove between nose and mouth, known to the Chinese as *jen-chung*, is accentuated in the Corpus Christi portrait by the moustache; it indicates in this case a period of conflict or uncertainty in childhood which has never quite gone away. The thicker lower lip indicates to the Chinese a man who is not to be fully trusted. Such people will try to reassure others with their 'naturally good command of speech'. Many professional artists and entertainers have this type of mouth. The round cheeks of the sitter denote command of power to the Chinese and the weak, receding chin, whereas it can mean a personality not prone to exert itself unduly, can also indicate 'a dramatic change of future'. We cannot see the sitter's ears, teeth or face in profile, so other secrets must remain locked away.

Does this apparent flight of fancy into eastern culture help us to identify Christopher Marlowe? Emphatically not, but *if* the Corpus Christi portrait is our man, then the Chinese secrets of his face are uncannily accurate in reflecting what we know of him. But there is a second potential portrait, and it predates the Corpus Christi find by nearly fifty years. The 'Grafton' portrait was discovered in February 1907 by Thomas Kay, who presented it to the John Rylands Library in Manchester. Before that it belonged to sisters called Ludgate whose family had been tenant farmers on the Grafton family estate in Northamptonshire. Grafton House became linked with royalty in the fifteenth century because it was here that Edward IV met Lady Elizabeth Gray (née Wydeville), who subsequently became his queen. In Henry VIII's reign the house was a hunting lodge that doubled as a conference centre for visiting dignitaries. Elizabeth is known to have visited it in 1568 on the most northerly of her many wanderings.

The portrait itself is believed to have been salvaged when troops of General Thomas Fairfax's New Model Army sacked the Royalist house in December 1643 and it was probably spirited away for safe keeping in the old priest hole in the nearby house of Anthony Smith, from whom the Misses Ludgate were descended. There is no geographical link between that part of the Midlands and Marlowe. Although there are infuriating gaps in the man's life during which he could have been *anywhere*, rural Northamptonshire seems an unlikely setting. Interestingly, however, the earliest published copy of his poem *Hero and Leander begun by Christopher Marlowe and finished by George Chapman* was found in the lumber room of Lamport Hall only 3 miles from Grafton Regis. The connection here is that John Isham, who once owned Lamport, was a Cambridge University man and collected first editions.

What is fascinating, bearing in mind the on-going 'Marlowe was Shakespeare' nonsense, is that the Grafton portrait was put forward by Thomas Kay in 1907 as a putative painting of the man from Stratford, which makes more sense geographically.

The Grafton portrait has not yet been professionally retouched, but it has been damaged by amateur cleaning. Even so, the change of colour of eyes from dark brown (Corpus Christi) to grey (Grafton) might ring alarm bells for some people. The Grafton portrait is certainly strikingly similar in other respects. The collar and slashed doublet are very alike; the buttons almost identical. The painting is dated 1588, the year of the Armada, and it bears the Latin inscription '*Ae suae* 24' (his age 24) which fits Marlowe of course as well as it fits Shakespeare. The nose is very similar, as is the general appearance of the moustache. There is a certain likeness in the 'cow' eyes, but the lips are less impressive and the chin is stronger with a definite point. Allowing for the passage of three years, it is possible that certain features (hair, moustache, beard, clothes) would change, but not the shape of the face. What seems more likely to us is that the Grafton portrait is a copy of the Corpus Christi one by an inferior artist, one who used the chiaroscuro style of light and shade associated with Spanish and Italian painting. Perhaps on a whim he decided to update the sitter's age and drop the tell-tale motto to avoid charges of forgery.

We come back to the obvious question – is the Corpus Christi face that of Christopher Marlowe, Walsingham's new man, in 1585? The 1884 Fitzwilliam Museum catalogue lists the following portraits from Corpus Christi – Thomas More, Thomas Cromwell, Queen Mary, two of Matthew Parker, John Foxe, Robert Cecil, John Jegon and two anonymous portraits, both of men and dated '1579 *Aetatis suae* 23'. If the Marlowe portrait came from the collection, originally it is presumed a wooden panel series decorating the Master's Lodge at Corpus Christi, then he was in illustrious company. Thomas More was the Chancellor who defied Henry VIII over the supremacy issue in 1534. Tried for treason, he was executed in the following year, but his kindness, courage and moderation were already bywords long before he was canonized by the Catholic Church. Thomas Cromwell was more of a self-made man than More, rising from artisan stock in Putney to become Henry VIII's Chancellor of the Exchequer, Lord Privy Seal and Vicar General. As principal architect of the dissolution of the monasteries in the 1530s, he earned the nickname *malleus monarchorum* (hammer of the monks) before incurring the king's wrath over the disastrous marriage to Anne of Cleves. In 1540 he met the same fate as More. Queen Mary was, of course, Henry's eldest child, by Catherine of Aragon. A zealous Catholic, she had attempted to stop the Protestant rot of the Reformation by marrying Philip II of Spain, champion of Catholicism throughout Europe, and by burning Protestants at East Smithfield. Matthew Parker's portraits are easily explained. Probably still today the most eminent of the Masters of Corpus Christi, his endowments to the college ranked at Bene't's alongside his difficult time as Archbishop of Canterbury. John Foxe died in the year that Marlowe left Cambridge (1587). More controversial than Cromwell and less saintly than More, he clashed with Elizabeth over the wearing of the surplices for church services and his preferment reached a dead end as a result. His book of martyrs, chronicling the often grisly deaths of Protestants since the fourteenth century, was translated into English from Latin in 1563 and quickly established itself as a best seller, second only to the Bible. Robert Cecil is a man we shall meet again, because he had a central role in Marlowe's death. If the portraits of both men did indeed hang in Dr Norgate's Lodge at Bene't's simultaneously, there is a deep irony there, although Cecil, the deformed son of Elizabeth's Secretary of State, was probably less than a year older than Marlowe and was not yet a central figure in politics. John Jegon was Master of Bene't's College between 1590 and 1603, brought in by Elizabeth personally to pull the place up by its bootstraps. Norgate's Mastership and that of his successor, John Copcot, witnessed a sharp financial decline and Jegon was a troubleshooter appointed to stop the trend. He did this well and saw four new scholarships and several endowments created before taking up the post of Bishop of Norwich.

Jegon and Parker have clear connections with Corpus Christi, but the others do not. Some biographers claim that Robert Cecil attended St John's, Cambridge, and while others doubt it, no one claims he was a Bene't's man. There is no link at all with More, Cromwell, Foxe or Queen Mary. So the paintings seem to be a fairly random collection of sixteenth-century portraits and we have no way of knowing who the anonymous men are.

Did Marlowe, perhaps with a streak of personal vanity and pride, have his portrait painted when he could first afford to do so[16] in 1585 and did he bequeath it to the college in 1587 or 1588, by which time he was a famous playwright? His subsequent death in dubious circumstances at Deptford and the burning of his overly erotic poetry in 1596–9 perhaps led to his portrait being taken down and 'dumped' prior to its accidental discovery in 1953. What this does not take into account is the nature of playwriting in Marlowe's day, nor the character of John Copcot, Master when the portrait was presumably received. Playwrights, especially in the increasingly Puritan world of the late 1580s, were accounted worthless at best. For a young man of promise, a brilliant scholar destined for the Church, to squander his talents in this way would not have sat well with the Cambridge authorities, especially since they had clearly clashed with him over the granting of his Master's degree. Copcot in particular, Master of Bene't's between 1587 and 1590, was a bookish pedant, to whom one of his friends addressed a letter, while he was still alive 'to the ghost of John Copcot'. He was not the sort of libertarian soul who would appreciate a playwright's talents however great, even if Copcot was an appointee of Lord Burghley, ultimately Marlowe's boss as the Queen's Secretary of State.

All this leaves us with uncertainty. The balance of probability is that neither the Corpus Christi nor the Grafton portrait is of Christopher Marlowe, yet there is something deep in all of us that needs a face with which to identify. We are drawn to Marlowe's portrait. Reading again the inquest of Coroner William Danby, we are drawn in particular to the portrait's right eye. It must surely be just the ravages of time that gave the unrestored Corpus Christi forehead a deep gash above the eyebrow.

As in a play, Ingram Frizer still had to make his entrance on to the stage of history. It is two years after Marlowe left Cambridge that we first find him, wheeling and dealing in Basingstoke.

Nicholas Skeres may have been part of Thomas Walsingham's entourage as early as 1581 when the spymaster's cousin was acting as courier to Henry Cobham, the English ambassador in Paris. In a letter to Francis Walsingham,[17] Cobham referred to 'another Englishman in his company, called Skeggs as I remember'. While this could be Skeres, equally, it could be someone else entirely. All we can be sure of is that he was definitely involved in espionage by 1586, the year of the Babington Plot. So too, was Robert Poley, who was working with Thomas Walsingham from 1584 in his house in Seething Lane, London. Two of the men in Widow Bull's house at Deptford Strand at the end of May 1593 had now met and were working, occasionally together, in the most dangerous business in the world.

That dangerous business found a focus in Anthony Babington, a handsome squire a little older than Marlowe who came from a Catholic family in Derbyshire. He had spent time in Paris where he had met that fomenter of intrigue, the renegade Welshman Thomas Morgan, and he carried letters from him to Mary, Queen of Scots. By 1586, Mary had been Elizabeth's prisoner for nineteen years and while she remained alive, she was the inevitable focus of Catholic plots. All commentators agree that the plots on the monarch's life – culminating in the best known of all, against Elizabeth's successor James I in November 1605 – were engendered by boundless optimism, Dutch courage and not a little naïveté.

By the summer of 1586, Babington was in regular negotiation with Father John Ballard, a Catholic convert unleashed on England with every intention of murdering the Queen as an act of God's vengeance.[18] Babington was to be the instrument, with a team of like-minded idealistic friends, and the Queen was to be hit while walking or riding in her coach. It says a great deal for Walsingham's secret service – or very little for Babington's security – that the spymaster knew of these plans by June and had Mary's letters to Babington intercepted from her new place of house arrest, Tetbury Castle in Staffordshire. In that same month, Babington applied for a passport, either as a genuine means of escape if he believed that Walsingham was on to him, or as an alibi when he killed the Queen. The cost was a staggering £300 and the broker to arrange it was Walsingham's man, Robert Poley.

Poley's job was to watch Babington, but he went further, organizing three meetings between the conspirator and the spymaster, in which Walsingham pretended to want Babington as an *agent provocateur*. It was a cat and mouse game, but Babington was very definitely the mouse and he seems unaware of Walsingham's duplicity. As the summer lengthened, Babington incriminated both himself and the Queen of Scots by writing openly to her of the murder plot. Walsingham's code-breaker Thomas Phelippes intercepted the letter and, in translating it, drew in the margin for Walsingham's grim sense of humour, a gallows. With touching naïveté, Babington asked Mary about Poley – 'I would gladly understand what opinion you hold of one Robert Pooley . . . I am private with the man and by means thereof know somewhat, but I suspect more.'[19] Unfortunately for Babington, he did not suspect enough.

Ballard was sent to the Tower on 4 August and the other conspirators panicked. Mary herself was arrested while hunting five days later and her correspondence and private papers handed over to Walsingham. Her staff was changed as the start of the whole process of tightening a metaphoric noose around her neck. Babington was found hiding in the hamlet of St John's Wood ten days after Ballard's arrest. He had already written to Poley, still essentially trusting the man:

> Farewell, sweet Robyn, if as I take thee, true to me. If not, adieu, omnium bipedum nequissimus [the worst thing on two feet] . . . the furnace is prepared wherein our faith must be tried. Farewell till we meet, which God knows when.
> Thine, how far thou knowest,
> Anthony Babington.[20]

Seven years before Deptford, Robert Poley was already instrumental in killing a man.

The bells rang out in thanks for the safe delivery of the Queen and the interrogations by her paranoid state officials began. The result was foregone. On 20 September the seven conspirators in the Babington Plot were dragged on sleds through the howling London mob from Tower Hill to the open square of St Giles in Holborn. At the express recommendation of the Privy Council, notably Burghley and Sir Christopher Hatton, the Queen's Chancellor, the execution was to be gruesomely prolonged. Beginning with Ballard, already crippled by torture, they were to be hanged one by one until they lost consciousness, then cut down and their genitals hacked off and waved to the crowd in front of them before disembowelling. Babington, understandably, cracked, screaming 'Spare me, Lord Jesus!' In the event, the Queen spared him, the worst at least, giving orders that the conspirators other than Ballard should be hanged until they were dead before the rest of the process continued. Lastly, Babington and his friends had their shoulder and hip joints sliced through before being pulled in four by horses.

Poley was sent to the Tower on 18 August, part of the government's round-up and an essential element of his cover. Astonishingly, he stayed in prison for nearly two years, re-establishing his old contacts with Joan Yeomans and continuing to inform Walsingham on the conversations of fellow-prisoners. His imprisonment was easy. Despite the Tower's grim reputation as a place of murder and execution, money softened the burden and the cost of Poley's 'board' has survived. He paid 5s to his keeper, 13s 4d for food and bed and 4s for fuel and candlelight. This is the sort of expenditure that may have come from Walsingham's own pocket.

The year 1585 was something of a watershed for England and her European neighbours. For over twenty years, Elizabeth had played a waiting game with the more powerful States of France and Spain, but by the mid-1580s things had changed. There was increasing pressure on the Queen, from both Walsingham and the Earl of Leicester in the Council for involvement against both countries: in France to aid the Hugenots; and to aid the Dutch Protestants in their on-going revolt against Spanish overlordship in the Netherlands.

Philip II likewise was under pressure from his advisers, notably Cristobal de Moura and Juan de Idiaquez, to take England in the name of Spain and the Counter-Reformation. Inexorably, if reluctantly, the former brother- and sister-in-law were being pushed towards war. On 20 August, Elizabeth signed a treaty at her palace of Nonsuch in Surrey authorizing Leicester to land with an expeditionary force in the Netherlands to check the increasingly successful Spanish forces under Alexander Farnese, the Duke of Parma. Leicester's tiny army, of 5,000 foot and 1,000 horse, would hardly stop the most powerful military force in Europe, but it was an irritation and it served to make a point.

In the meantime, Francis Drake was unleashed on the Spanish treasure fleet, dipping through the tropics on their way from the mountains of silver in the Americas. Drake was a privateer, operating with government backing and with orders to loot and pillage as long as the lion's share of the booty came home to Elizabeth. If things went wrong and Philip threatened war over these continuing insults, Elizabeth could always scream 'pirate' and wash her hands of Drake.

The all-important port of Antwerp fell to the Spaniards in August and it was not until December that Leicester landed at Vlissingen. Bearing in mind that we know Marlowe was in the same town in 1592 and that the plays of his about to burst forth on the London stage are full of military allusions, some commentators have claimed that the poet-spy accompanied the Earl's force. This seems unlikely, although we have no detailed knowledge of his movements after November when he read the will to Katherine Benchkyn in Canterbury. It simply makes little sense that an agent so useful to Walsingham should be trapped by the conventionalities of war. Marlowe was more useful as a free agent, moving as a civilian to Rheims and perhaps Paris on the Queen's business.

The Dutch Protestants were desperate. Their leader, the Prince of Orange, had been murdered the previous year and only four of the seventeen provinces held out against the renewed fury of the Spanish attack – Holland, Utrecht, Zeeland and Friesland were still free, but hardly united. Leicester, it quickly transpired, was neither general nor diplomat enough to handle the situation. He declared himself governor-general without the Queen's permission and clashed with half the Dutch leaders. His very presence in the field made open war with Spain inevitable and to cap it all, the courtier-poet Sir Philip Sidney, the darling of the Court and country alike, died pointlessly at Zutphen in November 1586 because he had left off his cuisses[21] and was hit by a chance shot.

The new Pope, Felice Peretti, who became Sixtus V in April 1585, also showed his impatience with England. An admirer in fact of Elizabeth and of the Protestant heir to the French throne, Henri of Navarre, and unhappy with the cloying domination of the Catholic League by Spain, he held off for as long as he could, but the Babington Plot forced a long overdue decision from Elizabeth on the fate of her cousin Mary of Scots; it was that decision that spurred Sixtus to back the Spanish Admiral Santa Cruz's 'enterprise of England'.

In the midst of all this rising tension, Christopher Marlowe went south, to London.

FIVE

The Muse's Darling

... by practice a playmaker and a poet of scurrilitie.
Thomas Beard, *Theatre of God's Judgements* (1597)

We know a great deal about Kit Marlowe's London thanks to the keen observation of a contemporary, John Stow. A tailor from Cornhill, Stow had been publishing antiquarian works since 1560, but his *Survey of London and Westminster*, produced five years after Marlowe's death, is the best. Stow was impelled by what he saw as the wanton destruction of a great city by greed and speculation. Tudor London, because of the Reformation, was the old religion's graveyard. Great religious houses were derelict and decaying, street stalls and even theatres springing up in their Gothic shells. The city's population, like that of the country generally, was growing. There was a frantic need to spread, to build, to occupy. And if none of this found favour with the Cornhill tailor, at least it pushed him into chronicling the moment with extraordinary detail.

What had dominated medieval London, physically as well as spiritually, was the Church. There were 119 spired churches in the pre-fire capital. The great monastic houses of the Friars, White, Grey and Black, were matched in size and splendour by the 'inns', the sprawling bishops' palaces that ran from Westminster Abbey to the Tower. It was this ostentatious opulence that had contributed to the Reformation's anti-clerical aspect in the eyes of most ordinary people. During the reigns of Henry VIII and Edward VI, a fever of land speculation had broken out. Secular landlords queued up to buy the ex-church properties from the government. Noblemen such as the Earls of Southampton and Bedford built lavish houses on ecclesiastical sites – the place names alone now survive to bear witness, Southampton Row and Bedford Square among them. Elizabeth gave presents of some church properties to her favourites –

Walter Ralegh graciously accepted the former 'inn' of the Bishop of Durham along the Strand from her. Few religious houses survived the 1530s and '40s and those that did focused on the public health role which was originally only part of their *raison d'être* – the hospitals of St Bartholomew at Smithfield, St Thomas south of the river and St Mary of Bethlehem at Bishopsgate.

By the time Marlowe reached London, some time in 1587, three areas in the capital were expanding particularly rapidly. Population figures are elusive. Various foreigners visiting between the 1530s and 1550 guessed at between 70,000 and 185,000 inhabitants. The more rational and conservative estimates of social historians like Roy Porter[1] put the figure at the time of Marlowe's birth at 85,000, one in fifteen of the entire population of England. Ten years after Marlowe's death, the figure may have reached 140,000 within the medieval walls and another 40,000 in the suburbs.

The City itself, first mapped by R. Aggas, a German cartographer in 1560, still retained its wall and was bounded by the river to the south and Moorfields to the north. To the west lay the old precincts of the Black Friars and to the east the Tower and the Hounds' Ditch. Within these walls was all the chaos of one of the largest cities in the world. Roy Porter visualizes how

The City . . . remained a mishmash, wealthy, middling and poor jostling wherever mazes of backyards and blind alleys led off main streets. Aldermen and a few aristocrats still lived within the walls; yet within spitting distance dwelt butchers, bakers and candlestick-makers with their stores and stables, fires and furnaces and rowdy apprentices under the eaves.

The City was dominated in Marlowe's day by the guilds, the exclusive companies of makers and sellers who doubled as chambers of commerce and nascent trade unions. The 'Twelve Great' – Clothmakers, Mercers, Grocers, Haberdashers, Fishmongers, Goldsmiths, Merchant Taylors, Ironmongers, Vintners, Salters, Drapers and Skinners – had their own coats of arms, liveries and ornate halls. They also provided half the City's governing elite, the aldermen and councillors of the Common Council and Common Hall.

To the west along the Strand, a more refined residential area was growing centred on the Queen's palace at Whitehall. As we have noted, Elizabeth was the last of the peripatetic monarchs, but pressure of business and lack of cash combined to lessen these 'progresses' and increasingly as she got older she spent more time at Whitehall and Greenwich. The noble houses of Somerset, the Savoy and Durham fronted the river, with their private boat moorings for speed of travel. The church of St Martin's was still just about in the fields to the north of Charing Cross and, south of that, ran the clerk-infested corridors of power at Whitehall – the Parliament House and Star Chamber. Here, too, were the Inns of Court, stretching along Fleet Street, spawning lawyers to deal with the ever-growing tide of paperwork that characterized an increasingly literate society. The Fleet itself was still an open tributary of the Thames, ever more polluted and a growing source of infection in an already overcrowded city. Of the Inns of Court, the Middle Temple (1571) and the Staple (1581) were the newest buildings to have appeared in Marlowe's time.

This area, from the bend in the river at Scotland Yard north to Holborn Bar, was far more homogeneous than the old City. It was the first of the suburban ghettoes, populated by the professions and the new breed of men elevated by the Tudors to positions of responsibility and power.

The third expansionist area of John Stow's and Christopher Marlowe's London was to the east and south, beyond the medieval construction of the City and its jurisdiction. These were the liberties; where land was cheaper, fields still a commonplace and regulations absent. Along Aldgate High Street grew the tenements and mean hovels detested by Stow – the 'nurseries and seminary places of the begging poor that swarm within the City'.[2] Beyond Bishopsgate, there were jerry-built cottages – 'with alleys backward, of late time too much pestered with people (a great cause of infection)'.[3] Out of the City to the east ran streets that followed the river's course through the mud-flats to Wapping. Here lived and worked the sailors and 'marine men' who also dominated Deptford further south and east with the growth of the royal shipyards. To the north-east ran the Ratcliffe Highway, to Shadwell and Stepney, then still villages surrounded by countryside. This area, Stow complained 'bee pestered with buildings, with Cottages, with Allies, even up to White chappel church and almost halfe a myle beyond it. . . .'4

All these areas shared one thing – the growth in the importance of money and trade. The opening up of the New World led to exploration and merchants followed in its wake, tentatively at first, then in a torrent.

The sense of growth, of power, of London as the new financial capital of the world, was crystallized in the official opening of Thomas Gresham's Royal Exchange in 1570. Stow recorded it:

In the year 1570, on the 23rd of January, the Queen's Majesty attended with her nobility came from her house at the Strand called Somerset House and entered the City by Temple Bar, through Fleet Street, Cheap and so by the north side of the Bourse [Exchange] through Threadneedle Street to Sir Thomas Gresham's in Bishopgate Street, where she dined. After dinner Her Majesty, returning through Cornhill, entered the Bourse on the south side; and after that she had viewed every part thereof above the ground, especially the Pawn [enclosed gallery] which was richly furnished with all sorts of the finest wares in the City, she caused the same Bourse by an herald and a trumpet to be proclaimed the Royal Exchange, and so to be called from thenceforth and not otherwise.

We do not know exactly when Marlowe left Cambridge, but it must have been before 10 November 1587 when, according to the Registrum Parvum, Bene't College's Order Book, a successor was elected to the Parker scholarship that Marlowe had vacated now that he had obtained his second degree. It is likely that the university authorities were glad to see the back of him. He had flouted their regulations by absenting himself and then getting no less an authority than the Queen's Privy Council to intercede on his behalf. He had spent money ostentatiously in the college Buttery, arousing who knows what animosity among students and Fellows poorer by far. He may or may not have worn the flashy clothes of the Corpus Christi portrait, but if he did, this was another gesture of defiance to authority and orthodoxy and some, like Gabriel Harvey, perhaps, were aware of his dabbling in the dubious works of Machiavelli and

Bruno, as well as the lascivious ones of Ovid. Like all Bene't scholars, Marlowe had been destined for a career in the Church, but clearly that was not about to happen.

From the north, Marlowe would have travelled, probably on horseback,[5] to Saffron Walden and Bishop's Stortford before riding through Epping Forest and on through Woodford and Leyton. Five years later, Frederick, Duke of Würtemberg, found himself on the same road – 'we passed through a villainous boggy and wild country and several times missed our way because the country thereabout is little inhabited and is nearly a waste . . .'. He would have crossed the Hackney marshes and ridden south-west through Shoreditch. His most probable point of entry to the City was through Bishopsgate and although there is no hard evidence we believe that his first lodgings were not far from here. Marlowe was a poet and a scholar – what more natural than that he should want to live near the heart of book-land? And that, in Marlowe's day, meant the churchyard of St Paul's. In one of the earliest publications of Marlowe's translation of Lucan, Thomas Thorpe, publisher, wrote: 'in memory of that pure elemental wit, Chr. Marlowe, whose ghost or genius is to be seen walk the churchyard in (at the least) three or four sheets.' The heart of it all was the central aisle of the great church, known as Paul's Walk. Forty years after Marlowe, John Earle wrote:

> Paul's Walk is the land's epitome, or you may call it the lesser isle of Great Britain. It is more than this the whole world's map . . . jostling and turning. It is a heap of stones and men, with a vast confusion of languages, and were the steeple not sanctified, nothing liker Babel. The noise in it is like that of bees, a strange humming or buzz, mixed of walking, tongues and feet. It is a kind of still roar or loud whisper. It is the great exchange of all discourse, and no business whatsoever but is stirring and afoot. It is the synod of all pates politic, jointed and laid together in most serious posture and they are not half so busy at the parliament. It is the antic of tails to tails and backs to backs, and for wizards you need go no further than faces. It is the market of young lecturers, whom you may cheapen here at all rates and sizes. It is the general mint of all famous lies, which are here, like the legends of popery, first coined and stamped in the church. All inventions

are emptied here, and not a few pockets. . . . It is the other expense of the day, after plays, tavern and a bawdy-house; and men still have some oaths left to swear here. . . . The visitants are all men without exceptions . . . stale knights and captains out of service, men of long rapiers and breeches . . . and traffic for news. . . . Of all such places it is least haunted with hob-goblins, for if a ghost would walk more, he could not.[6]

London was the heart of the book world. William Caxton had set up his first printing press at the sign of the Red Pale in Westminster Abbey as early as 1476. His foreman and successor, Wynken de Worde (Jan van Wynkyn), took over Caxton's business and set up two presses, one at The Sun in Fleet Street, the first tentative beginnings of the newspaper capital; and the other in St Paul's churchyard by 1509. St Paul's was probably the biggest church in the world, easily dominating the City skyline along with the Tower, even though the spire was destroyed by lightning in 1561 and the fire had affected part of the south aisle. This incident itself affords an early example of London journalism; within a week of the event, broadsheets describing the calamity were circulating all over the City.

By the year that Marlowe went to London, there were twenty-five printers working in and around Paternoster Row (now Paternoster Square), where dozens of stationers (publishers) and booksellers sold their wares. The Company of Stationers established in 1557 gave them an effective monopoly of printing, which explains why Catholic and other 'heretical' texts had to be printed in secret or imported from Europe. Acceptable works – The Bible, Foxe's *Martyrs*, moralistic fables – sold well. Ballads cost a penny, almanacs twopence, chap-books threepence. Marlowe's friend the poet Thomas Nashe wrote *Pierce Penniless* in 1592 and described one of the regulars in the churchyard:

If I were to paint Sloth . . . by Saint John the Evangelist I swear, I would draw it like a stationer that I know with his thumb under his girdle, who if a man comes to his stall and ask him for a book, never stirs his hand or looks upon him but stands stone still and speaks not a word; only with his little finger points backwards to his boy, who must be his interpreter, and so all the day, gaping like a dumb image, he sits without motion, except at such times as he goes to dinner or supper: for then, he is as quick as other three, eating six times every day.

The other reason we believe that Marlowe lived in Shoreditch was his new association with the theatre. The whole issue of the date of plays is a tortuous one, given the fact that the Stationers' Company's monopoly of printing was so complete and that all plays had also to be vetted by the Queen's Master of the Revels, nominally responsible for all forms of public entertainment. Writers like Marlowe would have to find an impresario like Philip Henslowe or an actor like Edward Alleyn or Richard Burbage and persuade them of the work's commerciality. Copies of the script would then have to be written out in longhand, often by candlelight and always with a quill. In that sense, Marlowe's plays, like Shakespeare's, were more like modern film scripts; they represented works in progress and were often altered to suit individual players or adapted to accommodate technical difficulties.

For the rest of his life, Marlowe was bound up with the theatrical life of London and this, rather than the rest of his colourful existence, is his legacy to us. We believe, however, that there was more to Marlowe's creativity – what Ben Jonson called his 'mighty line' – than the mere acquisition of a groat or even a desire for fame.

Theatrical performances were well known in the Middle Ages in the form of mystery or miracle plays. Coventry, Chester and many other cities performed these routinely in town squares or cathedral cloisters. Many of them were performed by the guilds and they always showed virtue triumphant over the forces of evil. From the late sixteenth century, travelling companies of actors, usually attached to great households, went on the road, bringing their religious or secular performances to wider audiences. Early London theatres, like the Swan and the Globe, had movable stages and were open to the elements, a silent reminder of these origins. By Marlowe's day, these companies had become far more professional and were the plaything of the aristocracy. Moreover, troupes *had* to have a patron before being allowed to perform. Leicester's Men, Worcester's, the Lord Chamberlain's, the Lord

Admiral's, Arundel's and the Queen's vied with each other to find the best playwrights, the most dramatic tragedies, the most entertaining clowns.

Marlowe, who may well have finished his play *Tamburlaine* by the time he left Cambridge, gravitated towards the Lord Admiral's company. It was formed in 1576 under the patronage of Charles Howard, later Elizabeth's Lord High Admiral. It probably toured the provinces, perhaps Cambridge where Marlowe may have seen a performance, before the first surviving record of it in London in 1585. When Edward Alleyn joined the company, probably in that year, it had become, with the Queen's Men, the most famous and elite of the theatrical troupes.

Alleyn, who was to play all of Marlowe's anti-heroes in the next six years, was born the son of an innkeeper in the parish of St Botolph's, Bishopsgate. He was two years younger than Marlowe and, with Burbage, dominated the theatrical scene at the end of the century. Thomas Nashe wrote in awe that he was the best actor since before Christ was born and Ben Jonson was equally lavish in his praise – 'others speak but only thou dost act.' In keeping with the tradition, and indeed law, of the time, Alleyn may have played female roles (women were not allowed on stage) with Worcester's Men before making the switch to the Lord Admiral's. Alleyn became the richest actor of his day, later founding the College of God's Gift at Dulwich (it helped of course that his step-father-in-law was the nearly as well-off Philip Henslowe).

The Elizabethan theatre played to mixed reviews. On the one hand, Henslowe, Alleyn, Burbage and eventually Shakespeare made serious money and filled houses with a surprisingly wide social range of audiences from the Queen to the groundlings. On the other, the increasing Puritanism of the age brought sharp and obsessive criticism. Philip Sidney, the doyen of scholar-knights, felt obliged to defend poetry against the Puritans in 1581. The anonymous writer of *A second and third blast of retrait from plaies and Theatres* in 1580 was in full cry:

The writers of our time are so led away with vainglory, that their only endeavour is to pleasure the humour of men . . . the notable liar is become the best poet; he that can make the most notorious lie, and disguise falsehood in such sort that he may pass unperceived, is held the best writer.

Thomas White thundered from the open-air pulpit of St Paul's cross outside the cathedral in 1578 – 'Look but upon the common plays in London and see the multitude that flocketh to them and followeth them. Behold the sumptuous theatre houses, a continual monument of London's prodigality and folly.' He went so far as to blame not merely the theatres for the spread of the plague but the plays themselves – 'The cause of plagues is sin, if you look to it well; and the cause of sin are plays; therefore the cause of plagues are plays.' Young Marlowe was on his way to Cambridge when this sermon was preached. One wonders what his Professor of Logic would have made of it!

John Stockwood, however, went further. In the same place, in the same year, he ranted, 'Will not a filthy play, with the blast of a trumpet, sooner call thither a thousand, than an hour's tolling of a bell bring to the sermon a hundred? . . . What should I speak, of beastly plays, against which out of this place every man crieth out?' Three years before Marlowe went to London however, the most hysterical Puritan attack came from Philip Stubbes:

> Do not they [plays] maintain bawdy, intimate foolery and renew the remembrance of heathen idolatry? Do they not induce whoredom and uncleanness? Nay, are they not rather plain devourers of maidenly virginity and chastity? For proof whereof but mark the flocking and running to Theatres and Curtains, daily and hourly, night and day, time and tide . . . where such kissing and bussing, such clipping and culling, such winking and glancing of wanton eyes . . . is wonderful to behold. Then, these goodly pageants being ended, every mate sorts to his mate . . . and in their secret conclaves (covertly) they play the sodomites or worse. . . .[7]

Plays, Stubbes maintained, were the breeding ground of every kind of sin and depravity:

> If you will learn cozenage; if you will learn to deceive; if you will learn to play the hypocrite, to cog, to lie and falsify; if you

will learn to jest and fleer, to grin, to nod and mow; if you will learn to play the Vice,[8] to swear, tear and blaspheme both heaven and earth; if you will learn to become a bawd, unclean, and to devirginate maids, to deflower honest wives; if you will learn to murder, flay, kill, pick, steal, rob and more; if you will learn to rebel against princes, to commit treasons, to consume treasures . . . to deride, scoff, mock and flout, to flatter and smooth . . . and finally, if you will learn to contemn God and all his laws, to care neither for Heaven nor Hell . . . you need to go to no other school. . . .

In Kit Marlowe's day, men like Stubbes, riding on the backlash of the Counter-Reformation and fear of Catholics, were increasing in number and beginning to inherit the earth.

We do not know precisely where *Tamburlaine* was first performed. Alleyn usually used The Theatre, in Shoreditch to the north of Finsbury Fields, but a rift with James Burbage, who owned it, in May 1591 led to Alleyn and the Admiral's Men decamping to The Rose, Henslowe's theatre south of the river on Bankside. Derek Traversi writes:

What the new theatre needed was a figure of outstanding genius capable of firing the imagination of audiences in the process of creating fresh dramatic worlds. Such a need was met in the short and meteoric career of Christopher Marlowe. . . .[9]

And J.B. Black:

But it was Marlowe who invented the true medium of the Elizabethan drama. His 'drumming decasyllibon' and 'bragging blank verse', coupled with the spirit of revolt and defiance which animated all his plays, took the public by storm. . . . More than any of his contemporaries, Marlowe displays the *terribilita* of the Italian renaissance.[10]

It is a mistake to ignore Marlowe's works as irrelevant to the cause of his death. If for no other reason, the meteoric rise which Marlowe's plays brought about for the man made him enemies. And enemies have motives for murder. In The *Epistle to Perimedes* entered in the Stationers' Register 29 March 1588, the ever-bitter Robert Greene railed against the contemporary fad for tragedy – 'daring God out of heaven with that Aetheist Tanburlan.' Men who wrote such drivel, he calls 'mad and scoffing poets, that have propheticall spirits as bred of Merlin's race'. This phrase is important in our understanding of Marlowe's death and it gives the lie to the official publication date of *Tamberlein the Cithian shepparde* at the Stationers' Hall on 14 August 1590. Marlowe's name does not appear on any early edition. The two parts of the play were published by Richard Jones in 1593 and 1597 and later by Edward White in 1605 and 1606.

If the incident described by Philip Gawdy which took place on 16 November 1587 involving the Admiral's Men refers to *Tamburlaine*, then clearly the first production was already under way by then, probably within three months of Marlowe's leaving Cambridge. In the second part of the play, an actor is tied to a tree and shot dead, but in pre-blank firing days, when the petronels of the time were notoriously unreliable, one or more members of the audience died instead.

What can we learn of Marlowe the man from his first venture on to the London stage? His choice of hero fascinated the Elizabethans. Timur-i-lang, the lame, was born in 1336, the son of a chief of the Berlas tribe, in Kash, near Samarkand. Marlowe's 'Scythian shepherd' gives a totally distorted view of a rags to riches story and even a whiff of the pastoral so common and popular in classical culture. The Berlas were nomadic warrior-tribesmen who followed their flocks, and this was as close as the play gets to reality. A general of some distinction, he invaded neighbouring Karashan in 1358 (Marlowe was the same age in fact as his hero when he wrote about him) and was made governor of the province. It was the Machiavellian mix of courage and cunning that Elizabethan audiences liked and it was these qualities that won Timur the crown of Samarkand by 1369. His armies smashed westward towards the Caspian, clashing with the Persians and routing the lords of the Golden Horde. In 1398 he turned south to India, sacking Delhi and carrying home mountains of booty. By 1402 he had defeated both the Turks and the Egyptians, capturing Aleppo and Damascus. His planned invasion of China never happened because he died of natural causes on 17 February 1405.

There is nothing historically in Shakespeare's plays to compare with Timur. The 'upstart crow' from Stratford specialized in Roman history and the appallingly biased Tudor version of English history before the sixteenth century. Timur falls between both stools. Neither a barbarous thug nor a ruler of great sophistication, Timur was a combination of the two. Like Marlowe himself, he was an over-reacher, an ambitious man who made too many enemies and took on too much. The sources that Marlowe probably used were Thomas Fortescue's *The Forest*, an English translation of 1571 of Pedro Maxim's *Siva de Varia Leccion* written in Seville in 1543; more current and possibly a book that spurred Marlowe to write was George Whetstone's *English Mirror*. Equally, he could have read Petrus Resondimus' *Magni Tamerlais Scytharum Imperatis Vita* published in Florence in 1553. The only significant areas in which Marlowe departed from these sources for the sake of dramatic effect were the characters of Zenocrate and her son Calyphus. The two parts of the play went into print in August 1590, having astonished audiences already. Richard Jones 'neere Holborne Bridge' produced the typset:

> Tamburlaine the Great, who, from a Scythian shepherde by his rare and wonderful conquests, became a most puissant and mighty monarque, and (for his tyrrany and terror in Warre) was termd the Scourge of God. Divided into two Tragicall discourses, as they were sundrie times shewed upon stages in the Citie of London by the right honourable the Lord Admyrall, his servants. Now first and newlie published.

Marlowe's 'mighty line' burst on to the London stage and took the world by storm. One of the problems of studying Marlowe the man is that most writers feel they too have to be poetic. So Charles Norman[11] writes of his style 'like combers making towards the land, treading the offshore deeps with flashing, rhythmic thunder, the music of his marching iambics surges forward, thundering harmony to the shores of consciousness.'

There are themes in *Tamberlaine* which need to be understood if we are to understand what happened at Deptford. Dissent is a common idea in the prologue – 'threat'ning the world with high astounding terms'. No writer can be divorced from the personal experiences of his life or the broader experiences of his nation. So, 'Unhappy Persia, that in former age/Hast been the seat of mighty conquerors . . .' may well be a nostalgic farewell to the English empire in France, lost finally under Mary Tudor. And was Marlowe firing a barb at explorers like Ralegh, Hawkins and Drake in

> Trading by land into the Western Isles
> And in your confines with his lawless train,
> Daily commits incivil outrages . . . [?]

The Spaniards are parodied as the enemies of England – 'With costly jewels hanging at their ears/And shining stones upon their lofty crests.' And surely, in Tamburlaine's own arrogance, there is an echo of Philip, the most powerful ruler in Europe – 'All through my provinces you must expect/Letters of conduct from my mightiness.' Tamburlaine's character is flesh and blood, however, and the detail makes it possible that here was a real individual whom Marlowe knew and admired. Is he Ralegh, whom Marlowe may already have met in Cambridge? Or Walsingham, on whose service he had already been?

Running throughout both halves of the play is an anti-Christian element which is more apparent in Marlowe's later works. Tamburlaine the atheist sees Christians as a common enemy, akin to Moroccans as examples of pure evil:

> Now hear the triple region of the air,
> And let the majesty of heaven behold
> Their scourge and terror tread on emperors.

> Come let us march against the powers of heaven,
> And set black streamers in the firmament
> To signify the slaughter of the gods.

There are ideas in *Tamburlaine* which we would expect to find in a play about a non-Christian conqueror; conquest itself, empire, monarchy and the role of kings. In the realms of internal conflict and dissent, especially perhaps of atheism linked with this, Marlowe was treading increasingly dangerous ground.

One thing is certain: *Tamburlaine* was an overnight success, establishing Marlowe as perhaps the foremost playwright of his day. He was feted among the university wits, fellow poets who had made their way from Cambridge or Oxford. Perhaps closest to Marlowe in the years of his fame was Thomas Watson, whose lodgings he shared in Norton Folgate. Best known for the infamous fight in Hog Lane, Watson was some six years older than Marlowe and a Londoner, dying in September 1592 and commemorated by their mutual friend George Peele – 'To Watson, worthy many epitaphs for his sweet poesy, for Amyntas' tears and joys so well set down.' 'Witty Tom Watson' wrote sonnets in the mid-1580s from which Shakespeare borrowed – *Ekatompathia*, *Amintas* and *Amintae Gaudia*. Widely read, he translated from French, Italian, Latin and Greek and wrote plays (none of which has survived) for which Puritans like Francis Meres criticized him – 'he could devise twenty fictions and knaveries in a play, which was his daily practice and living.' 'He was a man,' wrote Thomas Nashe, 'that I dearly loved and admired, and for all things hath left few his equals in England.'[12] They drank together at the Nag's Head in Cheapside.

But there is more to Watson than a fellow literatus of Marlowe's. A Wykehamist at a time when the school at Winchester was pro-Catholic, he went to school with Henry Garnett, later to lead the Jesuits in England. Having attended Oxford University, Watson travelled widely in Europe in a 'grand tour' that lasted seven years. He was at Douai, the English seminary, in 1576 and lodging with a preacher named Beale in London three years later. We need not read anything into the contemporary phrase 'lie with' as it simply meant shared lodgings in what was, after all, an expensive and overcrowded city. It is possible that Watson joined Sir Philip Sidney's literary circle Aeropagus for a while. By 1581, Watson's Catholic leanings were being monitered by the authorities. He appeared in an official description as a yeoman of St Helen's, Bishopsgate as one of the 'strangers that go not to church'. The term usually referred to continental Europeans and the enormously cosmopolitan Watson would have fitted that bill closely enough. An extraordinary link, though an unprovable one, is that the poet's sister may be 'one

Watson's daughter' who married the intelligencer, Robert Poley. Since Watson wrote an elegy on the death of Francis Walsingham it is at least possible, given his knowledge of the Continent, his linguistic ability and his Catholic leanings, that he too was a spy for the secret service. This would make perfect sense to explain his being drawn to Marlowe; the two shared the same literary skills and perhaps the same secrets.

From Marlowe's friend George Peele comes the title of this chapter, 'And after thee [Watson] Why hie they not, unhappy in thine end, Marley, the Muses darling, for thy verse fit to write passions for the souls below.' It was a dedication published some months after Deptford and addressed to another mutual friend, the Earl of Northumberland in *The Honour of the Garter*. Some of the poetry that Peele, graduating from Oxford in 1579, has left behind deals with the occult and the emerging science of his day – 'following the ancient revered steps/of Trismegistus and Pythagoras.'[13] Warned to repent by Robert Greene, Peele lived the typical Bohemian life of a 'roaring boye'. He flattered the Queen in his *Arraignment of Paris* in 1584, and the Earl of Essex in *Ecologie Grantulatory* five years later; like any self-respecting Elizabethan poet, he was always on the lookout for a likely patron. His plays include *Edward I* and *The Old Wives' Tale*. He died of the pox three years after Marlowe.

George Chapman was described by Anthony à Wood in the seventeenth century as 'a person of most revered aspect, religious and temperate – qualities, rarely meeting in a poet.'[14] A graduate of Oxford and Cambridge, Chapman's deep intelligence led him to spend years on an epic translation of the works of Homer, published in 1616. He was probably encouraged to write by Marlowe who no doubt introduced the older man to Thomas Walsingham, whose protégé at Scadbury he became after Marlowe's death. It was Chapman who finished Marlowe's last work, the poem of *Hero and Leander*, left three quarters complete when the playwright set out for Deptford. He was not always the stolid poet-scholar, however. In the year of the Gunpowder Plot, he did time with Ben Jonson (always a reckless friend to have) for scurrilous comments about James I in a play called *Eastward Ho!*[15]

Matthew Roydon was a lawyer from Thavies Inn. We have seen already that he knew Nicholas Skeres as early as 1582 and was perhaps already living in the same shoemaker's house in Blackfriars that he was still occupying in the year of Marlowe's death. In that year too, Roydon was writing poetry with Thomas Watson and it seems logical that this was the original link between Roydon and Marlowe. He wrote flattering poetry in 1586 for Philip Sidney – *A Friend's Passion For His Astrophel*, and was probably a member of Aeropagus. Three years later Thomas Nashe was talking about Roydon's 'most absolute comic inventions', but none of his comedy has survived. What, again, makes us believe that 'good Mat' was more than just a literary friend to Marlowe is a rather cryptic letter from Lord Burghley dated May 1591:

> I have cause to thank you, and so I do heartily for your good, kind letter, sent to me by our countryman, Mr Roydon, who maketh such good report to you, as doth every other man that hath had a conversation with you.[16]

The letter was written to Edward Kelley, the charlatan associate of the magus John Dee, then in Prague. What Roydon was doing in distant Bohemia is anybody's guess, but the fact that he was carrying letters to Burghley speaks volumes. It is likely that he, like Marlowe, was on the Queen's business in the twilight world of the intelligencer.

The last of the 'university wits' to remain Marlowe's friend, even when the heat was on in 1593, was Thomas Nashe. He does not seem to have been as close as Peele, Chapman and Roydon, perhaps because he had no known connection to the School of Night, but he wrote an elegy to Marlowe, and, like all the playwright hopefuls in London in the late 1580s, was knocked sideways by the instant success of *Tamburlaine*. It is difficult for us to imagine the effect of the 'mighty line' and blank verse on a literary set untrained to it and an audience for whom the thrilling experience was new; the first radio, cinema and television audiences would have understood.

'Idiot art-masters,' Nashe stormed (he never took the higher degree) in the Preface to Robert Greene's *Menaphon*, published in 1589, 'that intrude themselves to our ears as the alchemists of eloquence, who (mounted on the stage of arrogance) think to outbrave better pens with the swelling bombast of a bragging blank verse.' Although Nashe would go on to deny that he ever 'abused Marlowe' this is surely an attack born of sour grapes. After Marlowe's death, Nashe edited the play *The Tragedy of Dido, Queen of Carthage* which in the original version contained the Latin elegy 'a diviner muse than him, Kit Marlowe'.

Robert Greene deserves a special place in Marlowe's circle because he left it spectacularly, first because he resented Marlowe's success far more than did Nashe and second because, after a dissolute life, and knowing he was dying from syphilis, he turned belatedly to God and slammed those who had not in *A Groatsworth of Wit Bought With a Million of Repentance*. It was Greene, through his publisher Henry Chettle, who libelled Marlowe over his homosexuality. He was to die in a shoemaker's house near Dowgate by the Thames, not, according to Gabriel Harvey, who visited and stole his notes, 'of the plague or the pockes . . . but of a surfeit of pickle herring and rennish wine.' The nauseating Harvey wrote, almost while Greene was still warm,

> Who in London hath not heard of his dissolute and licentious living; his foul disguising of a Master of Arte with ruffianly hair, unseemly apparel, and more unseemly company: his vaineglorious and Thrasonicall braving; his pipely Extemporizing and Tarletonizing;[17] his apish counterfeiting of every ridiculous and absurd toy; his fine coosening[18] of Jugglers and finer juggling with cooseners; his villainous cogging and foisting;[19] his monstrous swearing and horrible forswearing; his impious profaning of sacred Textes; his other scandalous and blasphemous ravings. . . .

Harvey continued to rant, accusing Greene of frequenting brothels in Southwark, pawning his belongings, moving on frequently without paying his rent. It is difficult, bearing in mind the petty, petulant attacks made by both men, to decide who is the more despicable, Harvey or Greene.

The most difficult relationship to fathom is that between Marlowe and William Shakespeare. Rejecting as we do that they were the same man (at least after 1593), we have no way of measuring their friendship. There is no actual documentation to tell us whether the pair ever met, but given that they arrived in London in the same year, both wrote for the theatre and were only two months apart in age, it seems unlikely that they never did. The first part of *Henry VI*, now usually attributed to Shakespeare alone, was probably co-written by Marlowe and there were likely to have been other collaborations in what is now the Shakespeare canon. For a time in the early 1590s, both men were chasing the same patron, Henry Wriothesley, Earl of Southampton. It is the implied rivalry for a common love which is evident in the series of Shakespearean sonnets numbered 78 to 86.

The story the sonnets tell is a tortuous one and by no means certain, but the likelihood is that they were written in two sections, the first in 1592–3 when Shakespeare was hit especially hard (as actor as well as playwright) by the closure of the theatres because of plague. Along with almost everybody else involved with the young lord (Southampton), Shakespeare seems anxious to get him to do the correct thing and marry. The fact that Southampton was only twenty, quite possibly homosexual and not ready to settle down, made all this rather difficult. Shakespeare met the 'dark lady' to whom the sonnets refer at this time and among a host of likely contenders, the most likely is Emilia Lanier (née Bassano), the half-Italian mistress recently discarded by Henry Carey, Baron Hunsdon, Privy Councillor and the Queen's chamberlain. This is certainly A.L. Rowse's theory and it makes a degree of sense. Every line of Shakespeare's reveals his awe of the more famous and superior poet.

> I grant, sweet love, thy lovely argument
> Deserves the travail of a worthier pen.
> (Sonnet 79)

And

> O, how I faint when I of you do write,
> Knowing a better spirit doth use your name . . .
> . . . He of tall building and of goodly pride;
> Then, if he thrive and I be cast away,
> The worst was this; my love was my decay.
> (Sonnet 80)

And

> Was it the proud full sail of his great verse,
> Bound for the prize of all too precious you . . .
> . . . Was it his spirit, by spirits taught to write
> Above a mortal pitch, hath struck me dead?
>
> (Sonnet 86)

And, tantalizingly, is Shakespeare referring to Marlowe as Faustus in the supernatural implication of the last lines?

Recent works have implied different relationships. A new biography of Shakespeare[20] has the Stratford man visiting Deptford on the night of 30 May 1593 to view Marlowe's corpse and say his farewells (for which there is no evidence whatsoever).

There is no doubt that Shakespeare owed a huge literary debt to Marlowe. Despite the similarity in their ages, Marlowe's school and university background, not to mention the astonishing hit of *Tamburlaine*, made him very definitely the senior partner. Shakespeare probably went in awe of him, and if imitation is the sincerest form of flattery, Shakespeare went on to help himself not only to Marlowe's style of iambics, the blank verse which annoyed Nashe, but the notion of the *Jew of Malta* and the whole range of English history plays of the type of *Edward II*. Alone of his contemporaries, Shakespeare actually quoted Marlowe in *As You Like It* – 'Dead shepherd, now I find thy saw of might/"Who ever lov'd that lov'd not at first sight?"' In the same play, the character Touchstone makes a veiled reference, perhaps to Marlowe's death in Eleanor Bull's house at Deptford – 'When a man's verses cannot be understood, nor a man's good wit seconded with the forward child understanding, it strikes a man more dead than a great reckoning in a little room.' Shakespeare may have been overawed by the man; he may have owed him a great deal, but he was not Marlowe; nor was he one of his immediate circle. J.B. Black makes a valid point:

> But by a curious coincidence, chance and circumstance combined to eliminate all rivals from [Shakespeare's] path, when most he needed a free field for the development of his genius. Greene died in 1592, Kyd in 1594; Lodge gave up letters for medicine; Lyly

ceased work; and Peele plunged into dissipation. In fact from 1593 to practically the close of the century, Shakespeare had the stage to himself. . . .

Today, in their search for someone who might benefit from Marlowe's death, the police would look very closely at Mr Shakespeare!

We will never know all the people linked with Christopher Marlowe. The booksellers Thomas Thorpe and Edward Blount published his works posthumously and speak with affection of him. A lawyer on the fringes of the literary set, John Marston, calls him 'kind Kit Marlowe'.

The only name remaining is that of Thomas Kyd. A scrivener's son from London, he probably attended Merchant Taylor's School and wrote an earlier version of *Hamlet*, which Shakespeare later plagiarized. His revenge play *The Spanish Tragedy* was among the most popular of Elizabethan plays. He shared lodgings with Marlowe in 1591, probably in Shoreditch, and it was his testimony under the torture of Richard Topcliffe that led to Marlowe's arrest and subsequent death. Whatever brought down Marlowe, brought down Kyd too.

We do not know the exact sequence of Marlowe's success on the London stage. *Tamburlaine* was the first, a second part following on almost by popular demand. It would be a brave man who tried to chronicle the writing or even first performance dates of anything else. The time frame we have is the autumn of 1587 to the early summer of 1593. Within those years, Marlowe wrote five plays, although *Dido, Queen of Carthage* may have been completed by Nashe and *The Massacre at Paris* has only survived in a much hacked-about form and again may have been a collaboration with Nashe. *Edward II* was entered to William Jones in the Stationers' Register, which recorded all plays, on 6 July 1593. Marlowe had by then been dead six weeks. *The troublesome reign and Lamentable Death of Edward the Second, king of England, with the tragicall fall of proud Mortymer* was first published in 1594, attributed to 'Chri. Marlow'.

Like Shakespeare in his History plays, Marlowe's major source was Ralph Holinshed's *The Chronicles of England, Scotland and Ireland* of 1577, but one scene may well have been suggested by a passage in John Stow's *Annales*, which gives it a late date of 1592. It was first performed by the Earl of Pembroke's Men. *The Jew of Malta* was recorded at the Stationers' Hall by Nicholas Ling and Thomas Millington as 'the famouse tragedie of the Riche Jew of Malta' on 17 May 1594. Dating for this one is easier, because it refers to the death of the Duke of Guise, 23 December 1589, and we know it was performed by Philip Henslowe's company on 26 February 1592. It may be that the cutpurse character was lifted by Marlowe (perhaps a deliberate act to annoy him) from Robert Greene's underworld pamphlet *A Notable Discovery of Cosenage*, published in December 1591. The play was performed thirty-six times between February 1592 and June 1596, mostly by Lord Strange's Men.

There is a date structure of a sort in *The Massacre at Paris*. It must have been written after the death of the French king Henri III on 2 August 1589 and possibly after that of Pope Sixtus V, in August 1590. Its first recorded performance was in January 1593, with Marlowe at the height of his fame and only five months away from Deptford. Henslowe's company at The Rose performed it then and the Admirals' Men ten times the following year. *The tragicall history of the horrible life and Death of Doctor Ffaustus, written by C.M.* was based on an English translation of a German edition of 1587 not available in England until 1592. Edward Alleyn played Faustus for the Admiral's Men at The Rose twenty-four times between September 1594 and January 1597.

Edward II, *The Jew of Malta*, *Dr Faustus*, *The Massacre at Paris* – these are the plays, along with *Tamburlaine*, that resound with Marlowe's mighty line. With the likely exception of *Tamburlaine*, they were, indirectly but surely, the plays that killed him.

SIX

Tobacco and Boys

That all they that love not tobacco and boys were fools.
The Baines Note, May 1593

Three days before the end of Marlowe's life, an extraordinary document found its way into the hands of the Privy Council. It was written by Richard Baines, a shadowy figure whose denunciation of the poet-playwright would make his murder inevitable. He was a gentleman pensioner, in other words a rich undergraduate, at Christ's College, Cambridge in 1568 and transferred to Caius shortly after 1573. As we have seen, Caius was one of the most Catholic of the university colleges at a time of growing Puritanism and it comes as little surprise to know that Baines left for the English college at Rheims in 1578. Taking to the monastic regime like a duck to water, he became a sub-deacon on 25 March 1581 and an ordained Catholic priest on 21 September of the same year.

All this seems to be taking his part rather too far, because according to a confession he made later to Dr Allen who ran the college, Baines's role was actually that of projector: 'I found means,' Baines wrote, 'to insinuate myself to the familiarity of some of the younger set, that methought might be easily carried into discontentment.' Further, Richard Baines was an assassin. Of him, Allen wrote:

They resolved to begin another way of persecution, which was to put sedition among ourselves by sending over spies and traitors to kindle and foster [discontent]. Such a one was one Bayne, who besides other ill offices was to poison also Dr Allen at that time in the seminary.

Among nineteen accusations made by Baines against Marlowe in May 1593, number thirteen reads: 'That all they that love not

Tobacco and Boies were fooles.' Since the twelfth charge that immediately precedes it reads: 'That St John the Evangelist was bedfellow to C[hrist] and leaned alwaies in his bosom, that he used him as the sinners of Sodoma',[1] we must assume that Baines's thirteenth charge of loving boys is literal.

The projector's brief, according to some commentators, was to blacken Marlowe's reputation. We believe that in essence what Baines was reporting was the truth. Marlowe did smoke tobacco and he was probably a practising homosexual. Whereas only fanatics like James VI of Scotland loathed and denounced the 'noxious weed', homosexuality was a capital crime. It is important that we understand where this places Marlowe. More than simply a dissolute 'roisterer' on the lines of his friends Greene and Nashe, he was what he remained for the rest of his life: an outsider, a man on the edge, and dangerous company.

What do we know about Marlowe's relationship with the 'noxious weed'? King James's 'counterblast' was not the only attack on the substance. In 1628, John Earle wrote of tobacconists in *Microcosmographie* – 'No man opens his ware with greater seriousness, as challenges your judgement more in the approbation. His shop is the rendezvous of spitting, where men dialogue with their noses, and their communication is smoke.' The king went into print on the subject in 1604:

And for the vanities committed in this filthy custom, is it not both great vanity and uncleanness, that at the table, a place of respect, of cleanliness, of modesty, men should not be ashamed to sit tossing of tobacco pipes, and puffing of the smoke and tobacco one to another, making the filthy smoke and stink thereof to exhale athwart the dishes, and infect the air, when very often men that abhor it are at their repast? . . . Have you not reason then to be ashamed, and to forbear this filthy novelty, so basely grounded, so foolishly received and so grossly mistaken in the right use thereof? In your abuse thereof sinning against God, having yourself both in persons and goods and taking also thereby the marks and notes of vanity upon you: by the custom thereof making yourselves to be wondered at by all foreign civil nations, and by all strangers that come among you, to be scorned and contemned. A custom loathsome to the eye, hateful to the nose, harmful to the brain, dangerous to the lungs, and in the black stinking fume thereof nearest resembling the horrible Stygian smoke of the pit that is bottomless.

James sounds uncannily modern in his conclusion that tobacco was dangerous and he is also right when he refers to the revulsion to the weed among foreigners. Paul Hentzner, travelling in England in the 1590s, wrote:

> . . . the English are constantly smoking the Nicotian weed which in America is called Tobaca – others call it Paetum – and generally in this manner; they have pipes on purpose made of clay, into the farther end of which they put the herb, so dry that it may be rubbed into powder, and lighting it, they draw smoke into their mouths, which they puff out again through their nostrils, like funnels, along with it, plenty of phlegm and defluxion from the head.

In part, the reason for the aversion to tobacco of James and others was its sheer novelty. Like the theatres, it was new. Christoforo Colon, better known as Columbus, first saw the Arawaks of Espanõla smoking the nicotine leaves as early as 1492, either through inhalation via the nostrils or through a hollow tube called a tobago. The Arawaks used tobacco as a mild hallucinogenic and as an offering to their gods in religious festivals. Its first introduction to England seems to have been the year of Marlowe's birth, when John Hawkins, explorer and slave-trader, brought back a small amount from an American voyage. For twenty years smoking remained the pastime of sailors, although two scholars, Penn and Lobel, published a herbal containing drawings of the plant in London in 1570.

While Francis Drake brought back larger amounts of *Nicotinia tobacum* in 1573 European doctors (usually ahead of their British counterparts) were looking at the weed as a potential cure for a whole range of ailments and diseases including toothache, worms, lockjaw, migraine, labour pains, asthma, bubonic plague, cancer and halitosis! In the year in which Marlowe was recruited to Walsingham's secret service, Francis Drake introduced smoking to

Walter Ralegh. Three years later, Thomas Hariot wrote a treatise about the weed and is generally regarded as England's first recorded lung cancer victim as a result of his own addiction. Since Ralegh and Hariot were part of Marlowe's circle by 1588, their links with the man and his murder are important and extend to their use of tobacco.

Hariot visited Ralegh's colony of Virginia in 1585 or 1586 and brought back the clay pipe possibly invented for smoking by Ralph Lane, the colony's first governor. The astronomer and mathematician so extolled its virtues to Ralegh ('it purgeth superfluous phlegm and other gross humours, and openeth all the pores and passages of the body') that within a year, tobacco had become the new craze at Court. Years later, when James was king and counterblasting the weed with vigour, he focused the blame on Ralegh, whom he detested, as the instigator of the foul habit – 'it seems a miracle to me how a custom springing from so vile a ground and brought in by a father so generally hated, should be welcomed.'[2] To spite the sanctimonious hypocrite who had ordered his execution in 1618, Ralegh enjoyed one final pipe of tobacco on his way to the scaffold.

Edmund Spenser is probably the first poet to refer to tobacco, in *The Faerie Queen* written in 1590, but there are other references and they oddly revolve around Marlowe. Giordano Bruno, the atheist whom Marlowe may have heard lecture in Oxford and whose works he had certainly read, wrote *Work for Chimney Sweepers* and the verse that prefaced it ran 'Better be choked with English hemp than poisoned with Indian tobacco'. This piece refers to Giovanni della Porta, whose *De Furtivus Literarum Notis* was, as we have seen, the standard reference work for codification used by Walsingham's code-breaker Thomas Phelippes.

There is a sense that the substance which Ralegh, Hariot, Marlowe and others smoked was a great deal more powerful than the modern version with its low tar and government health warnings. Various accounts of its effects, not influenced by the antipathy of the Puritans, describe a light-headedness and loss of control more associated with cannabis-smoking. A French witness of the trial of the Earl of Essex for treason in 1601 spoke of English lords making themselves 'silly' by smoking. It may be that the tobacco imported in the 1580s and 1590s was of a particularly strong strain – or that it was not tobacco at all, but marijuana.

We have seen already, through the drama of his plays and the licentiousness of his poetry translations, that Marlowe loved to shock. His use of tobacco is simply another example of that, at a time when the revolutionary substance was the smart thing with which to be associated, exciting the senses and the Court. It was the stuff of Ralegh's and Hariot's School of Night and it smacked of the forbidden.

In the year before Marlowe died, Robert Greene went into print with his idea of what a poet was. Whether it was intended to refer to Marlowe himself we do not know, but it sums up the image of the man that has come down to us:

A poet is a waste-good and an unthrift, that he is born to make the taverns rich and himself a beggar. If he have forty pounds in his purse together, he puts it not to usury, neither buys land nor merchandise with it, but a month's commodity of wenches and capons. Ten pounds a supper, why 'tis nothing, if his plough goes and his ink-horn be clear. Take one of them with twenty thousand pounds and hang him. He is a king of pleasure. . . .[3]

And London provided plenty of places where pleasure might be taken. The bustling life of the city is most vividly recreated by Marlowe's fellow-dramatist Ben Jonson in *The Devil is an Ass*:

> I will fetch thee a leap
> From the top of Paul's steeple to the standard in Cheap
> And lead thee a dance through the streets without fail
> Like a needle of Spain, with a thread at my tail.
> We will survey the suburbs and make forth our sallies
> Down Petticoat Lane, and up the Smock-alleys,
> To Shoreditch, Whitechapel, and so to St Kather'n's,
> To drink with the Dutch there, and to take forth their patterns.
> From thence we will put in at Custom-house quay there,
> And see how the factors and prentices play there,
> False with their masters; and geld many a full pack
> To spend it in pies at the Dagger, and Woolsack.

Nay, boy, I will bring thee to the bawds and the roysters
At Billingsgate, feasting with claret-wine and oysters;
From thence shoot the Bridge, child, to the Cranes i' th' Vintry,
And see there the gimblets how they make their entry!
Or, if thou hadst rather, to the Strand down to fall,
'Gainst the lawyers come dabbled from Westminster Hall,
And mark how they cling, with their clients together,
Like ivy to oak, so velvet to leather.

London's underworld developed like a cancer in the growing city.
The area of the Savoy along the Strand was already one centre; so
was the no-go rabbit warren called Alsatia. Other places adopted
colourful names like Devil's Gap and Damnation Alley and there
was a plethora of taverns where 'roysters' or 'roaring boys' could
drink, smoke their tobacco and whore to their hearts' content. The
scale of the problem was huge and honest men worried about it.
George Whetstone wrote in 1584:

Now remaineth the discovery of the third sort of these haunts,
which are placed in alleys, gardens and other obscure corners out
of the common walks of the magistrate. The daily guests of these
privy houses are masterless men, needy shifters, thieves, cutpurses,
unthrifty servants, both serving men and prentices. Here a man
may pick out mates for all purposes, save such as are good. . . .[4]

Of particular concern to the authorities were the theatres and the
liberties, those areas, like Shoreditch in the north-east and Bankside
across the river which were beyond the City's official jurisdiction. At
the end of July 1597, the Lord Mayor and aldermen, clearly at the
end of their collective tethers, wrote to the Privy Council,
complaining about stage-plays – 'neither in polity nor in religion are
they to be suffered in a Christian commonwealth, specially being of
that frame and matter as usually they are, containing nothing but
profane fables, lascivious matters, cozening devices and scurrilous
behaviours.' Theatres, the City fathers agreed, 'give opportunity to
the refuse sort of evil-disposed and ungodly people that are within
and about this city to assemble themselves and to make matches for
all their lewd and ungodly practices'. They demanded nothing short

of 'the present stay and final suppressing of the said stage-plays, as well as the Theatre, Curtain and Bankside . . .'.

But the government had tried this before and to no avail. In June 1584, William Fleetwood, Recorder to the City of London, had written to Lord Burghley himself concerning riots outside the rival houses of The Curtain and The Theatre:

> Upon the same night I sent for the Queen's players and my lord of Arundel his players, and they all willingly obeyed the lords' letters. The chiefest of her highness's players advised me to send for the owner of the Theater [James Burbage] who was a stubborn fellow and to bind him. I did so. He sent me word that he was my lord of Hunsdon's man and that he would not come at me, but he would in the morning ride to my lord.

That was the problem. Although Fleetwood seems to have won that particular battle, men like Burbage believed themselves to be under the protection of great lords, which they were. Hunsdon was, like Burghley, a member of the Privy Council and a power in the land. So the theatre-owners, the actors in theatrical companies and quite possibly the playwrights who wrote for them, saw themselves, if not exactly above the law, at least alongside it.

South of the river lay the stews of Southwark, where professional card and dice cheats rubbed elbows and no doubt other parts of their anatomy with the 'Winchester Geese', the prostitutes who plied their trade on land formerly belonging to the bishop of that diocese. Southwark too was theatre-land, the home in the later 1590s of The Swan and The Globe. Marlowe was dead before they reached their zenith, but the theatrical link was already established. Philip Henslowe, who put on most of Marlowe's plays, and Ned Alleyn who acted in them, both owned brothels here. Alleyn's wife (Henslowe's stepdaughter) was dragged at the cart's tail through the streets in 1593; this was the traditional punishment for habitual prostitution.

The Elizabethans called such establishments 'stews' in a long forgotten folk memory of Roman baths where relaxation and prostitution went hand in hand. With deep irony, Henry VIII had outlawed such places, but then, as now, prostitution provided for a need and the ban was largely ignored. Lord Hunsdon was here again, owning Paris Gardens and farming them out to Francis Langley, who owned The Swan and who asked few questions when it came to nightly behaviour in the theatre's precincts. Such favours could be expensive. The author of *A Mirror for Magistrates of Cities* wrote in 1584 that a gentleman may need 'forty shillings or better' to buy his pleasures in 'some blind brothel house about the suburbs' which would include 'a pottle or two of wine, the embracement of a painted strumpet and the French welcome'. The 'French welcome' was the pox, gonorrhoea or syphilis which the English attributed to their ancient enemy, just as they attributed it to the English.

Robert Greene, as always bursting with rabid born-again indignation, gave an account of the methodology of these women in 1592 in a scene he had probably witnessed:

> I removed my lodgings and gat me into one of those houses of good hospitality whereunto persons resort, commonly called a trugging-house, or to be plain, a whore-house, where I gave myself to entertain all companions, sitting or standing at the door like a stale, to allow or draw in wanton passengers, refusing none that would with his purse purchase men to be his, to satisfy the disordinate desire of his filthy lust.[5]

Greene is describing his former life and, incidentally, the acquisition of the syphilis which was killing him. Theatres, drink, tobacco; these were as nothing when compared with prostitution in the Puritan canon of vice. Philip Stubbes railed against it in *The Anatomie of Abuses* in 1583:

> it dimmeth the sight, it impaireth the hearing, it infirmeth the sinews, it weakeneth the joints, it exhausteth the marrow, consumeth the moisture and supplement of the body, it rivelleth the face, appalleth the countenance, it dulleth the spirits, it hurteth the memory, it weakeneth the whole body, it bringeth it into a consumption, it bringeth ulcerations, scab, scurf, blain, botch, pocks and biles; it maketh hoar hairs and bare pates; it induceth old age, and, in fine, bringeth death before nature urge it, malady enforce it or age require it.[6]

If we accept the version of Marlowe's murder written by Anthony à Wood in 1691, we get a flavour of this world of the 'frail sisterhood' with their bare breasts under their velvet cloaks – 'For it so fell out that [Marlowe] being deeply in love with a certain Woman had for his Rival a bawdy serving man, one rather fit to be a Pimp . . .'. We know that Ingram Frizer does not fit this pattern, but it raises interesting questions on Marlowe's sexuality that we cannot answer. The Baines Note talks of tobacco and *boys* and on this, the most taboo of subjects in Elizabethan England, even the most rabid Puritans are silent.

In 1614 William Lithgow wrote his *Rare Adventures and Painefull Peregrinations* and describes an aspect of his visit to Padua, in the north of Italy:

> The Schollers here in the night commit many murthers against their privat adversaries, and too often executed upon the stranger and innocent, and all with gun-shot or else stillettoes: for beastly Sodomy, it is rife here as in Rome, Naples, Florence, Bullogna, Venice, Ferrara, Genoa, Parma not being exempted, nor yet the smallest village of Italy: A monstrous filthinesse, and yet to them a pleasant pastime, making songs and singeing sonnets of the beauty and pleasure of their Bardassi, or buggerd boys.[7]

There are fascinating echoes of Marlowe here: the link with murder, specifically by stiletto, the slim-bladed Italian dagger; the link with scholars; the link with sonnets. That Lithgow wrote this at all is, says G. Rattray Taylor, a testimony to the frankness of writing on such matters. This we doubt. Lithgow's 'frankness' probably has more to do with the facts that his king was James I, openly homosexual, as many of his courtiers could testify, and that the Scots traveller was writing, after all, about a foreign culture, albeit an admired one. On the same 'grand tour', Lithgow visited Malta and saw the authorities' punishment for the same activity he had witnessed in Padua:

> The fifth day of my staying here, I saw a Spanish soldier and a Maltese boy burnt into ashes, for the public profession of sodomy; and long or night there were above a hundred bardasses,

whorish boys, that fled away to Sicily in a galliot [boat] for fear of fire. . . .[8]

The sixteenth century was one of rampant 'patrism'[9] in which certain attitudes prevailed towards homosexuality, which explains why it was a capital offence. G. Rattray Taylor outlines twelve attitude systems, most of which fit the Elizabethan period, although some require qualification.

First, there was a restrictive attitude to sex. Virtually all of this stemmed from the Puritan zeal that grew throughout Elizabeth's reign. So normal sexual appetites became to Robert Greene 'filthy lust' and paved the way for the hysterical prudery of the following century which saw 'witches' hanged in Pendle, Lancashire and Salem, Massachusetts. In the latter case, one of the 'crimes' that most appalled the bigoted village community was that the teenaged girls concerned were dancing.

Second, there was a limitation on freedom for women. Here we have the curious anomaly of a monarch who was, by accident of birth alone, a woman, yet who treated her own sex as second rate. In fact, Henry VIII had gone to extraordinary lengths to prevent this situation from occurring. In her turn, almost as a subconscious effort to please him, Elizabeth had tried to prove more of a man than most of her male counterparts in Europe. Playing the little woman when she needed to, she was nevertheless notorious for her fierce temper and short fuse. The Queen aside, however, Elizabethan England was run entirely by men. Women could inherit titles, although these passed on marriage to their husbands, but every profession, even the dubious one of acting, was barred to them. So Eleanor Bull, in whose house Marlowe died, owned the property in Deptford Strand, but her clients were exclusively male and she held the position she did because of her links with important men.

Third, women were seen as inferior and even sinful. Both Puritan and Catholic ideologies reflected this. One of the most obnoxious books ever written, *Malleus Maleficarum* (The Hammer of the Witches) was the work of two misogynist priests, Heinrich Kramer and James Sprenger. For page after page these two, creating the bible of the sixteenth- and seventeenth-century witch-hunters, heaped every sort of guilt on woman. 'For as she is a liar by nature. . . . Her gait, her posture, and habit, in which is vanity of vanities. . . . All witchcraft comes from carnal lust, which is in women insatiable.' It is this ideology, deeply ingrained and viciously chauvinistic, that even today criminalizes prostitutes in Britain, but rarely their male clients. The unique publication, in 1589, of Jane Anger's pamphlet *A Protection for Women*, defending their honesty and integrity, made no impact at all.

Fourth, chastity was considered more important than welfare and was a virtue held in greater esteem than any other. Note the Queen's disapproval of Archbishop Matthew Parker's wife because she had been brought up to believe that the Church hierarchy should be celibate.

Fifth, the sixteenth century was politically authoritarian. We have seen already the stream of legislation and the monopolistic control that ran from the dissolution of the monasteries to the death of the Queen and beyond. The power of the Privy Council was immense; it literally held men's lives in its hands. The Church made and broke men. The Stationers' Company decided what literature Englishmen should read. The Master of the Revels opened and closed theatres at will. Elizabeth even prescribed the length of the rapiers carried by her subjects.[10]

Sixth, the age was conservative, opposed to innovation. This is one area that threatens not to fit Rattray Taylor's thesis. It was an age of adventure, exploration, novelty. Yet the argument holds because of the rising Puritan backlash against the shock of the new. The theatres were an innovation and detested by many; so was tobacco. The very novelty of the Protestant ascendancy and the eclipse of Catholicism smacked of conservatism once the move had been made.

The seventh point is linked with this – a distrust of research and enquiry. The whole nature of Ralegh's School of Night became suspect as a result – it was not only the Catholic Church that demanded total acceptance of every word of the Bible.

Rattray Taylor's eighth point, a sense of inhibition and fear of spontaneity, is difficult to fit into the Elizabethan age. Where it exists, however, is yet again among the Puritans, whose sense of wonder at the existence of God had become increasingly deist as the century drew to a close. Keith Thomas, in his superb thesis on the decline of magic, shows how the Protestants tried to deprive religion of its miraculous nature, an aspect which had characterized the medieval Church. Spontaneity came with the theatres and the power of drama and poetry to move men's souls. It was over this that Philip Sidney counterattacked the Puritans in defending his poetry in 1580.

The ninth point concerns a deep fear and loathing of homosexuality, and we will return to it in Marlowe's case.

The tenth is a maximization of sex differences, especially in dress. Whereas dandies ('gimblets') and some courtiers like Ralegh wore earrings and expensive finger jewellery, the actual shape of men's and women's garments differed widely. The 'peascod' doublet or stomacher was the only similarity. Ruffs were of different shapes for each sex and for a woman to appear in the hose, pantaloons and buskins (boots) of a man would have been unthinkable.

The eleventh point, again closely associated with the Puritans, is an asceticism amounting to a morbid fear of pleasure. Smoking, drinking, whoring, play-going, even dice and backgammon, were regarded as the Devil's practices. In the next generation, the innocent maypole would be dismantled from a thousand village greens, not merely because it represented a 'lewd' and pagan phallic worship, but because it was symbolic of people *enjoying themselves*.

Finally, the major hallmark of the patrist society is the association of religion with a father image. God was male, Christ was male, the disciples were male. All priests were male. Only one woman, Mary, was allowed elevation to sanctity – and that because the male Lord had sent his male angel Gabriel to tell her she would be the mother of the male saviour. And the only branch of Christianity which extolled womanhood via the cult of the Virgin Mary, the Catholic, was rapidly being expunged from England.

In this patrist society, homosexuality was a taboo not to be tolerated, but oddly, there was a dichotomy here that fitted the hypocrisy of Elizabeth's Court and government. Sexual matters were originally the concern of the Church, in that a sin had been committed and that God's laws, rather than man's, had been broken. The Ten Commandments given to Moses were fairly unequivocal, but homosexuality had no specific mention in the Bible. The word itself was coined by the daring pioneers of sexual psychology in the

1890s. Before that, a whole range of euphemisms, mostly classical, could be found in various forms of literature – sodomite, catamite, ingle, ganymede, pathic, cinaedus, and the much ill-used, bugger. In the Old Testament's version of the destruction of Sodom and Gomorrah, the compilers of the King James Bible in 1611 used euphemisms. 'All vices vile'[11] according to du Bartas, including rape, incest and heterosexual prostitution, led to the most depraved sin of all, sodomy. It is equally clear, however, that in the literary usage of the day, sodomy was equated with heterosexual sex and bestiality. Edward Coke,[12] one of the greatest jurists in English history (but, perhaps by definition, a man of the Establishment) defined it as a sin 'by mankind with mankind or with brute beast or by womankind with brute beast'.

Given the vagueness of definition, which may itself account for the very taboo of the subject, it is not surprising that double standards existed. On the one hand, there were prosecutions for homosexual acts. For example in 1580, Matthew Heaton, a priest from East Grinstead, Sussex, was put on trial for his relationship with a young male parishioner. Forty years before Heaton, Nicholas Udall, the future writer of the comic play *Ralph Royster Doyster*, was dismissed from his post as headmaster of Eton after it was discovered that he was having an affair with (and possibly being blackmailed by) a former pupil. Fourteen years after Heaton, as the dust began to settle on Marlowe's death, Mr Cooke, the headmaster of Great Tay in Essex, was up before the church courts as one who 'teacheth [his pupils] all manner of bawdry'; 'a man of beastly behaviour amongst his scholars'.

The ambiguity of attitudes and of English law is demonstrated by the fact that both Udall and Cooke got away with their offences. In an age far less hysterical than ours over the fate of children, Cooke did not even bother to attend court and Udall, although dismissed his post and imprisoned for a while, was made Prebendary of Windsor by Edward VI, where presumably he could continue to swish his cane with his usual fervour in charge of the chapel's choirboys.

Less lucky, however, was John Atherton, the Bishop of Waterford and Lismore, who was hanged in 1640 along with his lover and proctor John Childe. We are perhaps cheating a little with this example, as it took place in Ireland fifty years after Marlowe's death and probably reflects the changing attitudes of a different generation. As Alan Bray has pointed out, however, trials for sodomy tended to hit the headlines at times of other tensions. John Swan and John Lister were executed in Edinburgh in 1570 at the height of the Catholic–Calvinist tensions there. It is likely that Atherton and Childe were victims of the same sense of upheaval. The actual number of trials concerning homosexuality is small. Between 1559 and 1625 there were only four indictments for sodomy in the counties of Kent, Sussex, Hertfordshire and Essex put together.

The evidence that Marlowe was actively homosexual is circumstantial. We do not know enough about the relationships within his family in Canterbury to identify the classic patterns of homosexual development, but he was brought up in an essentially female household where he was the only boy. The all-male environment of the King's School, at a time when boys naturally experiment out of curiosity, may have had its influences on him, but a far more likely place was Cambridge. At Bene't's, as at other colleges, the practice was for Fellows to share rooms with scholars. At seventeen, Marlowe was older than most, but here was an environment, at once claustrophobic and incestuous, in which homosexuality may well have been practised. Was the atheist Francis Kett one such Fellow who engineered such bedroom-sharing for his own ends?

If we are right in that Marlowe was recruited to Walsingham's secret service while at Cambridge by Nicholas Faunt, this may explain how it happened. As we have seen, Faunt became a firm friend of Anthony Bacon, an active intelligencer for Walsingham, operating from Paris. The letters that have survived between the two while they travelled Europe separately reporting to the spymaster, are gushingly sentimental and may well be symptomatic of a homosexual relationship. In the summer of 1586, Bacon was accused, while monitoring the French Catholic–Huguenot situation in Béarn, of an act of sodomy with a young male servant. Servants were in a highly vulnerable position for the predatory homosexual in Elizabethan England (or Europe). Living in, with little approximating to human rights and utterly dependent on their masters for a living, an unknown number of them may have included bedroom games as part of their duties. Although there are no English documents relating to the case, Bacon's misogyny (he even avoided his mother and the Queen whenever possible) had made him enemies among the wives of the Huguenot aristocracy and they saw to it that the case came to court.

A series of witnesses testified before the royal historian Claude de la Grange that Bacon, oblivious to casual observers, kissed and fondled his page, Isaac Bougades, in exchange for sweets and cash. Other servants were involved and the evidence implies that Bougades was something of a rent boy in the local town of Montauban. As always, French society was even more hypocritical than English. Male prostitutes – Henri III's *mignons* – were an accepted part of court life but it was a *repeated* offence of sodomy that under French law could lead to execution. In the event, Bacon obtained financial support from (of all ironies) local Catholic lords and everyone seems to have turned a blind eye.

The link between Marlowe, Faunt and Bacon is tenuous, but the taint of homosexuality has lurked under the surface in male universities for centuries and it has also refused to travel far from the secret service.[13] A city like London, with its quickly growing population, much of it flotsam and jetsam, provided temptations too. One of the books (including Marlowe's works) burned by order of the Bishop of London at the Stationers' Hall in June 1599 was by John Marston and contained the following description of a man-about-town:

Rags [fashion], running horses, dogs, drabs [prostitutes], drink and dice
The only things that he doth hold in price.
Yet more than these, naught doth him so delight
As doth his smooth-skinned, plump-thighed catamite.

There were probably homosexual 'stews' in Southwark, but the problem with identifying homosexuality, in London as elsewhere, is that there was no discernible underground subculture of literature, clothing or meeting-places that could be called homosexual.

There were traditions, however, that may well have had an important influence on Marlowe; the first is classical culture. Ancient Greek society prized male relationships as being superior to heterosexual ones. The purpose of the latter was procreation whereas male–male bonding, seen in the homosexual pairings of the Spartan army and in Homer's *Iliad* in the love between Achilles and Patroclus, was on an altogether higher plane. It even found acceptance in the Old Testament relationship between David and Jonathan – 'passing the love of women'. Marlowe, like all scholars of his day, was brought up in the culture, borrowed from the cradle of civilization. When Marlowe's friend the playwright Thomas Kyd was arrested he wrote to Sir John Puckering, apportioning blame in all directions. Kyd's second indictment against Marlowe reads: 'He would report St John to be our saviour Christes Alexis. I cover [report] it with reverence and trembling that is that Christ did love him with extraordinary love.' Christ's homosexual leanings towards John the Evangelist are included in the Baines Note, but Alexis is the crucial word and refers to a character in Vergil's second eclogue, a beautiful youth loved by the shepherd Corydon.

This was the second influence on Marlowe's homosexuality – literature. John Marston,[14] Michael Drayton,[15] Ben Jonson,[16] Edward Guilpin,[17] Richard Brathwaite,[18] Thomas Middleton[19] and John Donne[20] all wrote satires which have a homosexual theme or references.

In the 1590s, John Donne was still a student at Lincoln's Inn and about to embark on Essex's expeditions to Cadiz and the Azores as part of the on-going war with Spain. He can have had no direct influence on Marlowe, but his description of Elizabeth's Court in his *Satires* is a vivid lightning flash illuminating those 'hypocritical asses' who surrounded the Queen – 'who loves whores, who boys and who goats'.[21] Both Ben Jonson and John Marston linked homosexuality and bestiality. In *Sir Voluptuous Beast* Jonson's character teases his wife – 'Telling the motions of each petticoat/And how his Ganymede moved and how his goat.' John Marston's *The Scourge of Villanie* has his hero, Luscus, turning for solace in his mistress's absence to his 'Ganymede' and 'perfumed she-goat'.

The other influence on Marlowe was of course the theatre. The Puritan Philip Stubbes was not alone in believing the London stage to be a centre of all kinds of debauchery. In *The Anatomie of Abuses* (1583) he wrote of audiences, 'And in their secret conclaves (covertly) they play the sodomites or worse.'

Again we are in the realms of the boy-actress and the whole androgynous world forced on impresarios and playwrights by the obsessive straitjacket of the Church's laws prohibiting women from acting. One of Ben Jonson's characters in *The Poetaster* asks, 'What? Shall I have my son a stager [actor] now, an ingle for players?' Another interesting link between Marlowe and the shadowy world of homosexuality is Robert Poley. There is circumstantial evidence for his homosexuality too.

In common with many English kings, Edward II was perhaps more sinned against than sinning. Modern biographies concentrate on the cultured man, fond of art and architecture, even if he was not the general his father had been. It was quite probably Edward's friendship with Piers Gaveston that fascinated Marlowe, although perhaps the fact that the king was an early patron of the theatre had an appeal too. Evidence for a homosexual relationship between Edward and Gaveston is almost non-existent, but it has come down to us in the form of a weak, idle monarch cavorting in unnatural frivolity while his country went to the dogs, humiliated by the Scots for example at Bannockburn. 'Obstinate sodomy' was prevalent among the clergy in Edward's day, but the strongest evidence of the king's leanings seems to come from the manner of his murder in Berkeley Castle, sometime in late September 1327. He was, according to one account 'slayne with a hoote broche putte thro the secret place posteriale'. If this is true, it is an early example of symmetrical reversal, the principle, still used in Elizabethan times and perhaps applicable to Marlowe's own death. Edward had sinned, according to gossip, by taking part in anal intercourse – it was only fitting that he should die the same way.

Those who see no homosexual overtones in *Edward II* have clearly not been looking. In the play, Mortimer says

> The mightiest kings have had their minions:
> Great Alexander lov'd Hephaestion;
> The conquering Hercules for Hylas wept;
> And for Patroclus stern Achilles droop'd;
> And not kings only, but the wisest men.
> The Roman Tully lov'd Octavius;
> Great Socrates, wild Alcibiades.

Horrified by the frivolity and self-seeking of the upstart Gaveston, the nobility's patience wears thin. 'The king,' says Mortimer, 'is lovesick for his minion', and this situation is not excused by the pedigree of homosexual love just described. Outmanoeuvred by his council, Edward is forced to let Gaveston go. It reads like a lovers' parting – 'But to forsake you, in whose gracious looks/The blessedness of Gaveston remains.' And Edward, lost, snaps at his queen, Isabella, 'Fawn not on me, French strumpet, get thee gone.'

Many commentators have noted that Isabella is the *only* important female character in any of Marlowe's plays – Helen of Troy in *Dr Faustus* for example, is a mere sex object, not a real person – and since he cannot portray women properly this proves that he was homosexual. In *Edward II*, of course, he is bound by the historical sources he used (Holinshed) and naturally, alongside the male power of Edward himself, Isabella pales. She is however the 'she-wolf of France', frequently unfaithful to her husband, and in his chauvinistic characterization, Marlowe does her justice by conveying her deviousness. Realizing that Gaveston has Edward's heart, she laments in a soliloquy, 'The cup of Hymen had been full of poison.'

Marlowe's murderer in *Edward II* is Lightborn, and the name is fascinating. Here is the carrier of light, Lucifer, with all the connotations of the unholy trinity of magic, homosexuality and heresy. In keeping with the galaxy of murderers we find in Shakespeare too, Lightborn is sympathetic and engages his victim in conversation. Prophetic souls like Robert Greene would have seen something portentous in this – a conversation between friends 'in quiet sort' at the house of Eleanor Bull in Deptford just before the 'hotte broche' struck. Lightborn, like Frizer at Deptford, needed help and two others enter – Matrevis and Gurney; another unholy trinity to augment the first. They carry a table and a spit. 'So,' says Lightborn, 'lay the table down, and stamp on it,/But not too hard, lest that you bruise his body.'

There is no mention of the heated poker through the anus and in all staged productions since, good taste dictates that the murder is carried out *behind* the table or in some other way. Unlike Deptford, where all the killers walked away, Gurney turns on Lightborn and stabs him. Frizer, it is true, went to prison, but merely to await the Queen's pardon; the analogy, ultimately, does not work. There is no symmetrical reversal here.

An acknowledgement of Christopher Marlowe's homosexuality is important because of the bearing it had in his time. Edward Coke wrote of it that homosexuality was a 'detestable and abominable sin amongst Christians, not to be named'. In his opinion, 'it deserveth death'[22] and it seems likely that Coke's (and therefore the Establishment's) attitude came about as a result of an increasing tendency by the late sixteenth century to equate homosexuality first with Catholicism and then with atheism.

There was an air of magic and the supernatural about homosexuality. It was, according to the poet Walter Kennedy, akin to the unnatural predations of the werewolf and the basilisk, mythical creatures who ripped out the hearts of men or turned them to stone with a single glance. As we shall see, Christopher Marlowe was linked in the minds of some people with the Black Arts because of his recreation of the Faust legend and of his membership of the School of Night.

On a more practical level, homosexuality was equated with the enemy that was Catholicism. Coke railed against the unholy trinity of 'sorcerers, sodomites and heretics'.[23] Rome was called, in England, 'new Sodom', 'second Sodom' and 'Sodom Fair'. William Lithgow, convinced that it lurked in the enforced celibacy of Catholic priests, wrote – 'Lo, there is the chastity of the Romish priests who forsooth may not marry and yet may miscarry themselves in all abominations, especially in sodomy, which is their continual pleasure and pastime.'[24] John Marston was even more specific, bearing in mind Marlowe's mission for Walsingham in 1585–6. In *The Times' Whistle* he wrote

> Hence, hence ye falsed, seeming patriots.
> Return not with pretence of salving spots,
> When here ye soil us with impurity
> And monstrouth filth of Douai seminary.
> What though Iberia yield you liberty
> To snort in source of Sodom villainy?

Douai of course was the home of John Allen's English seminary before its move to Rheims.

Robert Greene's *Groatsworth of Wit* was published posthumously by Henry Chettle. His accusations against Marlowe for his atheism and Machiavellianism are discussed elsewhere, but it is obvious from Chettle's later response that at least two of those libelled by the dead poet had complained. It is not known whether one was Nashe or Shakespeare, but the other is likely to have been Marlowe. It is clear that Chettle did not know him personally – 'With neither of them that take offence was I acquainted and with one of them I care not if I never be.'[25] In his own defence, Chettle explained that he had censored Greene's vitriolic purple prose – 'For the first [Marlowe] whose learning I reverence, and at the perusing of Greene's booke, stroke out what then in conscience I thought he in some displeasure writ; or had it been true, yet to publish it was intolerable. . .'.

That Marlowe was homosexual – or at least bisexual – cannot seriously be doubted. Was it also a motive for his murder?

On 18 February 1587, while Christopher Marlowe was probably still in Cambridge, Mary, the luckless Queen of Scots, went to her death at Fotheringhay Castle in Northamptonshire. Her cousin Elizabeth had agonized since the previous December over the death warrant which she alone could issue. The struggle between the queens had been going on for nearly thirty years and as long as Mary remained alive, as the Babington Plot and many like it had confirmed, she was a rallying point for discontented English Catholics stiffened by the bigotry of Rome.

'Mr Dean,' said Mary to the Dean of Peterborough, who was trying desperately to deliver the last rites to her in the castle's great hall, 'I shall die as I have lived, in the true and holy Catholic faith. All you can say to me on that score is but vain, and all your prayers, I think, can avail me but little.'[26] She prayed for all her subjects, both Scottish and English. She prayed for the soul of Elizabeth, who had brought her to this. And in her blood-red petticoat she knelt while the headsman swung his axe twice before the bald head rolled away from the auburn wig and the little lap-dog scampered away in terror from the dull thud and the seeping blood.

Her body was stripped and all the queen's clothes destroyed. There must be no relics of this martyr, those gruesome icons so beloved of the Catholic Church. The surgeons embalmed her body and on the orders of Francis Walsingham, it was placed in a lead-lined coffin, too strong for relic-hunters to break open.

While the bells of London rang and cannon roared on the Artillery Grounds in Whitechapel, Elizabeth flew into one of those rages for which she was notorious. 'Her countenance changed,' wrote the chronicler William Camden, 'her words faltered, and with excessive sorrow she was in manner astonished, insomuch as she gave herself over to grief.'[27] Her Privy Council fled to a man, knowing what would come. Walsingham hid at his home in Barn Elms and Burghley's grovelling letters to his queen were returned unopened.

While this grief was probably genuine and the result of thirty years' angst, Catholics were unimpressed. Philip of Spain, who saw himself as some sort of distant protector of Mary, wrote, 'It is very fine for the Queen of England now to give out that it was done without her wish, the contrary being so clearly the case.'[28] How much the execution was really a trigger to the 'enterprise of England' is difficult to say. Certainly by September, the Duke of Parma, Philip's highly capable general in the Netherlands, had orders from his king to assemble a fleet of barges for the invasion of England.

It is not known whether Marlowe, who was probably in London by this time, played any role in keeping Walsingham informed of these troop movements and logistical preparations.[29] Events moved quickly in 1587. On 21 April Francis Drake famously 'singed the king of Spain's beard' by sending his fireships into Cadiz to damage Parma's fleet, under construction. Thirty galleons and tons of supplies were lost by the Spaniards, delaying the 'enterprise of England' for fourteen months.

On land, however, the picture was less rosy. Leicester's men, despite being reinforced with fresh levies, made no impact on Parma's troops at all, even losing the important garrison town of Sluys on 25 July. By December, the disgraced Earl returned home, to die a broken man at his house in Cornbury, Oxfordshire, the following September, probably of malaria.

The campaign season of the next spring saw renewed vigour from Philip. Admiral Santa Cruz died from the typhus raging through the Spanish fleet and his replacement was the 'many-syllabled' Duke of Medina-Sedonia, who had clashed with Drake at Cadiz and *just* managed to save the town from total destruction. Medina-Sedonia was a brilliant administrator, but he had no naval experience and openly considered the invasion plan ill-conceived. The prospects in the summer of 1588 were not good: an inexperienced commander; a typhoid epidemic; a dubious welcome at best from English Catholics. The logistics of actually landing on England's shores were a nightmare that never, of course, had to be faced.

The Queen, on the other hand, was confronted by the most powerful enemy in Europe and a threat of the unthinkable – the invasion of England – which she had tried to avoid for thirty years. Lord Howard of Effingham, with his house at Deptford Green, had been appointed Lord High Admiral in December of the previous year, harbours were strengthened, old ships of the line refurbished and eleven new galleons built. Beacons were erected all along the south and east coasts as an early-warning system for the sighting of the Spanish fleet, which sailed down the Tagus on 20 May. Frantic talks held at Ostend between English and Spanish diplomats were proving fruitless. Howard of Effingham warned – 'For the love of Jesus Christ, Madam, awake thoroughly and see the villainous treasons around you, against your Majesty and your realm, and draw your forces round about you like a mighty prince to defend you.'[30] Peace talks were abandoned and London prepared for war. Some commentators assume that Christopher Marlowe was among the 10,000 men ordered to arms in the capital and that may be so, but there is no evidence for it. Leicester's headquarters were at Tilbury along the further reaches of the Thames and it was here the Queen famously appeared, in breast and back plate and riding a white horse, on 9 August and proclaimed

> I know I have the body of a weak and feeble woman, but I have the heart and stomach of a king, and of a king of England too: and think foul scorn that Parma or Spain, or any prince of Europe, should dare invade the borders of my realm. . . . By your valour in the field, we shall shortly have a famous victory over these enemies of my God, of my kingdom and of my people.

Were it not for the events that Elizabeth already knew had happened six days earlier, her 20,000 militiamen would have been no match for Parma's battle-hardened veterans.

On 3 August, the Armada, already lacking thirty-two of its ships because of squalls and bad navigation, was being driven by strong south westerlies up the English Channel, hotly pursued by Howard on board Walter Ralegh's ship, renamed *Ark Royal*. The tight crescent formation of Medina-Sedonia's fleet was broken up off the Isle of Wight by the four English squadrons commanded by Howard, Drake, Hawkins and Frobisher. Drake inflicted most damage and sent his fireships in again while the battered Spaniards anchored off Calais to recover three days later. Drake hit them again off Gravelines in an eight-hour sea fight and the bitter winds of the Channel did the rest. Of the 132 ships that had left Lisbon the previous May only 60 returned home; more than 11,000 men dead from thirst, hunger, drowning and battle. With a sense of irony not lost on those who loathed Elizabeth's police state, Spanish survivors were hailed as heroes on the orders of Philip, while their victorious English counterparts were left to die from gangrene.

The bells rang out and the whole country rejoiced. The Queen attended a service of thanksgiving at St Paul's, but not before she had been to a smaller one, at the church of St Nicholas in Deptford, entering through the 'Armada gate', just feet from where, five years later, anonymous sextons would bring the body of Kit Marlowe. 'God blew His winds and they were scattered.'

We next hear of Marlowe, now at the height of his fame in theatrical circles, in September 1589 in the infamous fight in Hog Lane. Thirty years later, Fynes Morrison had this to say of street-brawling:

Of old, when [Englishmen] were fenced with bucklers [small, leather shields] as with a rapier, nothing was more common with them, than to fight about taking the right or left hand, or the wall, or upon any unpleasing countenance. Clashing of swords was then daily music in every street, and they did not only fight combats, but cared not to set upon their enemy upon advantages and unequal terms.[31]

Duelling in all European countries was a national pastime. An estimated four thousand members of the aristocracy and gentry died

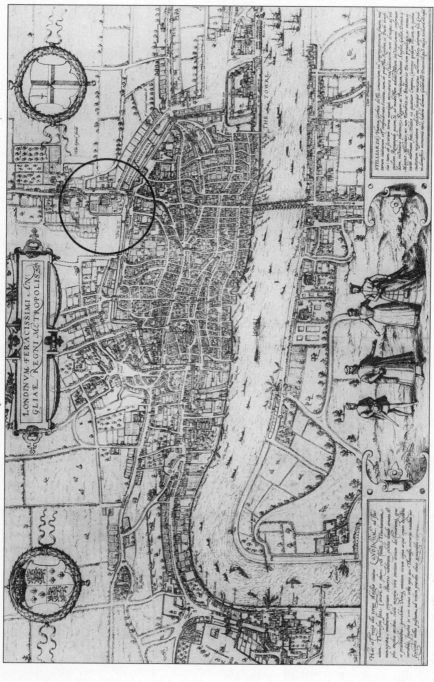

Map 2. Stilliard's Plan of London. Norton Folgate, where Marlowe shared rooms with Thomas Watson and later Thomas Kyd, is situated in the circled area top right, as is Hog Lane, where he fought on Watson's behalf with William Bradley. (Reproduced by permission of the Guildhall Library, Corporation of London)

in duels in France alone between 1560 and 1610. The cause was inevitably a sneer or casual remark, taken as an insult by one of the parties involved. The result was always a clash of steel, a loss of blood and, all too often, death. In *Romeo and Juliet*, Mercutio taunts Benvolio:

> Thou wilt quarrel with a man for cracking nuts, having no other reason but because thou hast hazel eyes. . . . Thou hast quarreled with a man for coughing in the street because he hath wakened thy dog that hath lain asleep in the sun.

The fight between Marlowe and William Bradley in Hog Lane, off Bishopsgate Street in the parish of St Giles Without Cripplegate is important because it establishes Marlowe as a man of violence and quick temper, character defects seized upon by those who wanted the man dead in the early summer of 1593. The Middlesex Session Rolls for the period 9 September to 2 October 1589 confirm that Christopher Marlowe and Thomas Watson, both of Norton Folgate and styled 'yeoman' and 'gentleman' respectively were arrested by constables and committed to Newgate prison by the Lieutenant of the Tower, Sir Owen Hopton, on suspicion of murder.

Norton Folgate was bisected by Bishopsgate Street midway between the open spaces of Spitalfields and 'Fynnesburie Field', where archery was practised. To the south, Moor Field was a tenter ground, where linens and wool were laid out to bleach in the sun. Hog Lane itself ran between Bishopsgate Street and Finsbury. Marlowe and Watson, most authorities presume, were either close neighbours or shared lodgings in one of these places, since both men probably had the money to rent somewhere quite substantial.

William Bradley was the son of an innkeeper of Gray's Inn Lane, Holborn and he was slightly older than Marlowe, at twenty-six. The man owed a £14 debt to John Alleyn, another innkeeper who was the brother of the famous actor. In keeping with the litigious spirit of the age, Alleyn threatened to sue Bradley in the Court of Common Pleas, using his lawyer Hugh Swift. Bradley countered this by getting a friend, George Orrell, to beat Swift up if this action went ahead. Swift was the brother-in-law of Thomas Watson and by September 1580 a regular feud was going on between Bradley and

Orrell on the one side and Swift, Alleyn and Watson on the other. Bradley was a known thug and was waiting for Watson in Hog Lane on the afternoon of the 18th.

It was then that Marlowe arrived and Bradley attacked him as a friend of Watson. We do not have the exact details of the weapon(s) involved, but it is likely that swords were drawn. Early in the sixteenth century, a scientific system of fencing moves was developing. Swordsmanship, like music, architecture, mathematics and astronomy, was regarded as part of a gentleman's education. Despite an attempt by George Silver to champion an English school of broadsword fighting, the Italians dominated the art, as they did so much else, and Marlowe probably used a variant technique of that promulgated by Achille Marozzo in 1536 which included tripping, kicking and shoulder barging. Several authorities believe that it was the Hog Lane fight that influenced Shakespeare's duel scene in *Romeo and Juliet*, even to the extent that the Stratford man may have witnessed it. Mercutio refers to Tybalt's Spanish style of swordsmanship – 'He fights as you sing prick-song, keeps time, distance, and proportion; rests me his minim rest, one, two, and the third in your bosom.' In *As You Like It*, Touchstone describes the formality of the Italian style of picking a quarrel – first came the 'retort courteous', then the 'quip modest', the 'reply churlish', the 'reproof valiant', the 'countercheck quarrelsome', the 'lie with circumstance' and the 'lie direct'. The point was that street-fighting was all about staying alive and the formal, highly stylized pirouettes of the later Italian, French and Spanish schools bore little relevance to that.

Marlowe probably carried a swept-hilt rapier, the most common sword available in the 1580s, and he may have used a dagger or cloak as well to deflect Bradley's blade. The fight, with thrust and parry (the lunge had probably not developed this early) continued up and down Hog Lane for some minutes before Thomas Watson arrived. According to testimony delivered later, Bradley shouted 'Art thou now come? Then I will have a bout with thee' and attacked Watson, who was subsequently wounded. Marlowe bowed out and Watson, driven to the edge of a ditch at the northern end of the lane, desperately drove Bradley back and killed him. The coroner for Middlesex, John Chalkhill, duly noted the dead man's wounds, 6 inches deep and 1 inch wide to the right side of his chest.

In an uncanny precursor to Deptford, neither Marlowe nor Watson made any attempt to run, but calmly waited to be taken into custody, sure in the knowledge (*unlike* Deptford) that they had both acted in self defence. The arresting officer was Stephen Wylde, a tailor from the area. The well-known characters of Dogberry and Verges in Shakespeare's *Much Ado About Nothing* remain close to the truth. William Bullein had the measure of them; in 1573, he wrote

> These are not only the constables with the watchmen in London, but also almost through this realm, most falsely abusing the time, coming very late to the watch, sitting down in some common place of watching, wherein some falleth on sleep by the reason of the labour or much drinking before.[32]

For all the great jurist Edward Coke expected honesty, loyalty, knowledge and ability in his constables, it is unlikely that he actually got any of these. In 1616, a constable in Wiltshire reported (presumably via an intermediary): 'I am unlearned, and by reason thereof am constrained to go two miles from my house to have the help of a scrivener to read such warrants as are sent to me.'[33] Constables were unpaid and untrained, doing their local duty out of some vestigial remainder of feudal service. The problem, as Bullein realized, was the criminality of Elizabethan society – 'too little wages, too many serving-men, too many tippling-houses, too many drabs, too many knaves, too little labour, too much idleness.' Overnight in Newgate was enough for many men, although as we have seen, some spent their lives there. Some, like Robert Poley, were in and out of prisons on the Queen's business. The prison where Marlowe and Watson waited was the second called Newgate, nicknamed 'The Whit' after Richard Whittington, the Lord Mayor of London who had left money for its building in his will. It was five storeys high with a condemned cell called 'Limbo', but it was the first such prison to reflect the social standing of its inmates, with a dining hall and airy rooms for those with the freedom of the City, subterranean caverns for the rest. *The Blacke Dogge of Newgate* published by Luke Hutton in 1600 described the hideous clattering of the prisoners' chains as they begged richer inmates for food. The con worked systematically by the turnkeys in Newgate was that the prisoners were obliged to pay when fetters and leg-irons were fitted and when they were taken off.

On 19 September, the inquest on Bradley took place and Coroner Chalkhill's twelve-man jury decided that Watson had acted in self-defence. Marlowe was technically not charged with murder as he had withdrawn from the affray when Watson arrived to confront Bradley. He was therefore able to obtain bail while Watson was returned to Newgate to await the official closure of the case. Marlowe applied to Richard Kytchine, a lawyer of Clifford's Inn and horner Humfrey Rowland of East Smithfield, who gave sureties of £20 each. He himself was bound over to the tune of £40 as long as he promised to attend the next court sessions, to be held on 3 December.

It is noticeable that the coroner here was the Middlesex county official, despite the fact that Hog Lane, like Deptford, is within 'the verge', i.e., 12 miles of the Queen's person, assuming that Elizabeth was at Placentia in Greenwich or Eltham, or Whitehall, or Nonsuch. There was no need for a royal coroner to attend the legal formalities following the killing of William Bradley, because there was no need, as yet, to cover anything up. That level of double-dealing would come later.

Who were Marlowe's sureties? Kytchine was a Yorkshireman who probably knew Marlowe personally, appearing for Philip Henslowe later. He frequented the Mermaid Tavern in Bread Street, where both Walter Ralegh and Ben Jonson drank. Rowland came from a lower rank altogether, a maker of lantern horns.[34] A constable of the watch in East Smithfield, he seems to have made quite a living out of standing surety for people and even had two servants. Intriguingly, they were Dutchmen from Antwerp and described as 'of no church'. One of the most polemic of the exiled Catholics in Antwerp was Richard Verstigan, whose real name was Richard Rowlands. Could he and the lantern-maker have been related?

It may have been with some relief that Marlowe recognized, when he appeared before the bench on 3 December, Sir Roger Manwood, now Chief Baron of the Exchequer, who had been the poet's patron as a boy in Canterbury. For all Manwood was 'the terror of the night-prowler' with a fine reputation for dealing with felons, there really was no case to answer against Marlowe and he was released. When Manwood died in 1592, leaving 'a one penny wheaten loaf every Wednesday and Sunday' and 'four cartloads of fuel' as well as gowns and shoes for his tenants in his will, Marlowe wrote his epitaph in Latin:

> Because of his many virtues, Envy, spare this man alone. Do not vent your insolence on the ashes of him whose countenance awed so many thousands of mortals. So may your bones lie happily at rest, and may your fame outlive the memorials on your marble tomb, when the bloodless messenger of Pluto wounds you.

It was in this year of 1589 when Marlowe crossed swords with Bradley and Manwood that Ingram Frizer was buying and selling property in Basingstoke. What of Nicholas Skeres? After his probable involvement in the Babington Plot, he disappears from the official scene for nearly three years, but by 1589 was one of the minions of the Earl of Essex.

Robert Devereux was born two years after Marlowe in Netherwood, near Bromyard, Herefordshire. The eldest son of the 1st Earl, he emerged with an MA from Trinity College, Cambridge at fifteen and although the two men were technically contemporaries at colleges only a few hundred yards apart, it is unlikely that Marlowe would have mixed with a boy at once so junior to him in terms of age and so senior in terms of rank. By the time Marlowe obtained his MA and was working for Walsingham, Devereux was already a soldier with Leicester's army in the Low Countries. He distinguished himself at Zutphen, and came home to ingratiate himself as one of the Queen's new favourites. As Leicester's stepson, he inevitably filled the man's shoes after Dudley's death in 1588.

It is possible that, by 1589, Robert Poley had met Christopher Marlowe. He may have married the poet Thomas Watson's sister in 1582, but had left her for the on-off affair with Joan Yeomans two years later. We have no idea if the two men remained friends in this situation – it seems unlikely. But if they did, and he and Poley continued to meet up in the late 1580s, then what more natural than that the agent should meet his fellow lodger, fellow poet and fellow spy Kit Marlowe?

It was in 1589 that the fourth member of the cast assembled at Deptford made her appearance for the first time – Eleanor Bull. She was born Eleanor Whitney of a Herefordshire family from Whitney-on-Wye who were local gentry. Any image the Puritans have left of Marlowe's death in a tavern run by a 'doxy' immediately disappears. Eleanor was, allowing for the patrism of the times, a woman of substance. And as if to prove it, she was left £100 by her cousin, Blanche Parry, in a will dated 1589. Another recipient of Blanche's generosity was another cousin, William Cecil, Lord Burghley. Yet another, though dead before Blanche Parry, was Dr John Dee, the Queen's magus. That the woman who owned the house in which Kit Marlowe died should be related to these men is no mere coincidence.

Eleanor had married Richard Bull, sub-bailiff at Sayes Court, the manor house in Deptford, at the church of St Mary-le-Bow in October 1571. Bull's superior was Sir George Howard, a kinsman of the Lord Admiral whose house stood on Deptford Green and who by 1589 was the destroyer of the Armada and a national hero.

Given all these interwoven connections, there could only be one house in the country where Kit Marlowe could have met his death.

SEVEN

Machevill

And let them know that I am Machevill,
And weigh not men, and therefore not men's words.
Admir'd I am of those that hate me most.

Christopher Marlowe, *The Jew of Malta*

The *Concise Oxford Dictionary* defines Machiavelli as an 'unscrupulous schemer; one who practises duplicity in statecraft' and blames it all on the Florentine of the same name.

Niccolo Machiavelli was a political philosopher born in Florence in 1469. Rising rapidly to power after the overthrow of the monk Savonarola in 1498, he served as diplomat for fourteen years and mixed with the most powerful rulers of the High Renaissance – Julius II, the warrior pope who commissioned Michelangelo; Louis XII of France, 'the father of the People', who married Henry VIII's sister, Mary; Cesare Borgia, captain-general of the papal armies; Maximilian I of Austria, who drove the Hungarians back from the gates of Vienna. Discredited, stripped of office and tortured by the Medici family who ruled Florence from 1512, Machiavelli spent the remainder of his life writing.

The fact that the Cambridge don Gabriel Harvey could find illicit readings of the man's book so appalling speaks volumes for the hypocrisy of Elizabethan England. As Marlowe was to pronounce to his friends in the School of Night, 'all Protestants are hypocritical asses'. Machiavellian realpolitik was practised by the Queen and her council, but everyone decried it, claiming they operated out of nationalism, love of sovereign or religious conviction. We find amoral attitudes to politics almost without exception among the great and good of Elizabethan England, especially in the statesmen who made up the Queen's Privy Council, Walsingham, Burghley,

Howard and the rest. It took a man of extraordinary courage – or recklessness – to tell it like it was; such a man was Kit Marlowe.

Robert Greene detested him – but then, Robert Greene detested nearly everybody. He was dying when he wrote *A Groatsworth of Wit Bought with a Million of Repentance* in 1592. The work, bitter and carping and based on envy, is addressed in part to Marlowe – 'To those Gentlemen his Quondam [sometime] acquaintance, that spend their wits in making plaies, R.G. wisheth a better exercise, and wisdome to prevent his extremities.' But Kit Marlowe loved extremities; he was a man continually pushing, always on the edge.

'Wonder not,' Greene seems to be writing directly to Marlowe,

> (for with thee I will first begin) thou famous gracer of Tragedies, that Greene, who hath said with thee (like the fool in his heart) There is no God, should now give glorie unto his greatness . . . Why should thy excellent wit, his gift, bee so blinded, that thou shouldst give no glorie to the giver: Is it pestilent Machiavelian pollicy that thou hast studied? O peevish follie! What are his rules but mere confused mockeries, able to extirpate in small time the generation of mankind. For if Sic volo, sic iubeo [I will, so I will command] hold in those that are able to command: and if it be lawful Fas & Nefas [right or not] to do anything that is beneficial; only Tyrants should possess the earth, and they striving to exceeding tyranny, should each to other be a slaughterman; till the mightiest outliving all, one stroke were left for Death, that in one age man's life should end.[1]

This dog-eat-dog hypothesis was unthinkable to Greene, terrified by approaching death and anxious to be seen as a believer against the day. This was a far cry from his attitude earlier, when he wrote the transparently Machiavellian *A Notable Discovery of Coosnage*. It was equally unthinkable fifty years later, when the playwright Thomas Heywood[2] penned *Machiavel, as he lately appeared to his dear sons* (1641) in which the Florentine is equated with all forms of sin and depravity.

The problem with works like *The Prince* is that once established – and misunderstood – they become a benchmark for someone to go further. That someone was Pietro Aretino, from Arezzo in Tuscany.

He was the illegitimate child of a nobleman, Luigi Bacci. Writing pornography – in sonnet form, of course – at the age of sixteen, he was banished from his native town for writing satires on papal indulgences, and worked for a while as a book-binder in Perugia. In Rome, however, between 1517 and 1527, he attached himself to Pope Leo X by reason of his wit, writing skills and sheer brass neck. The *sonetti lussuriosi* continued, however, and he was dismissed. Quite undaunted by this setback, Aretino went on to become the confidant of Giovanni de' Medici, of the same powerful family for whom Machiavelli had written, and of Francis I of France. At Venice in the 1530s he ingratiated himself via the local bishop with the Holy Roman Emperor Charles V who lavished presents on him. He is said to have died after falling off a stool, laughing at some joke![3]

Known as 'the scourge of princes', he was a blackmailer and intriguer in the sense in which the term 'Machiavellian' was used by men of the sixteenth century and it is to this that Greene alluded in *A Groatsworth of Wit*:

> The brocher of this Diabolical Atheism is dead, and in his life had never the felicitie he aimed at: but as he began in craft, lived in fear and ended in despair Quam inscrutabilia sunt Dei indicia? [How impenetrable are the judgements of God?] this murderer of many brethren had his conscience seared like Caine; this betrayer of him that gave his life for him inherited the portion of Judas; this Apostate perished as ill as Julian:[4] and wilt thou, my friend, be his disciple?

In *The Jew of Malta*, Machevill speaks the prologue to the play:

> Albeit the world think Machevill is dead,
> Yet was his soul but flown beyond the Alps,
> And now the Guise[5] is dead, is come from France
> To view this land and frolic with his friends.
> To some perhaps my name is odious;
> But such as love me, guard me from their tongues,
> And let them know that I am Machevill,
> And weigh not men, and therefore not men's words.
> Admir'd I am of those that hate me most.

> Though some speak openly against my books
> Yet will they read me, and therebye attain
> To Peter's chair; . . .

Marlowe was actually being very careful in referring to 'Peter's chair'. The clear inference was that Machiavelli's supporters were Catholic, and the duplicity of Catholics in England in the late 1580s/early 1590s was well known. Similarly, the central character of Marlowe's *Jew*, Barabas, who is clearly Machiavellian – 'grace him as he deserves/And let him not be entertain'd the worse/Because he favours me' – is also an outsider, more alien to England (the Maltese setting is irrelevant) than Catholics. Even his name was chosen with care; Barabas was the criminal released by the Roman Governor of Judea, Pontius Pilate, in preference to Christ, who was executed. Perhaps even there, Marlowe the over-reacher was trying his luck; among the Gospel writers, John refers to Barabas as a robber, and Matthew a 'notable prisoner', but Mark and Luke contend that he was a rebel who had killed a man in an uprising against Jerusalem (which can only mean Roman authority, the power in the land).

Machevill does not reappear in the play, but we are left under no illusion that Barabas's reprehensible behaviour is instigated by him. He, like Marlowe, was Machevill's disciple:

> As for myself, I walk abroad a-nights,
> And kill sick people groaning under walls;
> Sometimes I go about and poison wells; . . .
> Being young, I studied physic [medicine] and began
> To practise first upon the Italian;
> There I enrich'd the priests with burials,
> And always kept the sexton's arms in use
> With digging graves and ringing dead man's knells.

But mass murder by poison and for the Hell of it, is not the end of Barabas/Machevill's list of mayhem:

> And after that, was I an engineer,
> And in the wars 'twixt France and Germany,

Under pretence of helping Charles the Fifth,
Slew friend and enemy with my stratagems.
Then after that was I an usurer,
And with extorting, cozening, forfeiting,
And tricks belonging unto brokery,
I fill'd the gaols with bankrouts in a year,
And with young orphans planted hospitals,
And every moon made some or other mad. . . .

It has long been believed that Marlowe's work is clearly discernible in *Henry VI*, one of the history plays in the Shakespeare canon. If this is true, then Marlowe may well have referred to Machevill already. Into the mouth of Richard, Duke of Gloucester, he puts the words

I'll drown more sailors than the mermaid shall;
I'll play the orator as well as Nestor,
Decieve more slyly than Ulysses could,
And, like a Sinon, take another Troy.
I can add colours to the chameleon,
Change shapes with Proteus for advantages,
And set the murderous Machevill to school.
Can I do this, and cannot get a crown?
Tut, were it further off, I'll pluck it down.

One of the great problems for the Who Was Shakespeare? industry is that there were no laws over copyright in his day. Shakespeare's greatest genius lay in picking up other people's trifles, even, in the case of Marlowe, the exact rhythm of his 'mighty line'. And even though the author of Gloucester's speech very likely went on to recreate the same character in *Richard III*, the list of the man's dark doings are very similar to those of Barabas – two super-villains intent on doing the world harm. But whose villains are they? Shakespeare's or Marlowe's?

A careful study of the Machiavelli prologue in *The Jew* clearly shows a balance between the man's supporters and opponents; those who see Marlowe himself in Machiavelli have overlooked this.

There is ample scope in Barabas's asides, however, for Marlowe to malign Christians – he would rather be a hated Jew than a pitied Christian – 'This offspring of Cain, this Jebusite/That never tasted of the Passover.' Much of the play deals with racial slurs which were the currency of the time – 'And thus are we on every side enrich'd./ These are the blessings promis'd to the Jews' and 'To undo a Jew is charity and not sin.' Certainly Barabas is a deeply unpleasant character and does not elicit our sympathy in the way that Shylock does. Some writers use this as an example of Shakespeare's superior writing, but it is likely that Marlowe set out to create a double-dyed villain in Barabas. *The Merchant* is, after all, styled a comedy in the Shakespeare canon. So Barabas is prepared to lie, cheat, scheme and even poison his own daughter because she has betrayed him by becoming a Christian.

Marlowe's contempt for Christianity is seen most clearly in the supposed conversion of Barabas and his man Ithamore, who promise to do penance and take the cross for the sins they have committed. In *The Jew* the fact that Jacomo the priest simply encourages the conversion to obtain Barabas's gold underscores the duplicity and Machiavellianism of the Church. Again, by setting the play where he does and referring to the *Catholic* Church, Marlowe emerges as a patriot in an age when to be such could only be equated with Protestantism. Only if it was assumed that Marlowe was actually attacking the Anglican Church of Elizabeth was he sailing into dangerous waters.

In the context of Machiavellian realpolitik, A.G.R. Smith[6] sums up the role of Elizabeth herself admirably – 'by her economy the Queen avoided bankruptcy; by her moderation, especially in religious matters, she avoided the possibility of civil war; by her conservative attitude to the European situation, she avoided reckless foreign adventures.' We can be pedantic and point out the fact that she expected others to provide the cash she refused to supply – Walsingham paid his own spies and Drake had to attack Spanish silver convoys and give the lion's share to her. Her half-hearted commitment in allowing Leicester such a meagre force to aid the Dutch achieved nothing militarily, yet still angered Spain and led to the unleashing of the Armada. But in essence Smith is right.

None of this happened by accident, however. It happened because under Elizabeth was a group of brilliant, dedicated men who watched her realm, her friends and her enemies very closely. They were all Machevills and three of them at least had a great deal to do with the murder of Christopher Marlowe.

The Privy Council was in many ways the forerunner of the Cabinet. It was small and followed the Queen around wherever she went so that action could be taken quickly, especially on vital questions relevant to the security of the realm. When the Queen was present at Whitehall, which she was increasingly by the 1590s, the Council met in a chamber across the corridor from hers. Equally important for our thesis is the fact that she rarely actually attended their meetings, content to let the daily business of state devolve on to their ample and highly capable shoulders.

Although there were technically twenty-two members of the Council, in the 1590s the number who actually attended on a regular basis was thirteen. The key decisions, however, were increasingly taken by as few as four. Easily the most powerful of the Council were: William Cecil, Lord Burghley, the Lord Treasurer; Sir Francis Knollys, Elizabeth's cousin and Vice-Chamberlain of her Household; Sir Francis Walsingham, Principal Secretary from 1573; Sir Christopher Hatton, Lord Chancellor from 1587; Howard of Effingham, Lord High Admiral; and Sir Robert Cecil, Burghley's son, sworn in as late as 1591. Other officers of state, Sir John Fortescue, Chancellor of the Exchequer, Sir William Knollys, Comptroller of the Household and Sir Thomas Egerton, Lord Keeper of the Great Seal, took second place and their position on the Council was usually to back the others.

By the last decade of the Queen's reign, this small, tightly knit advisory group was highly professional and enormously powerful. It is interesting, in a reign and a century riven by religious unrest, that there was only one churchman on the Council – John Whitgift, the Archbishop of Canterbury.

The work of the Council is important to our understanding of what happened to Marlowe because in the days before his death he had been arrested and was bound over to report to them on a daily basis. The Council's brief was huge – too huge, in fact, because constantly between 1575 and 1595, there are attempts to foist some of the work on to other, lesser authorities. Delegation did not come easily, partly no doubt because men used to wielding large amounts of power were loath to lose any of it; and partly because of the natural tendency, especially among wealthy and important Elizabethans, to go straight to the top to get matters sorted out. An example provided by A.G.R. Smith, on one typical day, 5 July 1574, makes the point. Fifteen different items were dealt with, from deciding the outcome of a private quarrel between two gentlemen, through forcing four maritime counties in the south to provide supplies for the navy, to promoting good relations with Scotland. Although all of it could be classified as 'causes that concern her Majesty and the state of the realm', increasingly business fell into two categories – private and public.

In the early years of the Queen's reign, the Council met three times a week, on Tuesdays, Thursdays and Saturdays. By the 1590s, however, it met virtually every day, often mornings *and* afternoons, which reflects the growing complexity of government and perhaps, too, an increasing reluctance on the now ageing Queen's part to make decisions. Elizabeth's famous 'answers answerless' were not merely reserved for her increasingly frustrated parliaments, but for everyone else she met.

G.R. Elton, doyen of Tudor historians of an earlier generation, contended that the Privy Council was not a court and had no judicial functions. This overstates the case. It could only impose fines on miscreants and this via the public proceedings in Star Chamber, but it was the only body in the country allowed, with nominal royal consent, to use torture. And it was not slow to engage the formidable instruments of the Inquisition and men who knew how to use them.

One of the most accomplished was Richard Topcliffe, MP for Beverley in Yorkshire, who occasionally gave intelligence to Walsingham and was unofficially the Queen's rack master when Thomas Norton died. The rack itself was not unfamiliar to ancient history and may have been used on Christians by the Romans. Topcliffe applied it to Catholics or indeed anybody, like Marlowe's friend the playwright Thomas Kyd, sent to him by the Council. The rack, known in Elizabethan times as the Duke of Exeter's daughter, was a wooden platform with pulleys which could slide its ends further apart, stretching the victim who was tied by wrist and ankle to it. The result, after excruciating pain, was the dislocation of hips and shoulder joints. Thumbscrews, the iron maiden, strappado and Skeffington's Gyves[7] were all available to Topcliffe in the Marshalsea and the Clink, the notorious prisons south of the Thames in the liberty of Southwark. The Jesuit priest Edmund Campion described how he felt after such experience – 'Benumbed both of hand and foot, he likened himself to an elephant, which being down could not rise. When he could hold the bread he had to eat betwixt both his hands, he would compare himself to an ape.' Topcliffe was a sadist and there is evidence that he exceeded his brief, both in the nature of his use of torture and in his outspoken comments on the Queen he nominally served. While torturing a priest called Thomas Pormont, he told him

> that he was so great and familiar with Her Majesty that he many times putteth his hands between her breasts and paps, and in her neck; that he had not only seen her legs and knees, but feeleth them with his hands above her knees; that he hath felt her belly, and said unto Her Majesty that she hath the softest belly of any womankind.[8]

Even though Pormont reported this to the Council, nothing was done (probably because of Pormont's Catholicism). Lesser fry than Topcliffe were executed for suggesting who the Queen's successor might be, much less for claiming that she was a sex object!

Topcliffe's work represents the dark side of the Privy Council, and the dark side of the Queen. The paranoia of the state is exposed here in all its terror. After the early seventeenth century, such cruelty would never be seen again in England, but it was part and parcel of the reign of Gloriana and the gentlemen of the Privy Council kept it that way.

Smith and Elton are historians of the generation which believed that the Tudors behaved as they did due to circumstance. Henry VII had come to the throne by force after thirty years of civil war. His son tore apart the religious foundations of the State in order, essentially, to secure his dynasty. Opponents great and small faced the axe and the rope. All three of Henry's children, especially Mary, permitted burnings in the name of God. But all this was against a background of foreign and papal threat. The Tudors had no police force; they had no standing army. Law and order, the essential prerequisite of any successful State, was notoriously difficult to maintain in their situation.

It was an earlier generation altogether that talked of a 'Tudor despotism' and Elton, Smith, Neale, Bindoff and Dickens did their best to persuade us that this was wrong. Today, there is a tendency to swing back in that direction. Curtis C. Breight, in his fascinating *Surveillance, Mititarism and Drama in the Elizabethan Era* puts forward a revisionist view which strikes us as altogether more realistic. It doubts A.G.R. Smith's opinion that 'Elizabethan government was government by consent'. Her parliament was in no sense democratic and decisions were taken not by a female dictator but by a body of bigoted men jockeying for her favour and ultimately their own power.

The 'Gloriana' myth of Elizabeth's reign fabricates a 'Golden Age' only because it was a relatively settled period between the executions and burnings of the earlier Tudors and the convulsion of the Civil War. Aided by the blossoming of poetry, drama, the theatre, music, architecture and exciting adventures in the New World, the historians of yesterday saw this time as one of colossal achievement. And all of them were perfectly happy to go along with the nonsense that a would-be Elizabethan great, Kit Marlowe, died in a tavern brawl over a bill.

We view the decade of Marlowe's death in an altogether grimmer light. Earlier 'Gloriana' historians have pointed out Elizabeth's ageing, her unwillingness to cope with parliament or tackle the problems of her own succession or the monopolies tangle. Yet there is also the question of famine levels, the abandonment of the Queen's sailors after the Armada and a huge increase, especially in the luckless county of Essex, of witch persecution. Curtis Breight argues convincingly that Elizabeth's last years were marked by worsening class divisions and seething popular discontent in which local magistrates were struggling to stay afloat. He argues too that the Privy Council was bent on control at any cost and uses the word Machiavellian frequently in this context.

The lack of parties in a political sense in Elizabethan England meant that there was no true focus for an attack on the Queen and her government that was not launched from Rome or Rheims. The increasing outspokenness of MPs like Peter Wentworth, however, meant that the 'answers answerless' could not go on for ever. Elizabeth must change her outlook or die because her country was moving on without her, a prospect that only younger politicians like the Earl of Essex understood. It may be that Elizabeth herself was an irrelevance by the time of Marlowe's death and power had actually slipped to a *Regnum Cecilianum*, the rule of the Cecils, because in 1591, Robert, Burghley's deformed, clever son, was admitted to the Council.

Pertinently to Marlowe and the whole secret service world he still inhabited in 1593, treason laws were extended (for example the Surety of the Queen's Person Act in 1585), judicial torture was widely employed, house to house searches (like the one that led to Kyd's arrest) and government-sponsored scare campaigns like the Dutch libels were all designed to browbeat and *control* the people. Executions reached eight hundred a year in the last years of the Queen's reign.

Who were these men to whom power was so vital? First, in the sense of his years in office and his undoubted loyalty to the Queen, was William Cecil, Lord Burghley. He had been with Elizabeth since the beginning, appointed by her on 20 November 1558 while the new queen was still living at Hatfield House, which was to become one of Robert Cecil's principal residences in the years ahead. Thirty-eight years old to her twenty-five, Cecil was the perfect mix of solid Protestant and worldly politician the Queen needed to pilot her through the turbulent seas of sixteenth-century government. Above all, perhaps, despite a certain political quick-footedness in the reigns of Edward VI and Mary, he was what passed in the period for an honest man:

> This judgement I have of you that you will not be corrupted with any manner of gift and that you will be faithful to the state and that without respect of my private will, you will give me that council that you think best.[9]

Cecil continued to do that for forty years, giving Elizabeth his advice, arguing with her politely in private, backing her always in public. They essentially thought alike, both advocating religious compromise (although he was probably more Protestant than his queen), both wanting to improve the country's economy and both suspicious of foreign adventures. In the vexed questions of Elizabeth's marriage and Elizabeth's succession, Cecil got nowhere, but he was more successful in the issue of Mary, Queen of Scots, even though, as we have seen, he was banished from Court over it for a time. 'I have found such torment with the Queen's Majesty as an ague hath not in three fits so much abated.' In religion he steered more of a *via media* than did Elizabeth. 'He dissented,' wrote a contemporary, 'from papist and puritan, disliking the superstition of the one and the singularity of the other . . .'.[10] As David Cecil says, Burghley's 'was a public face and a public face is always a mask, hiding the inner man'. He had no friends, probably because he felt that the Queen's Principal Secretary and later her Treasurer could not afford to have any. He had 'no inward companion as great men commonly have, nor did any other know his secrets; some noting it for a fault, but most thinking it a praise and an instance of his wisdom. By trusting none with his secrets, none could reveal them.'[11]

So the private man is more difficult to find than the Privy Councillor, though he managed to keep the two quite separate. At home in Burghley, Northamptonshire or Theobalds in Hertfordshire, he ostentatiously laid down his staff and gown of office, especially at meal times with a 'Lie thou there, Lord Treasurer'.[12] He read avidly, especially astronomy and geography. He spoke French, Italian, Greek and Latin and carried a copy of Cicero in his pocket. He did not approve much of poetry or plays, in common with an increasing number of his contemporaries, but filled his houses with scholars and the sons of the aristocracy like the future Lords Essex and Southampton, who were anxious to soak up culture at the great man's knee. He was an avid collector of gold, coins and silver plate and had one of the finest collections of plants in the country, at a time when the science of botany was in its infancy. Bored by sport and the usual manly pursuits of Tudor gentlemen, his only exercise was gardening and riding the grounds of his houses on the back of a mule.

By the 1590s, however, the greatest statesman of Elizabeth's reign was tired out. He took to carrying a book with him at all times so that he could keep himself awake by reading. His clever, scholarly wife, Mildred, who seems to have played no part in his political work but ran his household very efficiently, died in 1589. Now he often ate alone and increasingly worked from his bed, complaining sadly, 'I am as lonely as an owl.'

His temper shortened and he snapped more often in Council meetings. Already by 1591 he was grooming his second son, Robert, to follow him. And once again, Cecil ambition was under threat from another lusty young favourite. In the 1560s, it had been the headstrong Earl of Leicester; now it was his stepson, another hothead, Robert Devereux, the Earl of Essex.

It was in 1590 that Francis Walsingham, the Queen's spymaster, died. The cause was purported to be a testicular tumour:

> The Secretary Walsingham, a most violent persecutor of Catholics, died never so much as naming God in his last extremities . . . in the end, his urine came forth at his mouth and nose with so odious a stench that none could endure to come near him.[13]

This is Catholic claptrap. The 'urine' was pleural effusion, excess fluid from the lungs. What actually killed Walsingham was pneumonia.

More of a Machiavellian than Burghley, his secret service was by now the envy of Europe. Philip of Spain was delighted with the news. In dispatches sent to him he read 'Secretary Walsingham has just expired, at which there is great sorrow' whereupon the king wrote in the margin, 'There, yes, but it is good news here!'[14] Walsingham had been the Queen's Principal Secretary since 1573 and it was a huge job. Nicholas Faunt, the homosexual who may have recruited Marlowe to the secret service in Cambridge, wrote in 1592 that

> amongst all particular offices and places of charge in this state, there is none of more necessary use, nor subject to more cumber and variableness, than is the office of principal secretary, by reason of the variety and uncertainty of his employment.

Robert Beale, another civil servant, like Faunt with ideas above his station, also leapt into print the same year and openly criticized

Walsingham now that the man was dead – 'Burden not yourself with too many clerks or servants, as Sir Francis Walsingham did. Let your secret services be known to a few; the Lord Treasurer Burghley, being secretary, had not above two or three. . . .' And, of course, Lord Treasurer Burghley was still alive. It is no accident that these men let their views be known in 1592 because immediately after Walsingham's death the post was vacant and Burghley himself filled it again *pro tem* while waiting for the Queen to accept young Robert's maturity, which she finally did in 1596. More combative and altogether darker than Burghley, Walsingham had allied himself with Leicester in a pro-war faction in the Council, urging the Queen to take on Spain in a no-holds-barred contest for supremacy in Europe. How far he was influenced in this position is difficult to say and historians are divided over the sincerity of his views. Certainly, he appeared the most Machiavellian of all Elizabeth's Privy Councillors and was not always as honest in his dealings with the Queen as she would have liked.

Even so, there is the unwritten feeling in the relationship between Walsingham and Marlowe that, had the spymaster lived, his agent would have survived too. It was not to be. Ill for many years and without any of the cash benefits bestowed by Elizabeth on other members of the Council, he died so heavily in debt, it was said, that the burial had to be kept secret to evade his creditors. The debt should have been the Queen's, for much of it was incurred in making Elizabeth and her realm safe.[15]

The poet Thomas Watson, who had known Walsingham since Paris in 1581, wrote an eclogue, *Meliboeus*, in the Secretary's memory. In flowery Renaissance style, Watson himself was Corydon, Thomas Walsingham Titymus and Walsingham's son-in-law Philip Sidney Astrophel, 'by cruel Fates cut off before his day'. The Queen was portrayed as the huntress Diana and England, of course, was Arcadia, the mythic land of fauns and shepherds.

Another member of the Council to have gone before Marlowe's death was Sir Christopher Hatton. Of an old Northamptonshire family, Hatton was typical of the squirearchy of the day who attended St Mary's Hall, Oxford, but took no degree. His acquaintance with the law was slight (odd, as contemporaries remarked, in a future Lord Chancellor) as he spent only a few months in the Inner Temple – there is no record of his being called to the Bar. Tall, handsome and an excellent dancer, he was performing in a masque at the Temple attended by the Queen in 1561 and so impressed her by his *gaillard* that he was made a gentleman pensioner three years later. Impressive at the tilt, he was made Captain of the Queen's Bodyguard and Gentleman of the Privy Chamber.

Hatton's relationship with Elizabeth was very intimate and certainly the rumour was that they were lovers, which neither of them denied. However seriously we take Elizabeth's famous determination to be wedded to England, Hatton was certainly her type. Historian David Starkey has recently[16] expressed the opinion that Elizabeth was sexually abused by her guardian, Thomas Seymour, Lord High Admiral and husband of Catherine Parr, Henry VIII's last wife. Starkey maintains that Elizabeth fell for Seymour and ever after looked for a similar type – athletic, powerful, bearded – and that this explains her attraction to Leicester, Hatton, Ralegh and even, though he was years younger, to Essex.

Few other members of the Council (Hatton was made a Privy Councillor and Vice Chamberlain of the Household in 1577) had as many gifts lavished on him. Still dispensing church properties to her favourites, Elizabeth showered him with estates, including the country house at Audley End and the huge town house in London known as Ely Place. When it was customary for courtiers to receive annual gifts of silver to the weight of between 50 and 100 ounces, Hatton never got less than 400! When he fell ill in 1573, she visited him daily and sent her own physician, Dr Julio, to Spa with him when he went there to convalesce. He wrote her sentimental letters:

Would God I were with you but for one hour. My wits are overwrought with thoughts. I find myself amazed. Bear with me, my most dear sweet lady . . . love me, for I love you.[17]

She in turn called him her 'mutton', 'bellwether' and 'pecora campi'.[18] Perhaps because he had it all financially, perhaps because he really loved her, perhaps because he had no greater ambition, Hatton rarely became embroiled in the increasingly frequent clashes over policy within the Council. He did go so far as to beg Elizabeth, characteristically in tears, not to marry the Duke of Alençon, but this was probably as a result of personal jealousy rather than acute statesmanship. He also persuaded the Queen not to appoint Leicester Lieutenant-General of England at the time of the Armada, but this may have been for the same reason. Certainly when Walter Ralegh arrived on the scene, Hatton left the Court and sulked on one of his many estates.

He seems to have had fairly strong Protestant convictions, perhaps on a par with Walsingham. As one of the commissioners at the trial of Anthony Babington and his co-conspirators in 1586, he savaged the Jesuit priest John Ballard – 'Is this thy religio Catholica? [Catholic faith] Nay, rather it is diabolica. [Devil worship].' As Lord Chancellor from April 1587, Hatton's legal pronouncements were not exactly earth-shattering. He liaised faithfully between Queen and parliament and it may be that his absence in the 1590s contributed to the increasing strain between these elements of government.

An odd incident had occurred in October 1573 when John Hawkins, the sea captain, was stabbed by a Puritan fanatic named Burchet in a London street. The Puritan had mistaken Hawkins for Hatton (perhaps mishearing his name) and had launched his attack believing the future Privy Councillor to be 'an enemy to the gospel'. Such a deranged sentiment was ignored at the time, but in the light of those members of the Council still ruling England in 1593, it has an odd echo of prophecy.

Hatton died of kidney failure in November 1591, owing his queen £56,000. She fed him 'cordial broths' in his last days at his house at Ely Place.

Sir Francis Knollys was easily the most rabid Puritan close to the Queen and she had to reprimand him for this more than once. He was Elizabeth's cousin and part of that incestuous coterie who invariably hang around royalty. The family origins lay in trade, reflecting the 'new men' whom the Tudors promoted. Thomas Knollys had been Lord Mayor of London twice in the early fifteenth century and Francis's grandfather had been a staunch supporter of both Henries. Francis became an MP in 1542, having spent some time at Oxford, probably at Magdalen, before being knighted by 'Protector' Somerset with the English army in Scotland. Like Hatton, he took part in tournaments but was more outspoken,

'hat which feeds me destroys me' – e unretouched 'Marlowe' portrait, s it was found in 1953. Reproduced by permission of the Master and Fellows of Corpus hristi College, Cambridge, who nnot vouch for the portrait's uthenticity)

'That pure elemental wit' Kit Marlowe – the retouched Corpus Christi portrait. (Reproduced by permission of the Master and Fellows of Corpus Christi College, Cambridge, who cannot vouch for the portrait's authenticity)

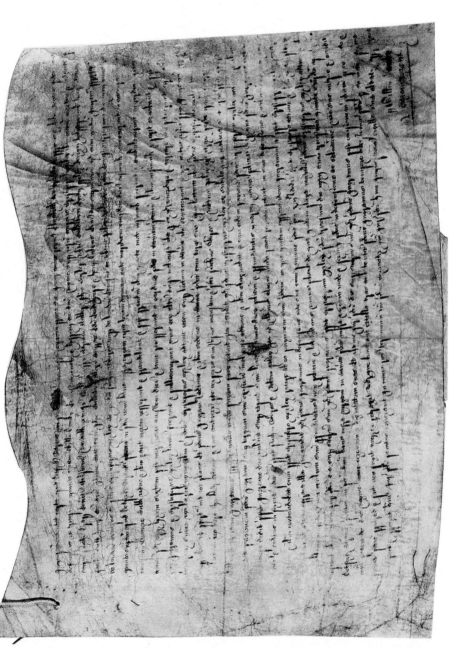

'Within the verge' – Sir William Danby's Inquest, exposed as a cover-up by J. Leslie Hotson as long ago as 1925. (PRO C260/174 No. 27. Reproduced by permission of the Public Record Office)

That great Lucifer'. Sir Walter Ralegh soon after his arrival at Court. He was accused later of atheism in the School of Night. (Reproduced by permission of Kunst-historisches Museum, Vienna)

The Wizard Earl – Henry Percy, 9th Earl of Northumberland and member of the School of Night, from a miniature by Nicholas Hilliard, c. 1595. (Reproduced by permission of the Rÿksmuseum, Amsterdam)

Thomas Hariot, 'conjuror', mathematician and physicist of the School of Night, may have been the first victim of smoking-induced lung cancer. (Reproduced by permission of the President and Fellows of Trinity College, Oxford)

A Note Containing the opinion of one Christopher Morley as composed by the informer Richard Baines. (Harley 6848/185. Reproduced by permission of the British Library)

William Cecil, Lord Burghley, the Queen's Lord Treasurer and elder statesman. (Reproduced by permission of the Marquess of Salisbury)

SERO, SED SERIO

Robert Cecil, Elizabeth's 'pygmy', who succeeded his father, Burghley, as the power behind the throne. (Reproduced by permission of the Marquess of Salisbury)

Howard of Effingham, the hero of the
Armada, who took his secret to the grave.
Artist unknown. (Reproduced by courtesy
of the National Portrait Gallery)

The centre of the Gloriana Myth –
Elizabeth I at the time of the Armada,
1588. Painting by George Gower.
(Reproduced by kind permission of the
Marquess of Tavistock and the Trustees of
the Bedford Estate)

Mr Secretary Walsingham, Elizabeth's spymaster, from the painting by Johann de Critz, *c.* 1585, the year in which Walsingham recruited Marlowe to the secret service. (Reproduced by courtesy of the National Portrait Gallery)

Henry Carey, Baron Hunsdon, who h Berwick for the Queen. His son George wa member of the School of Night. (Reprodu by permission of Berkeley Castle Charita Trust)

Robert Greene, dying at Dowgate and already in his winding sheet, warne Marlowe in 1592 'for lit thou knowest thou how the end thou shalt be visited'. Title page woodcut from *Greene in Conceipt*, 1598. (Reproduced by permission of the Bodlei Library, University of Oxford)

especially in religious matters. Wisely in Germany during the reign of Mary, he returned to be made Chamberlain of the Household, Captain of Halberdiers and Privy Councillor in December 1558.

Frequently accompanying Elizabeth on her famous progresses and acquiring honorary MA degrees from both Oxford and Cambridge as a result, his most difficult duty was to act as jailer to Mary, Queen of Scots intermittently during her long imprisonments in England. Knollys taught her to speak and write English and attempted, until Elizabeth ordered him to stop, to convert Mary to the Puritan faith. His wife was Catherine Carey, the sister of Henry, Baron Hunsdon, a fellow councillor; she was also first cousin to the Queen and she died in 1569 of an illness brought on, it was said, by her husband's prolonged absence in the north.

By far the most outspoken critic of the Queen, he distrusted her statesmanship, especially in the early years when Elizabeth responded to flattery and flirtatiousness. He wrote her stern letters, warning against such sycophants – 'King Richard II's men' he called them – and told her to support the Dutch in the Spanish Netherlands, put the Scots followers of Mary in their place and sort out the English Catholics.

In the 1580s Knollys was at the forefront of the movement against Catholicism, a prominent commissioner at the trials of the Jesuit Parry and the traitor Babington. In December 1581 he attended the execution of Edmund Campion and asked him on the scaffold if he renounced the Pope. Like most of the Council, he urged Mary's execution on Elizabeth, but went further than his peers in rooting out heresy of all types. In September 1581 he begged Burghley and Leicester to suppress the 'anabaptisticall sectaries'[19] of the Family of Love, but turned more harshly still on Catholics. He accused John Whitgift, the Archbishop of Canterbury, of being over-zealous in his attempts to control the Puritans and despite the fact that the man had Calvinist leanings, charged him with 'treading the highway to the Pope'. In 1586, Knollys demanded that all recusants should be exiled and all who married recusants should be excluded from office. In the year of the Armada he railed against the bishops, demanding that their power be curbed.

Knollys may have been second rate to Burghley and Walsingham in terms of intellect and far less charismatic than Leicester or Essex, but his fanaticism knew few bounds. If he believed a tenth of the nineteen accusations made against Marlowe in the Baines Note, he would have hanged him out of hand. As it happened, other hands and other methods were found.

Another kinsman of the Queen was Charles Howard, later Baron Howard of Effingham and Earl of Nottingham. He was both sponsor of the Admiral's Men, for whom Marlowe wrote and Alleyn acted, and naval commander against the Armada. Like many Tudor acolytes, from a Welsh family (his mother was Margaret Gamage of Coity, Glamorgan), he was given a post at Elizabeth's Court as her cousin once removed and was made General of Horse under the Earl of Warwick in the suppression of the rebellion in the north in 1569. Having served at sea with his father in Mary's reign, he commanded a naval squadron covering the Queen of Spain's departure from Flanders the following year, which, according to the geographer Richard Hakluyt, 'environed the Spanish fleet in most strange and warlike sort and enforced them to stoop gallant and to vail their bonnets for the Queen of England.'[20] Howard's ascendancy to naval heights occurred in the year that Marlowe was recruited into the secret service. With the death of Edward de Clinton, Earl of Lincoln, Howard was made Lord High Admiral and by December 1587, as open war with Spain looked ever more imminent, he was made Lieutenant General and commander in chief of the navy 'prepared to the seas against Spain'. His flagship was the 800 ton *Ark Ralegh* sold to the Queen by Walter Ralegh and renamed the *Ark Royal*.

Ralegh was impressed with Howard. He found him 'better advised than a great many malignant fools were that found fault with his demeanour'.[21] And certainly in an age when commanders tended to regard their men as cannon fodder (Elizabeth included) Howard kept his fleet together at his own cost when the government wanted to break it up and he paid personally for doctors to deal with the typhus epidemic among his crews.

The assumption was made later that the hero of the Armada was a secret Catholic, in that the Howards clung to the old religion throughout. He certainly did not give any hint of this in his lifetime; in fact, there is a lot of evidence for his working actively against them. He crossed them in the revolt of the north and collected evidence in the Babington Plot. Along with all others on the Privy

Council, he urged the death of the Queen of Scots. In the State Papers for August 1598 is the sentence 'The recusants say that they have but three enemies in England whom they fear, viz. The Lord Chief Justice [Sir John Popham], Sir Robert Cecil and the Lord High Admiral.'

On the Council with Howard was another of the Queen's cousins, Henry Carey, Baron Hunsdon. His father had been Esquire of the Body to Henry VIII and Carey, whose education is unknown, was knighted by Elizabeth on her accession and made Captain of the Gentlemen Pensioners. Prominent in court jousts in 1559 and 1560, he became a member of the Privy Council in 1561 and was involved in various state visits to France, conferring in the Queen's name an honorary order of the Garter on Charles IX. Elizabeth was very fond of her cousin. When she thought she was dying in 1562 she let it be known that she wanted Hunsdon to run the Council, even though Burghley was Principal Secretary and Leicester her undoubted favourite. In the late 1560s he was appointed Governor of Berwick, a key town on the marches of Scotland. The revolt of the north at one point hinged on Berwick and Hunsdon defeated the rebels near Carlisle in February 1570.

In the case of Thomas Percy, rebel Earl of Northumberland, it was different. Percy was handed over to Hunsdon by the Scots, but Hunsdon refused to hang him as was the plan and he tried to intercede with Burghley on the Earl's behalf. That failed and Percy was hanged (the final insult for a nobleman, a felon's death at the end of a rope) by John Forster at York in August.

Hunsdon clearly hated his time in the north, keeping the Scots at bay and hanging thieves, as is evident from his extant letters to Walsingham asking to be allowed home, which are numerous. In 1582 he was made Lord Chamberlain of the Household, but refused to return to Berwick in 1583. Elizabeth was furious and threatened to have him replaced and 'set him by his feet'.

Active against the treasonable Henry Percy, Earl of Northumberland, who shot himself in the Tower in 1585, he was also one of the commissioners at the trial of Mary, Queen of Scots. In Hunsdon's case, however, while other Councillors hid from Elizabeth's ultimate anger, he had the unenviable job of going north to placate the Scots. It did not help that Hunsdon disliked Mary's son, the shifty James VI, and believed him quite capable of betraying Elizabeth.

In the year of the Armada, Hunsdon was made Earl Marshal and commanded the troops at Tilbury when the Queen made her famous speech there. In the early 1590s he was commissioner for the trials of William Parry, Philip, Earl of Arundel, Sir John Perrot and Patrick O'Cullen, all victims of Elizabeth's paranoid State.

Hunsdon was a blunt man with few of the refinements of other courtiers. He kept himself aloof from the political infighting of the Council, although his prolonged absence in Berwick probably accounts for much of this. His one intellectual interest seems, like Burghley's, to have been botany.

By the 1590s, the old order of Elizabeth's Privy Council was changing. Walsingham and Hatton were dead by 1591 and new, untried faces replaced them – Walter Mildmay, Thomas Randolph, James Crofts. So it was the perfect time for the old guard – Burghley, Knollys, Effingham and Hunsdon – to be assailed by the meteor that was Robert Devereux, Earl of Essex.

Essex was Knollys's grandson and Leicester's stepson, but it was in the footsteps of the latter that he appeared at Court. Handsome, mercurial, athletic, brave, he was everything that the Queen looked for in a favourite. But Elizabeth was nearly sixty, her scrawny chest and thin face plastered with the white lead-based make-up fashionable in her day. With hindsight, Essex appears almost an irrelevance, the last in a long line of gentleman-adventurers who burned themselves out trying to outdazzle their rivals. The other irrelevance in political terms, though not in relationship to the Queen, was Walter Ralegh, 'that great Lucifer'. The on-going struggle between these two has been blamed for Marlowe's death, but it is not a motive for murder.

A far more dangerous rival to them both was the second son of Lord Burghley, Robert Cecil, to the extent that Alison Plowden refers to the 1590s as 'The War of the Two Roberts',[22] which would culminate in Essex's execution in 1601. Burghley's eldest son, Thomas, was a disappointment to him, without the old man's intellect or devotion to duty. Robert, however, was another matter. Articulate and clever, he was an MP at eighteen, a student of law at Gray's Inn and probably spent some time at St John's College,

Cambridge, where the authorities were impressed by 'his godly vigilance both at sermons and disputation'.[23] About a year older than Marlowe, Cecil was infinitely more secretive than his father, but his aloofness was probably the result of his deformity. His exact height is not recorded, but he was probably no more than 5 feet tall. The French called him 'M. le Bossu' (Mr Hunchback), Elizabeth (who never let an unpleasant nickname stand in her way), her 'pygmy', later softened to her 'elf' and in an extraordinary list of ten points which Burghley wrote by way of advice to his son, he said 'neither make choice [of a wife] of a dwarf or a fool; for by the one you shall beget a race of pygmies, the other will be thy continual disgrace . . .'.

It is clear from portraits that Robert Cecil did not suffer from achondroplasia (dwarfism) with its obvious facial and other characteristics, and the family stories that he was dropped as a baby may well describe the accident that affected his pituitary development, restricting normal growth or damaging his spine in some way. The point was that Cecil was a diminutive freak in a world of men as tall as we are and the Elizabethans either laughed at such people or believed them evil. Cecil, like Shakespeare's Richard III, ploughed a lonely furrow as a result.

In an age of nepotism, it was natural that Burghley should want his boy on the Council with him he and spent the 1580s giving advice and grooming him for eventual stardom. First came the selection of a wife, then the maintenance of a household, then the bringing up of children – the domestic side of life with which young Cecil would have to cope. In the context of European politics in general and of Marlowe in particular, Burghley was clearly very wary of Italy, with its Papal influence – 'And suffer not thy sons to pass the Alps, for they shall learn nothing there but pride, blasphemy and atheism.' Burghley was clearly thinking of his own eldest, Thomas, who got into expensive scrapes on the Continent.

The eighth of his ten points touched on the situation as it was in the early 1590s:

Towards thy superiors be humble, yet generous, with thine equals familiar, yet respective; towards thine inferiors show much humanity and some familiarity; as to bow the body, stretch forth the hand and to uncover the head, . . . The first prepares thy way to advancement, the second makes thee known for a man well bred; the third gains a good report, which once got is easily kept . . . yet I advise thee not to affect or neglect popularity too much. Seek not to be Essex; shun to be Ralegh.

By 1591, Cecil was already an experienced politician. He had spent two years in Paris on the Queen's business and, despite having no actual brief, became central in the abortive peace negotiations with Spain on the eve of the Armada. He was knighted at his father's house at Theobald's in 1591 and became a member of the Privy Council in August of the same year.

So began Curtis Breight's *Regnum Cecilianum*, the formidable father and son act that would see off adventurers like Essex and Ralegh – and a writer of 'scurillous poetrie' called Kit Marlowe. The younger Cecil did not have the intellectual depth of his father, although he was fascinated by architecture, but he was the most Machiavellian of all the Council. His private life is a blank canvas and Cecil was at pains to keep it so. He believed, however, that politics was a game played for high stakes. Men were merely players on a board to be swept aside if necessary without regret and without a backward glance.

EIGHT

The Sorcerer's Apprentice

Despair in God and trust in Belzebub.
The Tragicall History of Doctor Faustus, Christopher Marlowe

In the same year that Cyril Tourneur wrote his play *The Atheist's Tragedy*, a new version of the Bible appeared. Authorized by the King, it replaced the earlier Geneva edition which James considered seditious. Fifty-four scholars had spent seven years working on this translation from the Hebrew and Greek. Their work had been monitored by a committee of twelve and finally Thomas Bilson and Miles Smith corrected the proofs to give it unity of style. Among the most famous words in the King James Bible were those of Exodus 22:18 – 'Thou shalt not suffer a witch to live.'

James I was an expert on witchcraft, producing his *Daemonologie* four years after Marlowe's death. It may be more than coincidence that two of the forbidden things in which Marlowe, according to Richard Baines at least, was involved – tobacco and the Black Arts - were points of obsession with James. The third forbidden thing – boys – was another obsession of the King's, but in a different way.[1]

James had first-hand experience of witchcraft in 1591 in connection with the witches of Berwick. Intriguingly, Berwick, the vital fortress that guarded the Scots frontier, served as a centre for secret service activities north of the border. Robert Poley was there at the time of the witch hysteria. What brand of mayhem he added to the scene we can only guess. In the previous year, the Scots king was sailing home from Norway with his new bride of fourteen, Anne of Denmark. The unappealing young king, with his large head, rolling eyes and lolling tongue, wrote his bride-to-be passionate, if awful, poetry and married her in the old bishop's palace at Oslo. Four black slaves died of pneumonia after dancing in the snow during the festivities and if James did not see anything portentous in that, he certainly did as his little fleet was buffeted in a sudden storm off Bass Rock, near Berwick. He saw hares, well known as witches' familiars, standing on sieves as the waves overwhelmed them.

Landing at Leith, James immediately organized a search in the Berwick area. The ability to raise storms was one of the notorious skills attributed to witches and James wanted names. One he was given was that of Francis Stewart Hepburn, the Earl of Bothwell, whose father, the lover and eventual husband of the Queen of Scots, had died insane in Denmark thirteen years earlier. At the church of St Andrew, James himself witnessed a witch's sabbat in which ninety-four women, bare breasted and frenzied, danced with six wizards, all of whom took turns to kiss the arse of their goat-masked leader.

In the sensational trial that followed in April 1591, a wizard named Richie Graham testified on oath that black masses were held regularly in North Berwick and that the instigator of a demonic plot on the life of the king was the 4th Earl of Bothwell. A round-up of the usual suspects produced Johanne Fane, tortured and burnt on Castle Hill, Gilly Duncan who had the power to heal the sick and Agnes Sampson, who was interrogated by the king himself. 'She was fastened to the wall of her cell by a witch's bridle, an iron instrument with four sharp prongs pressed against the tongue, and the two others against the cheeks. She was kept without sleep.'[2] She was also stripped, her head and pubic hair shaved and her body searched, probably in James's presence, for the devil's mark. Agnes Sampson was a literate woman with an unblemished reputation and she was probably over sixty years old. Much of the evidence at the Berwick trial comes from her and it set the pattern, with hares on sieves, storms at sea, attempts on human life, naked cavorting in churchyards and desecration of all that was holy, for over a century of persecution throughout Britain.

But the roots of the Black Art go back much further and they have a very definite bearing on the death of Christopher Marlowe.

Many historians of the Reformation differentiate between Catholicism and Protestantism by referring to the former as 'the old religion'. But there was another way, an older religion still which is usually translated today as Wicca. There is no doubt that English witchcraft was a deeply ingrained social phenomenon. Most villages had their cunning men or women who acted in an unscientific age as doctors, nurses and midwives. Much of their 'magic' was sympathetic and involved herbs with curative powers such as foxglove, with its digitalis, for heart conditions. Because such medicine or white witchcraft was hit and miss, failure was as common as success, but there were a thousand and one excuses a witch could give, just as the rare and expensive doctors of the day did. To the Church the solution was prayer and penance; to the white witch it might be a dead rat hung around the sufferer's neck.

What changed the relatively quiet acceptance of witchcraft was the Reformation. The spread of Lutheran and Calvinist ideas from Europe introduced an element of devil-worship almost wholly lacking in Britain in earlier centuries. Appalled by the unparalleled attack on its structures, its dogma, its buildings and its priests, the Catholic Church launched the Counter-Reformation from the 1540s, resorting to desperate measures to reclaim lost souls. It is no accident that the first statute against witchcraft was passed by Henry VIII's parliament in 1542, two years after the creation of the Society of Jesus and three before the Council of Trent[3] sat to coordinate anti-Protestant strategies. The revocation of this Act in 1547 meant that a second had to be introduced, this time by Elizabeth in the year before Marlowe was born. It was this legislation that demanded the death by hanging (as opposed to burning in Scotland and Europe) of witches, enchanters and sorcerers. In the years of the Jesuit mission spearheaded by Campion and Parsons a number of fugitive Catholic priests wandered the country carrying out exorcisms. The whole issue of demonic possession is missing from earlier English witchcraft, but the hysteria of the Reformation brought it in with a vengeance. Between October 1585 and June 1586, John Ballard and William Weston conducted a whirlwind campaign to root out the devil, pursued in their turn by Walsingham's agents. One afflicted soul was a servant of Anthony Babington and the whole story was written up by Anthony Tyrell in *The Book of Miracles*. With this mind-bending and subversive subculture in existence, the Privy Council was never far behind. One eyewitness of an exorcism told Burghley that he had seen devils swimming like fishes under the skin of the possessed.

It was a superstitious age. The plays of Shakespeare and of Marlowe himself are littered with the strange, the supernatural. Elizabethan audiences loved them, because the Protestant Church had not quite extinguished the notion of magic. The Catholic Church preached transubstantiation, that the wine and bread miraculously became the blood and body of Christ at the communion altar. The Protestants took the low ground, that all this was mere symbolism; and in doing so, they destroyed the magic and the wonder. The gullible groundlings flocked to witness the last remnants of magic, wherever they found it – in the plays of Marlowe and Shakespeare, in the prognostications of Michel of Notre Dame as in the 'real' world. In Loch Fyne, Strathclyde, a monster with two crowns on its head was seen in the loch's murky waters in July 1570, a sure sign of troubled times for Scotland. In Oxford seven years later, nearly three hundred died from a mysterious fever that did not affect women or children. Death stalked the city – 'Think you on the solemn 'sizes[4] past/How suddenly in Oxfordshire/I came and made the judges all aghast.' And in the same month in Suffolk, a huge black dog chewed the church door of Bungay, before hurtling round the nave and tearing out the throats of two of the congregation. Whatever the reality of these incidents, in the sixteenth century men accepted them as supernatural. The only decision that had to be made was the source – God or the Devil?

The Devil was real enough in Marlowe's *The Tragicall History of Dr Faustus*, to the extent that legends circulated early in the seventeenth century to the effect that the incantations executed on stage to raise him had really worked, terrifying the actors. Marlowe's hero (the first time he appeared in English) may be based on a real character practising magical arts in early fifteenth-century Cracow in Poland. Marlowe transferred the scene to Wittenberg with its associations with Martin Luther, who sparked the Reformation in 1517. For this reason, the German states were seen as the centre of dissent and it was precisely this anarchic rejection of God that Marlowe wanted to discuss in *Dr Faustus*. Faustus, like Marlowe, is a scholar. He uses Latin tags as part of everyday speech and his natural bent is away from the traditional religious philosophy of the universities towards science, medicine and alchemy. Faustus's character is flawed and greedy. He wants riches, he wants power and he sees magic as the way to get them – 'A sound magician is a demi-god.' And he denounces religion – 'Divinity is basest of the three/Unpleasant, harsh, contemptible and vile.' It was this hatred of all that is holy that actually conjures up Mephistophilis, but it was the heretical Latin incantations that probably frightened Marlowe's audiences and perhaps some of his actors. *Ignei, aerii, aquatici, terreni spiritus, salvete!* (Hail, spirits of fire, air, water and earth!) In conjuring up the four humours, Marlowe is merely referring to the physical world of his day, in that it was believed that these four, together with their bodily fluid counterparts of bile, phlegm and melancholy, shaped a man's personality and even predicted the length of his life.

'*Belzebub, inferni ardentis monarcha*' chants Faustus ('Beelzebub, eternal king of the inferno') and at his appearance, audiences quaked. Unlike Barabas, however, Faustus is not a double-dyed villain, but is apprehensive and torn between good and evil. Only with reluctance does he make his 24-year pact, signing with his blood. Such a document supposedly exists – the document signed by the priest Urbain Grandier at Loudon in 1632. Like most other accusations against Grandier, this is clearly a forgery.

The powers that Faustus receives from Mephistophilis are typical of those given to witches – he can change the weather and his own shape and, the alchemists' dream, he can conjure gold. He longs for learning – of astronomy and herbalism in particular. 'The only sin,' Marlowe famously wrote, 'is ignorance.' The anti-religious theme is strong once again – 'Now, friars, take heed/Lest Faustus make your shaven crowns to bleed.' And when the invisible Faustus makes mischief like a poltergeist, stealing food, priests are sent to exorcise him: 'How now? Must every bit be spiced with a cross?' In the list of 'miracles' that Faustus makes happen – he is viciously attacked by Benvolio and Frederick, yet survives; his horse turns to straw; his amputated leg grows back – is Marlowe lampooning, as he was to do on many occasions, the sleight of hand of the prophet Moses?

Faustus's end is telling. His twenty-four years up, hated by almost everybody, he conjures up Helen of Troy as a last gasp of his power. An old man, who may perhaps be synonymous with Marlowe's erstwhile friend Robert Greene (certainly old before his time) implores Faustus to repent – 'Oh gentle Faustus, leave this damned art,/This magic that will charm thy soul to hell. . .'. Faustus is threatened by Mephistophilis in a strongly prophetic echo of Marlowe's visit from the Privy Council in May 1593 – 'Thou traitor, Faustus, I arrest thy soul/For disobedience to my sovereign Lord.' 'Sweet Helen,' Faustus begs, having been allowed to conjure up her spirit for one last time, 'make me immortal with a kiss.' In the end, three devils come for the soul of Faustus and, screaming in agony, he is carried off to Hell:

> My God, my God, look not so fierce on me.
> Adders and serpents, let me breathe awhile.
> Ugly hell, gape not; come not, Lucifer!
> I'll burn my books. Ah, Mephistophilis!

Finally the chorus arrives to speak the lines carved in stone in St Nicholas Church, Deptford:

> Cut is the branch that might have grown full straight,
> And burned is Apollo's laurel bough
> That sometime grew within this learned man.

The witch fever began in Essex when Marlowe was two. In Chelmsford, Elizabeth Francis and Agnes and Joan Waterhouse were accused of bewitching a child. Their confessions contain all the classic components of later witch trials which can be interpreted as natural incidents hitched to the Devil's star.

Essex was the focus of witch trials for the next eighty years,[5] with mass executions in 1579 and again ten years later, when Marlowe was in London and something of a celebrity. By this time, the essence of English witchcraft was changing rapidly thanks to the European influences crossing the Channel. The bible of the witchhunters – *Malleus Maleficarum* – had been in existence since about 1486 and ran to fourteen editions between 1487 and 1520 and sixteen more up to 1669. Most of them emanated from presses in Germany, Italy and France. As the twentieth-century occultist Montague Summers wrote

The Malleus lay on the bench of every judge, on the desk of every magistrate. It was the ultimate, irrefutable, unarguable authority. It was implicitly accepted not only by Catholic but by Protestant legislature. In fine, it is not too much to say that the Malleus Maleficarum is among the most important, wisest and weightiest books in the world.

It is also one of the most pernicious, chauvinistic and dangerous ever written, because, as Summers contends, it was accepted as fact.

Witch hunting had begun in northern Italy and Germany, the home of Dr Faustus, in the late fifteenth century, spurred on by the *Malleus* and the papacy.

Later, in the panic that ensued when the Catholic Church was under attack during the Reformation, this supposed mass movement to Devil worship took hold, exacerbated by the novelty of Renaissance science and the recurrence of serious economic depression, in which crops failed and animals died in unusual numbers.

The reason that the 1560s and 1590s should see concentrations of witch activity in England is, according to one theorist, the result of a government wishing to show its authority over the State. In the 1560s, Elizabeth's government was new. It, and especially its religious settlement, had to impose itself firmly and quickly on a people bewildered by the speed of religious change and counter-change. In the 1590s, the same government used the same tactics to disguise its tottering nature. England was still at war with Spain; the Queen was old and heirless; rampant Puritanism which produced James VI's *Daemonologie* was replacing the rampant Catholicism that had produced *Malleus*.

In the super-charged hysteria of the witch trials, the normal use of evidence was disregarded. Hearsay was accepted, and accounts for well over 90 per cent of convictions. Children, given no status under the law in other circumstances, were placed on the witness stand and their coloured imaginings accepted as hard fact. Alibis were useless, because it was well known that witches, with the devil's help, could change shape and fly; the hares that James VI swore he saw bobbing about in the sea off Berwick were clear proof of this.

By Marlowe's day, the concept of witchcraft was actually two separate ideas merged by the existing law into one. To that notoriously elusive character, the average man in the street, a black witch was one who carried out '*maleficium*', either for money or the hell of it, which usually involved crop failure, sudden deaths of animals or occasionally children – in other words, incidents and events that were actually part of everyday life. To the scholar, however, and that included all churchmen, magistrates, judges and legislators – in effect, the important men who made the decisions – witchcraft was Devil worship, with pacts with Satan written in blood, the services of familiars and rampant sex at sabbats.

Christopher Marlowe has no direct link with witchcraft, but in the public mind, and the mind of the government by the 1590s, heresy and devil worship were one and the same. And Christopher Marlowe was a member of the School of Night.

When Marlowe was five years old, the pamphleteer Nicholas Allen attacked the prevalent obsession with almanacs. In *The Astronomer's Grave* Allen compared three sets of predictions to expose the whole charlatanry, as he saw it, of prophecy. Like Reginald Scot who wrote his eminently sensible and modern *Discoverie of Witchcraft* in 1584, Allen was sadly out of joint with the times. The mathematician Robert Recorde wrote, 'No dearth and penury, no death and mortality, but God by the signs of heaven did premonish men thereof.' This was the scholar's answer, the educated man's belief. Just as the shoemaker John Marlowe may have consulted the stars in February 1564 at the birth of his first son, so courtiers, aristocracy, the Privy Council, even the Queen herself, made no crucial decision without such consultation.[6] Almanacs came in three varieties: there was the Almanac proper, listing astronomical events, eclipses, conjunctions and so on; the Kalendar, which listed days, months and church festivals; and the Prognostication, which gave a prediction of the coming year's events. These were hugely popular; Keith Thomas in his *Religion and the Decline of Magic* believes there were over six hundred different Almanacs available in England by the end of the sixteenth century. Their popularity is explained by the craze for astrology which was sweeping Europe.

The Earl of Leicester was particularly fascinated by the subject and through him, the Queen. Richard Forster and Thomas Allen both offered Dudley their astrological expertise. Burghley wrote notes on it and the Earl of Essex owned treatises on it. Sir Christopher Hatton, the Lord Chancellor, owned an astrological textbook and Marlowe's friend and later bitter enemy, Robert Greene, dedicated his *Planetomachia* to Leicester in 1585.

King of the astrologers, however, in the 1560s and '70s was John Dee, and his work and the attitudes to it are illustrative of the body of charges building against Marlowe in the early 1590s. Born in London in July 1527, Dee attended St John's, Cambridge and travelled widely in Eastern Europe, especially that traditionally occult country, Bohemia. Here he experimented in spiritualism, crystal-gazing and astrology, in fact with the whole pseudo-science called, in his day, alchemy.[7] Back in England, Dee was consulted by Leicester over the most propitious date for the Queen's coronation. She consulted him again over the appearance of the comet of 1577; his advice was that she should not look at it, as it was an omen.[8] On the practical side, all that remains of Dee's work is the Gregorian calendar, not actually adopted until 1751, which he presented to the Queen nearly two centuries earlier.[9] It is the negative side, however, that is remembered. In the 1580s, Dee was touring Europe with an unscrupulous assistant called Edward Kelly. Accused, among other things, of necromancy and attempting to raise the devil, the pair were kicked out of no less than four countries. During his absence, while a desperate Burghley tried to secure the man's aid for defence against the Armada, a furious mob destroyed Dee's house at Mortlake, burning his books and smashing his chemical apparatus.

Dee was a magus, a master magician and sorcerer who was believed by many, high and low, to have genuine powers. Men like him spread wonder and terror among their peers. It took someone as brave and level-headed as the playwright Ben Jonson to write

> Sir, I'll believe that alchemy is a pretty kind of game
> Somewhat like tricks o' the cards, to cheat a man
> With charming . . . What else are all your terms
> Whereon no one o' your writers 'grees with other?[10]

Less well-associated than Dee, but no less a good example of a magus was Simon Forman, from Quidhampton in Wiltshire. Twelve years older than Marlowe, Forman received a basic education in Salisbury before claiming, in 1579, that he had acquired miraculous powers. These landed him with a jail sentence of fourteen months but after his release he set up as a doctor in London. There was a College of Physicians by this time and it did its best to keep Forman out of what was actually a monopolistic guild. Almost the whole of his first year in London, 1583, was spent in prison, for he lacked a physician's licence and continued to pour scorn on the current practice of blood-letting and urine examination – 'paltry piss' he called it. Modern scientists of course would applaud Forman – blood-letting achieved nothing but loss of blood, based as it was on the spurious premise of the four humours. And even examination of urine was pointless unless it led, which it did not in Forman's day, to correct diagnoses based on chemical and microbiological analysis.

The range of Forman's activities, as much as John Dee's, illustrates the fact that no line was drawn between science and magic, and that between wisdom and charlatanry was an eminently fine one. Bishops, merchants and sea captains visited him to divine the future. Lady Hawkins, wife of the explorer and Armada hero, sought out Forman in March 1595 to learn the fate of her husband. That was the adventurer's last voyage – neither he, nor his cousin, Francis Drake, returned. Forman was a finder of stolen goods as well as missing persons and seems to have acted in this context as a sort of early private detective. Quack, scoundrel, womanizer and possibly poisoner,[11] Forman's reputation as a practitioner of the Black Arts was summed up, in a contemporary ballad – 'Forman was that fiend in human shape,/That by his art did act the devil's ape.' The fact that Forman stayed in London during the plague year of 1592–3 when 15,000 people died and many members of the College of Physicians made off for the safety of the countryside was conveniently overlooked by his detractors; this was not the behaviour of the devil.

A devil of a different kind was Walter Ralegh, and his links with Christopher Marlowe explain a great deal about the death in Deptford. The most universal of Renaissance Englishmen; courtier, statesman, explorer, he was also a fine poet, answering Marlowe line by line and producing some of the most effective literature of the era. In *The Conclusion*, he wrote

Even such is Time, that takes in trust
Our youth, our joys and all we have,
And pays us but with age and dust;
Who in the dark and silent grave,
When we have wandered all our ways,
Shuts up the story of our days:
And from which earth, and grave, and dust,
The Lord shall raise me up, I trust.

Ralegh (like Marlowe, there are many spellings of the man's name) was born in 1552 at Hayes Barton, near Sidmouth in Devon. His half-brother and fellow explorer was Humphrey Gilbert, who would drown during his return from America in 1585. Ever a man to put action before words, Ralegh left Oriel College, Oxford to fight for the Huguenots in France, at Jarnac and Moncontour, but his greatest love was the sea. In 1578 and again in 1583 he was involved in his half brother's expeditions to Newfoundland and Virginia. In 1580, he showed the cruel side of his nature by putting down the rising of the Desmonds in Ireland. The revolt by James Fitzgerald in the previous year was merely one of several bloody incidents there in Elizabeth's reign. When an army of 2000 Irishmen assembled under the papal banner, they were defeated in Connaught and a systematic slaughter was carried out. Those who had joined Fitzgerald in the Pale[12] had their property confiscated and were hanged, drawn and quartered, the traditional end for traitors.

The storybook meeting of Ralegh and the Queen, when the unknown young soldier fresh from the Irish wars threw his cloak down over a 'plashy place', as Fuller described it in 1662,[13] is almost certainly apocryphal. More likely, he attached himself in an age of patronage to Leicester, as had John Dee, which, in the words of the contemporary chronicler Naunton, 'would have done him no harm'.[14] And, in any case, he was the nephew of Kat Ashley, the maidservant and close confidante of Elizabeth when she was still a princess.

Ralegh had the same dark good looks as Leicester and the Queen's other favourite Christopher Hatton and he soon became 'the darling of the English Cleopatra'.[15] He was made Captain of the Guard and, like Hatton, was showered with lands and preferments. He had the 'farm of wines', a monopoly whereby all vintners had to pay him for the privilege of importing and by the year that Marlowe joined Walsingham's secret service, he was Lord Warden of the Stanneries and Vice-Admiral of Devon and Cornwall. His sponsorship of Gilbert's expedition to Virginia and the doomed settlement of Roanoke[16] led to his name being linked indelibly with the introduction of both tobacco and potatoes into England.

Ralegh may have met Marlowe at Cambridge. There was trouble here in 1585 when one of Ralegh's agents, Richard Browne, clashed with the university authorities over the cost of wine. Ralegh intervened personally, renegotiating his licence with the Queen and sacking the luckless Browne, who had already been imprisoned by the university's Vice-Chancellor. Riots had ensued over this clash between town and gown and Ralegh had to use all his considerable charm to smooth ruffled feathers. How he would have met Marlowe, who was not in Cambridge for much of that year, cannot be known and we believe that the two probably became acquainted in London two years later. We know that Ralegh – and Shakespeare and Jonson – frequented the Mermaid Tavern in Bread Street and perhaps this was a haunt of Kit Marlowe's too.

In the context of Marlowe's death, of the tragical history of Dr Faustus, of magic and 'bugbears' and 'hobgoblins', it is Ralegh's and Marlowe's connection with the School of Night that matters most. We do not know exactly who belonged to this group but we can make an informed guess. The exiled Jesuit Robert Parsons wrote in 1592

> of Sir Walter Ralegh who keeps a school of atheism much frequented with a certain necromantic astronomer as schoolmaster where no small number of young men of noble birth learn to deride the Old law of Moses and the New Law of our Saviour with ingenious quips and jests and the scholars taught among other things to spell 'God' backwards.

Parsons accused Burghley of similar behaviour, the upright old man who carried a prayer book with him wherever he went. Many commentators, even at this distance of time, regard Parsons as 'the enemy' in an ideological sense and disregard his views as vitriolic propaganda. Clearly, he seemed to believe that Ralegh's scholars were actually children or at least teenagers and that their lessons were pretty basic. The fact that Parsons was writing from France within a few months of Marlowe's death indicates how widespread knowledge of Ralegh's activities was and makes nonsense of Kalbe's assertion that Ralegh had Marlowe murdered to keep these very activities quiet.

That Ralegh discussed philosophical matters best left alone in an age of rabid Christian bigotry is not contested by any of his biographers. In March 1594, ten months after Marlowe's death, an ecclesiastic commission sat at Cerne Abbas in Dorset, a stone's throw from Ralegh's house at Sherborne. On the hillside overlooking the town loomed the Giant with his huge war club and erect penis as an ancient monument to the god of fertility. It is likely that on the hilltop above the Giant's head, still in Ralegh's day, stood a maypole with its phallic/fertility associations that the Puritans would soon destroy. The ever-rabid Philip Stubbes had his views on this:

This May pole (this stinking idol rather) is covered all over with flowers and herbs, bound round about with strings from the top to the bottom. . . . Then fall they to leap and dance about it, as the Heathen people did at the dedication of their idols, whereof this is the perfect pattern, or rather the thing itself.[17]

The hill was an appropriate setting for Ralegh to be accused of 'atheism' and bringing 'the Godhead in question and the whole course of Scriptures'. As in the vast majority of witchcraft accusations, there was a great deal of personal jealousy and malice in this. Ralegh had been a royal favourite, loaded with honours from the Queen; such men make enemies. The panel he faced were: Sir Ralph Horsey, deputy lieutenant of the county; John Williams, the sheriff of Dorset; Francis Hawley, vice-admiral of Dorset; Thomas, Lord Bindon and Dr Francis James. The first three were Ralegh men and the case of Ralegh's atheism was officially dropped. The essence of the attack revolved around a casual after-dinner conversation at Sir George Trenchard's house in nearby Wolverton within two months of Marlowe's death. It is likely from this that

Ralegh was teasing the rather po-faced local vicar, Ralph Ironside of Winterbourne, when the churchman clearly could not explain what a man's soul was. Aristotle had said that the soul was *ens entium*, a thing of things and Ironside's version of this was that the thing was God. Ralegh, like Marlowe a man of restless enquiry, wanted answers, not dogma and claptrap; and clearly the evening had rankled with Ironside and probably Mr Whittle of Fortnington, the other churchman present.

Ralegh believed that the soul, which was immortal, came from God with the first breath of life and gives biblical 'evidence' to prove it and yet his work disappoints on two levels. First, it shows him, despite his deserved reputation as a dazzling man of action and a noble spirit, very much a man of his times; unlike Marlowe, he did not have the nerve to challenge the Gospels. Second, his orthodoxy did not work and for the rest of his life that taint of atheism stuck, ensuring that he would never again reach the eminence he had at Court in the late 1580s.

Accused with him at Cerne Abbas, and, unlike Ralegh, a genuine scientist, was Thomas Hariot. The contemporary of Galileo and Copernicus, he was probably more able and original than either. Without doubt he was the most gifted member of the School of Night and a close associate of Marlowe. Born in Oxford in 1560, he attended St Mary's Hall as a commoner and in a life barely chronicled other than this, drifted to London, probably in 1581 and soon after met Ralegh. In 1585, he accompanied John White on his epic voyage to Virginia and made copious notes of the flora, fauna and constellations he saw.

Hariot's downfall in terms of posterity was that he did not publish his work. His telescope had a magnification of fifty times and he was the first astronomer to record Haley's Comet when it appeared on 17 September 1607. His scientific appetite was enormous: optics, lunar appearance, the rainbow, mechanics, gravity, magnetism, geometry, hydrostatics, harmony and, of course, astronomy. He was virtually the creator of modern algebra.

Anthony à Wood, admittedly a century later, said that Hariot 'made a philosophical theology wherein he cast off the Old Testament'.[18] At Cerne Abbas, three subsectional questions were put to Hariot which had a direct bearing on Marlowe's death:

Whom do you know, or have heard to be suspected of Atheism or Apostacy? And in what manner do you know or have heard the same? And what other notice can you give thereof?

Whom do you know, or have heard, that have argued or spoken against, or is doubting, the Being of any God? Or what or where God is? And to swear by God, adding if there be a God, or such like; and when and where was the same? And what other notice can you give of any such offender?

Whom do you know or have heard that hath spoken against God His providence over the world? Or the world's beginning or ending? Or of predestination, or of Heaven, or of Hell, or of the resurrection, in doubtful or contentious manner? And what other notice can you give of any such offender?[19]

It was the language of the Inquisition, the language of the witch-fever.

Parsons's jibe against the School of Night refers to 'young men of noble birth', and three of those stand out. First, Henry Percy, 9th Earl of Northumberland, the 'Wizard Earl', described by Lord Henry Howard as one of three – 'the infamous Triplicity that denies the Trinity'.[20] Like Philip Sidney, who founded the intellectual circle Aeropagus, not dissimilar to the School of Night, Percy was one of the scholar-knights who littered Elizabethan England. An exact contemporary of Marlowe, he was a shy, introspective figure, perhaps because of his stammer, and he looks at us in resigned sadness from the two surviving portraits. The odder of the two was painted by the superb miniaturist Nicholas Hilliard about two years after Marlowe's death. It shows the melancholy Earl lying on his right side in an artificial grove of trees, a book and a pair of gloves beside him, a handkerchief in his hand. Dangling from a tree over his head is a globe (the moon?) and the single in this context untranslatable word TANTI.

Percy's family was legendary in the north and over centuries had acquired formidable power, not to mention a huge private army, as the defenders of the border against Scots attacks. After 1569, when Henry was still a boy, his family fell from royal favour for their involvement in the revolt of the north. Thomas Percy, the Earl, took Durham and marched south with the intention of rescuing the

Queen of Scots at Tetbury. The courage of his Catholic supporters failed and after months of evading capture in Scotland he was executed at York in August 1570. Henry's father, who succeeded to the title, was implicated in the Throckmorton Plot of 1583. He was found dead in his cell in the Tower on 21 June 1585, apparently the victim of suicide; since his chest contained three balls from a dag (pistol) this seems unlikely![21]

Like Hariot, the 'wizard Earl' had a voracious appetite for study and owned one of the largest libraries in the country. There were perhaps two thousand books at his country house at Petworth, Sussex. There was a bed in the room, four globes and a chest of mathematical instruments. He employed Hariot on the then excellent stipend of £100 a year, plus house and laboratory, and his own interests included: botany, architecture, politics, military science and fortification, chemistry, geometry, geography, medicine and poetry.

Ferdinando Stanley, Lord Strange, who would later become the Earl of Derby, was another of the noble 'scientists' of the School of Night. As another of the northern Earls, like Percy he was a closet Catholic. It has been suggested that Stanley was not Catholic, but since his brother Edward was officially noted as a 'dangerous person' in 1592 and his cousins William and Rowland were openly Catholic, together with several friends who had harboured the fugitive Jesuit Edmund Campion, this seems unlikely. Stanley was a patron of the arts and despite a thirst for knowledge almost as wide as Percy's, put most of his energies into literature and the theatre. No mean poet himself, he was the patron of Lord Strange's Men, a theatrical troupe first appearing in the early 1580s and amalgamating in 1590 with the Admiral's Men to become the most brilliant company in the country. Will Kempe was their comedian and Richard Burbage their tragedian. Among the formidable range of writers sponsored by Strange were Thomas Nashe, Edmund Spenser, Robert Greene and Thomas Kyd. Since three of these men were friends of Marlowe, it is reasonable to assume that Strange was Marlowe's patron too; certainly *The Jew of Malta* was in the company's repertoire in 1591–2.

The last noble member of the School of Night was Henry Brooke, 9th Baron Cobham, Warden of the Cinque Ports, another of those long-suffering servants of the Queen who spent years away from home in her service.

Other members of this magic circle may have included Robert
Hues, Walter Warner, George Carey, Matthew Roydon, Thomas
Allen, George Peele, George Chapman and John Marston. Roydon,
Peele and Chapman were friends of Marlowe's on the literary scene,
but there is little to connect them with the School of Night. The
point is that, contrary to Parsons's accusation, the School was not a
school at all, but an unofficial gentlemen's club in which, quite
possibly, social status was disregarded, so that shoemaker's sons
such as Marlowe could stand on equal terms with peers of the
realm, men who were broad-minded enough to know genius when
they saw it. These men would meet casually in each other's houses in
London and discuss all sorts of issues, both commonplace and
taboo. This was the essence of the after-dinner conversation that led
to the inquisition at Cerne Abbas. It is perfectly likely then that
Marlowe brought the odd friend occasionally, so that Peele,
Roydon, Chapman, perhaps even Kyd and Marlowe's last patron,
Thomas Walsingham, joined the School as transitory guests. There is
nothing we could produce in a court of law to link Marlowe with
any certainty to the School of Night. His known links with Hariot,
Ralegh and the poets, however, not to mention the charges of
atheism brought against him by 1593, make his membership highly
probable.

Robert Hues was a graduate of Brasenose and Magdalen Hall,
Oxford, who sailed, in the same 'discovering' capacity as Hariot, on
Thomas Cavendish's circumnavigation of the globe in 1586–8. He
became tutor to Percy's son and was employed on an annuity, as was
Hariot. Since Hues was a close friend of Hariot and Peele, he must
have known Marlowe as well. With Hariot and Warner, he was
known jokingly as one of the 'three magi', although it is not certain
whether Ralegh or Percy christened them thus.

There is confusion over Warner. The surname comes from the sad,
grovelling letter written by Thomas Kyd to Sir John Puckering after
torture and as only the surname is used, it could be William the poet
or Walter the alchemist. William was the protégé of George Carey,
whose involvement in the School of Night is fascinating and central
to our thesis concerning Marlowe's death. Born in London and
educated at Oxford, William was a lawyer who also wrote poetry,
his first success being *Pan his Syrinx Pipe* in 1585. He translated

Plautus and – like George Chapman working on his monumental Homer – produced the colossal history *Albion's England* in fourteen syllable verse over a twenty-year period!

Walter is another of the philosopher-magicians patronized by Percy and, like Hariot, lost out to later, better self-publicists. His work on the circulation of the blood was probably appropriated in the years that would follow by William Harvey, physician to Charles I. Warner's left hand was deformed, a delicious opportunity for those convinced of the power of witchcraft – 'he had only a stump with five warts upon it' and 'wore a cuff on it, like a pocket' the inveterate gossip John Aubrey remembered.

The most intriguing member of the School of Night from our point of view was George Carey. George Chapman went into print with Marlowe's encouragement in *The Shadow of Night* in which he wrote a dedication to their mutual friend Matthew Roydon:

When I remember my good Mat how joyfully oftentimes you have reported unto me, that most ingenious Darby [Stanley] deepe searching Northumberland [Percy] and skill-embracing heir of Hunsdon had most profitably entertained learning in themselves, to the vital warmth of freezing science, and to the admirable lustre of their true nobility, whose high-deserving virtues may cause me hereafter to strike fire out of darkness which the brightest Day shall envy for beauty.

The 'heir of Hunsdon' was George Carey, son of Henry, Baron Hunsdon, who was Elizabeth's Chamberlain and a member of the Privy Council. He matriculated fellow-commoner of Trinity College, Cambridge in May 1560 and served under his father in various diplomatic and military missions, including the revolt of the north. Here he was knighted by the Earl of Sussex and delighted the Queen by his challenge to personal combat with Lord Fleming at Dunbarton. Receiving lands and duties in equal measure, he was empowered in 1580 to use torture against the Jesuits of Campion's mission who arrived in England that summer. In 1589 he was on an embassy to Scotland and in the year of Marlowe's death was investigating, with Richard Young, Owen Edmondes, an Irishman placed in the Bridewell and charged with 'treasonable practices'. As

Captain-General of the Isle of Wight he reinforced Carisbrooke Castle in 1597–1600 against a projected invasion by Spain. It was Carey's place among the cognoscenti of the School of Night that provides one of the most direct links to what happened at Deptford.

All the philosophers of the group, including Marlowe, were influenced by John Florio and through him by John Dee and Giordano Bruno. Florio was a distinguished Italian at a time when the culture of the Renaissance elevated all things Italian and explains why so many of Shakespeare's plays are set there. Roger Ascham, Elizabeth's tutor when she was a girl, wrote in *The Schoolmaster* in 1570, 'Time was, when Italy and Rome have been, to the great good of us that now live, the best breeders and bringers up of the worthiest men . . . that ever was in the world.' Florio was born in London to Italian Protestant parents and by the mid-1570s was a languages tutor at Oxford. His first published work, *First Fruits* and *A Perfect Induction to the English and Italian Tongues* appeared in 1578. *Second Fruits*, containing 6,000 Italian proverbs, followed in 1591 and by this time he had both the Earls of Southampton and Pembroke as his patrons. He played host to Giordano Bruno during his stay in England in the mid-1580s.

We have met 'the Nolan' (from Nolano in Naples) before and speculated that Marlowe may have made the journey from Cambridge to Oxford to hear him lecture. The Italian was described by the Inquisition court that tried him 'of average height, with a chestnut beard, in age and appearance about 40'. Bruno's writings have come down to us largely in the form of philosophical dialogues, for example in *La Cene de le Ceneri* (The Ash Wednesday Supper) his characters Theophilo, Prudentio and Fulla (all Bruno, in fact) debate the earth's movement at some length. Hariot in his scruffy, abandoned notes wrote 'Nolanus de immenso mundi' and was clearly enormously impressed by the man. Bruno believed that there was an infinite universe (*immenso mundi*) beyond the stars that Hariot could see with his telescope. He wrote

The one infinite is perfect in simplicity of itself, absolutely, nor can ought be greater or better. This is the one Whole, God, universal Nature, occupying all space, of whom nought but infinity can give the perfect image or semblance.

And in this 'soul world' in which he believed, Jesus Christ was just a man. This heresy would kill him.

Sir John Macdonnell, 'Sometime King's Remembrancer', wrote in 1927 that the sixteenth century was 'a bad time for men who thought and spoke freely and it was a time which tempted bold spirits to do so'.[22] It cannot be accidental that Marlowe gave the name Bruno to the rival pope in *Faustus* – the man who was infamous in England. The Nolan had said (at an address to the university of Oxford which Marlowe had perhaps heard) that he was 'a wakener of sleeping minds, tamer of presumptuous and obstinate ignorance'. Bruno was a man after Marlowe's own heart. Arrested in Venice on 23 May 1592, Bruno had to languish in jail for seven years before facing his execution.

The most common method of prosecution by the Inquisition was to accept the word of an informer. And informing is precisely what Richard Baines was to do against Marlowe the following year, ably abetted by the cowardice of Thomas Kyd. Such informers remained anonymous as part of the system. There was no public trial, no production of defence witnesses, no opportunity to cross-examine prosecution witnesses, no right to a lawyer – in short, none of the panoply of modern justice.

Examined continually over a period of time by his Inquisitors, Bruno admitted to praising various heretic leaders, including Elizabeth. He was burnt 'without effusion of blood', rejecting at the last the crucifix they offered him. As MacDonnell says, 'Bruno was guilty of heresy and apostasy; guilty of offences which in those days were capital; guilty in modern language of thinking freely; guilty of not being afraid to go into the light . . .'.[23]

Several writers have dismissed the School of Night as misunderstood, which it was. They have pointed to the astronomy, botany and algebra of Hariot, the architecture and medicine of Percy and Warner and have seen the first struggling flickerings that would be fanned into a flame by the scientific revolution of the next century and the Age of Reason after that. They have found the after-dinner chats of Ralegh and Bruno fascinating in a patronizing kind of way, noting how Bruno hated the evil-smelling mob and philistine Englishmen in general, appalled by the rudeness of the Thames watermen.

And these writers have consistently missed the point. As we write, a review of a recent book *A History of Terror* by Paul Newman reads, 'Newman traces the secularisation of terror back to the sixteenth century, when homicide and conspiracy began to replace demons as objects of fear; just think how unscary the supernatural is in Shakespeare compared to the unfathomable evil of his human villains.'[24]

Newman is both right and wrong. He is right in the sense that homicide and conspiracy haunt the Elizabethan era – the story of Kit Marlowe is about both. But he is wrong in that Shakespeare's and Marlowe's contemporaries *believed* in demons in a way that we have forgotten.

To the sixteenth century, Giordano Bruno, John Florio, Walter Ralegh, Thomas Hariot, Henry Percy, Ferdinando Stanley and, not least, Christopher Marlowe, were all part of that dark world of magic which genuinely terrified them. *That* was why the mob ransacked John Dee's house at Mortlake, *that* was why Thomas Hariot published nothing in his own lifetime and that, in an indirect way, was why someone wanted Kit Marlowe dead.

Of the leaders of the School of Night, Ferdinando, Lord Strange, by that time Earl of Derby, died an agonizing death from poisoning in April 1594. He was 'seized and tormented by vomiting matter of a dark rusty colour . . . so violent and corroding that it stained the silver and irons in the chimney of his room.' Poisoned by Catholics said some – yet he *was* a Catholic. Others said he was the victim of witchcraft. Henry Brooke, Baron Cobham, was accused of a plot to kill James I and place Arabella Stuart on the throne. At his trial and on the block facing execution he implicated Ralegh and this 'turning king's evidence' was rewarded with life imprisonment. He died rejected by everyone on his way to Bath to take the waters, having been released on licence from prison to get there. Henry Percy, the 'Wizard Earl' was imprisoned by James I in 1606 over his alleged involvement in the Gunpowder Plot, and spent sixteen years there. Walter Ralegh, fingered by Brooke, faced the axe with cool disdain in 1618. And Giordano Bruno, supporting the 'heretical' ideas of fellow astronomer Copernicus, was imprisoned by the Inquisition in the year before Marlowe's own death and spent eight years there before the Catholic Church burned him.

So were the enemies of the rabid State removed, the libertines, the free thinkers. That these men were merely curious and restless spirits was not acceptable in an age as totalitarian as anything produced in our own time.

And there was one other member of the School of Night – the informer Richard Baines.

NINE

God's Judgement

. . . See what a hooke the Lord put in the nostrils of this barkinge dogge.

Thomas Beard, *The Theatre of God's Judgements* (1597)

Almost all of Marlowe's biographers have quoted the infamous Baines Note, one of the four surviving documents that explain his death. Recent writers, however, have skated over Baines' charges, either because they have convinced themselves that someone of Marlowe's brilliance would not pen such puerile statements or because Baines was a liar, or both.

What convinces us that Baines was essentially telling the truth in his Note is the fifteenth charge:

That he [Marlowe] has as good a right to Coine as the Queene of England, and that he was acquainted with one Poole[1] a prisoner in Newgate who hath great skill in mixture of metals and having learned some things of him he meant through help of a Cunninge stamp maker to Coin ffrench Crownes, pistolets and English shillings.

At first sight this entry makes no sense. Except that it is an example of potential treason in stating that Marlowe has as good a right as the Queen herself to mint money, it bears no relation to the atheistic comments that make up the rest of the Note. Thanks to the excellent detective work of Charles Nicholl, we now understand the context. Baines was certainly in this instance reporting what Marlowe said, but what Marlowe said was a cover for something else.

In January 1592, Marlowe was staying in Vlissingen, at the mouth of the River Scheldt in the Spanish Netherlands. The town itself was garrisoned by the English and its governor was Robert

Sidney, younger brother of Philip, the 'Astrophel', whose death was still much lamented in court circles. Three prisoners from the jail there were deported, in irons, on 26 January: Evan Flud, Gifford Gilbert, a goldsmith and 'Christofer Marly, by his profession a scholar'.[2] Flud is irrelevant to our story, but Gifford Gilbert is, confusingly, an anagram of one of Walsingham's best known agents, Gilbert Gifford, working in France. The information concerning these men was conveyed in a letter from Sidney to Burghley and it contains another name we know:

> The matter was revealed unto me the day after it was done, by one Ri: Baines, whom also my ancient [old friend – David Lloyd] shall bring unto your lordship. He was their chamber-fellow and, fearing the success [of counterfeiting] made me acquainted withal.

Baines also told Sidney that Marlowe intended to defect to 'the enemy or to Rome'. This is language we have heard before, in connection with the granting of Marlowe's degree at Cambridge. Perhaps this time there was more to it. If Curtis Breight is correct about the Privy Council's paranoia in running to having Marlowe watched towards the end of 1591, this would explain Baines's presence at Marlowe's elbow. It also gives us an insight into Marlowe's contempt for Baines. It makes no sense for a man clearly once more on government business in the Low Countries, possibly paid by the State and with another income from his writing, to resort to the highly dangerous game of coining. It was a dismal failure. Only one coin was produced, a Dutch shilling (not a coin, interestingly, which Baines refers to in the Note, although such currency was legal tender in England) and this was a very bad pewter copy which would have fooled no one.

Marlowe and Baines accused each other of the same thing. Each man claimed the other 'induced' the goldsmith and intended to go over to the enemy. 'Coining' was a hanging offence. In an age of symbol and talisman, defacing the Queen's head was akin to striking the sovereign herself. Marlowe and Baines risked death.

It is likely that both men were interrogated by Burghley himself at the end of January. There is no record of this and no record of any subsequent trial, perhaps because Marlowe had the backing of

Henry Percy, the 'Wizard Earl' and Ferdinando, Lord Strange. Perhaps Burghley knew exactly what Marlowe was really doing in Vlissingen and the interrogation took the form of a cosy chat. We can only speculate on what was said. But we believe the line taken to Baines was very different from that adopted in the case of Kit Marlowe. Baines's other charges against Marlowe can now be seen in an altogether different light. If the 'coining' episode really happened (which it clearly did), then what of the rest? And the rest concern atheism.

The modern definition of atheism (from the Greek *a* meaning not and *theos*, God) is 'disbelief in the existence of God; godlessness'. As a thought system, it did not develop until the late eighteenth century and in Marlowe's time had a broader connotation than its official definition today. Most Elizabethans used the term, as Greene did of Marlowe's *Tamburlaine*, to mean immoral or corrupt or even nonconformist. Pure atheism in its modern sense was rare, but it is not true that it did not exist or that it was confined to intellectuals like the members of the School of Night. In this context, Keith Thomas argues that what we really have is deism, religion without revelation; in this context the soul is not immortal, Heaven and Hell are not real places and sometimes the extreme position is taken that Christ was just a man. On this basis, it is unfair to brand Walter Ralegh a deist, much less an atheist, because in his *Treatise on the Soul*, he clearly says 'The soul liveth and abideth for ever after the body is dissolved.' Unless we take the view that Ralegh was a liar and a supreme hypocrite (and there is no evidence for this throughout his life) then we can understand why the charges against him were dropped after the Cerne Abbas hearing in 1594.[3]

In this context of atheism, English intellectuals followed the lead of humanists like Erasmus of Rotterdam and even more so of his Italian and French imitators. Marlowe himself expressed one view commonly held among the group in *The Jew of Malta* where the prologue, Machevill, says – 'I count religion but a childish toy,/And hold there is no sin but ignorance.' This was a shocking revelation to Christians and to Puritans in particular, who recognized at least seven sins that were deadly[4] and a great many more as only slightly less lethal.

Beyond the parameters of the School of Night, the charge of atheism was levied against George Gascoigne, Nicholas Bacon, John

Caius and the Earl of Oxford. What is fascinating is that the taint of homosexuality also clung to one of them, the Earl of Oxford, and to the son of another, Anthony Bacon.

Gascoigne was born about 1525 in Cadington, Bedfordshire. He studied at Trinity College, Cambridge and Gray's Inn and sat for two years as MP for Bedfordshire as Elizabeth came to the throne. A notorious spender of money, he was disinherited by his father for his fecklessness and even marrying a rich widow could not save him. He fled to Holland in 1573 where he spent four years in the service of the Prince of Orange before being captured by a Spanish patrol and serving four months in a prison cell. On his release he came home, settled in Walthamstow and began to devote himself to poetry and philosophy, finding time to take part in Leicester's famed festivities for the Queen at Kenilworth and Woodstock. His *Jocasta* was only the second tragedy to be written in blank verse (the first was *Gorboduc* in 1560) and Gascoigne wrote what is perhaps the first essay on poetry writing in the English language. He experimented with various poetic forms and out of this experimentation came the ideas which some called atheism. The fact that much of his work was, even in his own day, indescribably dull, may literally have saved his life.

John Caius was born in Norwich in 1510 and became a student at Gonville Hall, Cambridge in 1529 before taking up a fellowship there four years later. He studied medicine at Padua under the great Andreas Vesalius and lectured in London on anatomy until 1564. President of the College of Physicians nine times, he was doctor to all three of the royal children, Edward VI, Mary and Elizabeth. In the first full year of Elizabeth's reign, he was given a charter to enlarge Gonville and was allowed to add his name to it. As a medical man, and especially as an expert in anatomy, Caius was chancing his arm in religious terms. Vesalius himself, like da Vinci and other 'universal men' of the Renaissance, had to carry out dissections in secret lest he was discovered and accused by those who believed that the soul of man, which they thought resided in the head or the body cavity, was being destroyed. No doubt Caius conducted such experiments too, but what brought about the charge of atheism against him was, ironically, his devout Catholicism. He fell foul of his fellows and students over this at college. The students burned his mass vestments (a huge bone of contention in the 1560s) and he put the students into the stocks.

Edward de Vere, the 17th Earl of Oxford, was born in 1550, the only son of the 16th earl whose title and estates he inherited on his father's death in 1562. Two years later, he obtained a degree from St John's, Cambridge and entered Gray's Inn. Renowned, like Marlowe, for his hot temper, he killed a servant at Cecil House (he had been made William Cecil's ward on his father's death), but the Queen's councillor was able to hush it up. In the early 1570s, by this time a royal favourite, dark and handsome in the Leicester mould, he had served with Sussex against the Catholic Scots, impressed in royal tournaments and married the newly ennobled Anne, Burghley's daughter. In 1574, hot-headed as ever, he went to Flanders with Leicester's army and had to be taken back by the Queen's agents. The next two years brought whirlwind change. His travels in Padua, Venice, Florence and Sicily led to his adoption of Italian fashions and ways. More seriously, he came to believe that his new daughter, Elizabeth, was not actually his and quarrelled with the Burghleys, abandoning the Court and mixing with the literary set in London. Clashes over religion and the Queen's proposed marriage to the French prince led to a near-duel with Philip Sidney, which the Queen intervened to ban.

By 1580, de Vere had formed his own theatrical troupe touring the provinces; the still unknown William Shakespeare may have seen their production at Stratford. Trouble and violence continued to dog him. In 1581 he did time in the Tower for his connection with Catholicism and it is likely that the vague charge of atheism came out of this, as it had with Caius. Wounded in a duel with Thomas Knyvet, uncle of his mistress, he was pardoned by the Queen in 1583 and effected a reconciliation with Burghley. Three years later, to seal his loyalty to Elizabeth, he presided over the trial of the Queen of Scots and in 1588 fitted out and served in a ship against the Armada.

With Oxford, we have accusations of atheism, however weak, perilously close to the throne. The man was, for all their on-off relationship, the son-in-law of the Lord Treasurer and brother-in-law of Robert Cecil, the two most powerful members of the Council. With Nicholas Bacon, it was even closer.

The father of Francis and Anthony, the 'golden lads', was born of a Suffolk family about 1510 and was educated at Marlowe's college of Bene't's[5] before being called to the Bar in 1533. Receiving monastic lands at the Dissolution, he was appointed attorney of the Court of Wards and Liveries. Despite his Protestantism, he kept this post during Mary's reign and in 1558 on Elizabeth's accession was made a Privy Councillor and Lord Keeper of the Great Seal. Bacon's second wife was Anne Cooke, the sister of Mildred who had married Burghley and was Robert Cecil's mother. Their two dazzling sons, Francis and Anthony, went to Trinity, Cambridge at the ages of thirteen and fifteen. Francis went on to become Lord Chancellor, probably the most truly brilliant mind of sixteenth-century England, while Anthony worked for Walsingham as an intelligencer.

It is difficult to know where the charge of atheism against Nicholas Bacon comes from, but it probably has to do with his early years under Mary. In contrast to those Protestants who resigned royal service or even left the country during her reign, Bacon stayed and prospered. Such behaviour was Machiavellian at best and atheistic in the sense of its amorality.

The Spanish ambassador estimated in 1617 that there were nine hundred thousand atheists in England, but given the strained relations between those countries, this figure is hardly surprising and was probably plucked from thin air. Keith Thomas, however, gives graphic details from ordinary people, barely literate, who had no links with intellectuals, humanism or the School of Night. It would be fascinating to know whether Marlowe's 'blaspheming' sister Ann could be counted among the godless in this context.

In 1597, Lady Monson, the wife of the naval commander Sir William, who served under Essex, consulted an astrologer because she could not sleep. 'She had many ill thoughts and cogitations . . . she thinks the Devil doth tempt her to do evil to herself and she doubteth whether there is a God.'[6] Leaving aside the philosophical argument that if there is a devil, there must be a God, Lady Monson was clearly an unhappy person, made unhappier by the religious straitjacket of conventional thought of her day.

The Reformation produced extremist sects like the Anabaptists who believed that the soul slept until Judgement Day and this fitted dangerously well with a widely held Tudor belief that ancient heroes like Arthur were merely sleeping somewhere against the day when their country had need of them. As early as 1573, churchmen in the diocese of Ely went on record as claiming that Hell was an allegorical, not a literal notion.[7] In the same year Robert Master of Woodchurch, Kent 'denied that God made the sun, the moon, the earth, the water and that he denieth the resurrection of the dead.' Thirty years earlier, in Dartford, Kent, a local had stated under oath that 'the body of Christ which he received in the womb of the Virgin Mary did not ascend into Heaven nor is not in Heaven.' The vicar of Tunstall in the mid-1550s believed that Christ did not, in fact, sit on the Lord's right hand. In Norfolk in 1576 someone claimed that there were 'divers [several] Christs'. He is referred to by the authorities as a 'desperate fellow' but whether this means his behaviour or his views is uncertain. Edward Kelly, the charlatan associate of John Dee, was notorious for his deistic views; and three years after Marlowe's death a prisoner appeared before the Star Chamber having maintained that 'Christ was no saviour and the gospel a fable'. Three years later the Bishop of Exeter was appalled to find that in his diocese it was 'a matter very common to dispute whether there be a God or not', and there were similar discussions in Bishop Bancroft's London.

Although ideas like this were to increase in acceptance and extremity during the next century, 'the world turned upside down', their origins lay in the sixteenth, the century of the Reformation when men's beliefs and orthodoxy were shaken for the first time. As Keith Thomas points out, the cases that he quotes above are probably the tip of the iceberg. Historian L. Stone has called the reign of Elizabeth 'the age of greatest religious indifference before the twentieth century'.[8] This diagnosis is unprovable, because most men kept quiet, fully aware of the penalties for heresy, blasphemy and atheism in all its forms. As C. Geertz wrote in 1966, 'If the anthropological study of religious commitment is underdeveloped, the anthropological study of religious non-commitment is non-existent'.[9]

We have seen that in the sixteenth century, religion and politics (and therefore religion and *control*) went hand in hand. A terror of Hellfire was a convenient way for the Church, and behind it the government, to keep order and ensure a modicum of the rule of law.

Some recklessly ignored the law, both God's and man's. One who did was Matthew Hamont, a ploughwright from Norfolk who was burned in 1578 for his belief that the Bible was 'but mere foolishness, a story of men, or rather a fable'. His end was horrific. As David Starkey reminds us, the auto da fé was relatively merciful in Italy and Spain, where the day's heat fanned the flames, but on a damp, cold Norwich morning, death could take two hours. Another who dared God out of his Heaven was Kit Marlowe.

Not since Paul Kocher in 1946 have Baines's nineteen charges been analysed in depth, yet they are crucial to an understanding of why Marlowe died. Kocher writes

> For free thought was stirring in England in a vague, unorganized way during the last fifty years of the [sixteenth] century. Underneath the intonations of the orthodox writers, one can hear it rising, this matter of revolutionary dissidence . . . in Marlowe we can see the quintessence of it drawn together and revealed . . . of whom among the Elizabethans have we such another record? Not Ralegh, not the scientists, nor any of Marlowe's fellow dramatists, nor any other literary Englishman whose works we know.

The Baines Note is not in Marlowe's handwriting. It is not in Marlowe's 'mighty line', his explosive blank verse and, no doubt, it is Baines's shorthand composed from what he remembered of Marlowe's conversations in the School of Night, so that the subtleties of argument of which we know Marlowe was capable are lost. We agree with Curtis Breight that Marlowe was a marked man, possibly for the last six months of his life or longer, and that he was being watched. One of the watchers was Baines.

In the note he gave to the Privy Council towards the end of May 1593 'containing the opinion of one Christopher Morley Concerning his Damnable Judgement of Religion and the scorn of God's Word' Baines knew he was signing Marlowe's death warrant and that he was doing so at the behest of the Council.

That indefatigable researcher Charles Nicholl followed up Frederick Boas's article in the *Times Literary Supplement* in 1949 to find an earlier Baines Note dated 13 May 1583, which at first sight casts doubts on the later one concerning Marlowe. It was unsigned and formed part of *A True Report of the Late Apprehension and Imprisonment of John Nicol*. Remarking on the Spartan regime at Rheims, where he was then posing as a Catholic convert, Baines wrote 'how far this devil [within him] would have driven me, who now wholly occupied my heart in hope of advancement in England', and that he had

> an immoderate desire of more ease, wealth and . . . more delicacy of diet and carnal delights than this place of banishment was like to yield unto me . . . I most delighted in profane writers and the worst of them such as either wrote against the truth, or had the least taste of religion . . . the next step of this stair is atheism and no belief at all.

It was 'the highway to heresy, infidelity and atheism, as to my great danger I have experience in mine own case.' This was precisely the point. Baines's own case in 1583 was that he had been caught as a double agent. Lucky to escape with his life from Dr Allen's English college, this confession was no doubt the deal which he struck for his freedom. The fact that he was on 'the highway' to Marlowe's ideological position by 1593 does not detract from the veracity of the Note of that year. Baines was either *actually* an atheist ten years earlier (and his being given the post of Rector of Waltham, Lincolnshire in no way precludes this!) or he was simply saying precisely what Allen told him to say to blacken his own – and, by association, all Protestants' – reputation.

Baines's first charge reads – 'That the Indians and many Authors of antiquity have assuredly written above 16 thousand years agone whereas Adam is proved to have lived within 6 thousand yeares.' Marlowe's knowledge of American Indians almost certainly came from Thomas Hariot's expedition to Virginia. Magnificent drawings of these tribesmen were produced by John White, the expedition's captain. These watercolour illustrations, which provide our earliest view of native Americans, appeared in a folio engraved by Theodor de Bruy in 1590 and took the publishing world by storm. It is possible that the originals hung in Thomas Walsingham's manor of Scadbury, Chislehurst, where Marlowe spent his last days. The

Indians whom White and Hariot met were part of the Powhatan confederacy of tribes of the Algonkian people. They were not the most civilized or powerful of native Americans, but they showed white explorers how to plant corn (maize), bake clams, eat pumpkin and squash and, of course, how to smoke tobacco. White's drawings showed feasts of succotash, a stew of fish, corn and beans and ceremonies in which fires blazed and gourd rattles were shaken.

We cannot know how much of the Algonkian culture could be communicated to Hariot, but it may be that their creation myths were among the stories the Powhatan told and they did not feature Adam or Eve or a garden called Eden or a Devil disguised as a serpent. Marlowe's date-structures are hopelessly wrong, a reminder that the Elizabethans were unable to empathize accurately with earlier cultures – hence Shakespeare's anachronisms, the famous clocks in Caesar's Rome or Cleopatra playing billiards with her maids. Today, despite constant shifts in date structures, most experts agree that *homo erectus*, the direct ancestor of modern man, dates from about 600,000 years ago. Interestingly, it is a measure of how indoctrinated Marlowe had been by the Church's teaching that he claims that Adam is *proved* to have lived within 6,000 years.

We do not know which 'authors of antiquity' Marlowe, through Baines, is taking about. In his university course at Cambridge, he was studying Plato and Aristotle, from a mere 3,000 years before his time. There are in fact no recorded works from over 16,000 years ago, the simple (and as yet untranslatable) cuneiform of the Sumerians being stamped on clay tablets some 10,000 years ago, more recently than Marlowe's guess. No doubt, had Marlowe been given the benefit of the Star Chamber to defend himself rather than a confined space in 'a little room', his inquisitors would have challenged these figures with contempt. The point at issue is that Marlowe is attacking the story of Genesis, the story of the Creation. The Bible is a house of cards – remove one and the whole edifice collapses.[10]

Baines moves on – 'He [Marlowe] affirmeth that Moyses was but a Jugler and that one Heriots being Sir W. Ralegh's man can do more than he.' We should not be surprised at the formality of 'one Heriots' – it was a conventional mode of address at the time (and remember, this is Baines writing, who probably knew Hariot slightly, and not Marlowe, who knew him well). The Book of Exodus in the Old Testament, dealing with the deliverance of the Children of Israel from slavery in Egypt, portrays Moses as a hero and to modern Jews he is still a patriarch of formidable reputation. Moses did God's bidding by forcing the pharaoh (Rameses II) to release the Israelites. This was done by a series of miracles. For example in Exodus 4:2–3, 'And the Lord said unto him [Moses], "What is that in thine hand?" And he said, "A rod." And he said, "Cast it on the ground." And he cast it on the ground, and it became a serpent; and Moses fled from before it.' A whole series of weird experiences follow in which God shows Moses how he can argue effectively with pharaoh, using a multiplicity of signs from God which will culminate in the plagues of Egypt, the deaths of the first born and the parting of the Red Sea.

Interestingly, Marlowe was not the only 'atheist' to challenge Moses' place as a quack and a charlatan. A common belief in the sixteenth century was that Adam's God-given knowledge of all things was passed down through certain 'magicians' including Moses. Because the man had been brought up by the Egyptians, following on from the bullrushes story on the banks of the Nile, he was also 'learned in all the wisdom of the Egyptians'. Moses was a stock character in many of the mystery plays performed all over the country during the Middle Ages. Magicians of Marlowe's day, from the highly regarded John Dee downwards, claimed to have inherited their special powers from men like Moses and some of them tried to reconstruct magic apparatus, for instance Moses' famous rod.

Whereas Walter Ralegh is on record as saying 'the art of magic is the art of worshipping God',[11] Marlowe clearly disagreed. It is this that makes him unusual in the School of Night; more than perhaps any of its members, he was prepared to take logic to its extremes – the Bible was a work of fiction, like any other. We do not know what Marlowe had seen his friend Hariot do in terms of 'juggling' but science, with its fascinating potions and powders, was in its infancy. All the plagues of Egypt can today be explained by rational, natural phenomena.

To cite Baines again:

That Moyses made the Jewes to travel xl [40] yeares in the wilderness (which Journey might have bin Done in less than one yeare) ere they Came to the promised land to thintent that those who were privy to most of his subtelties might perish and so an everlasting superstition Remain in the hartes of the people.

The Bible makes it clear that Moses was never to see the promised land and the Books of Exodus, Numbers and Deuteronomy explain the problems he and his brother Aaron had in keeping order among the people of Israel. Starving, thirsty and with the Egyptians on their tail, they panicked, erecting images of golden calves to worship while Moses was away, as he was often, communing with God on the nearest high ground. It was an age of maps. Marlowe might well have known that the distance from the Nile to Gilead was not all that great (about a thousand miles as the crow flies) and that the journey would indeed have taken far less than a year. The accusation is petty and has caused most commentators to contend that this is unworthy of Marlowe. What it does once again, however, is to challenge the Bible's orthodoxy – if the length of the journey is wrong, what else is? Doubly, Marlowe was once again criticizing Moses the lawgiver and Moses held a special place, not just among Jews (whose sensibilities all Gentiles ignored in the sixteenth century) but among Christians too. After Moses' death, says Deuteronomy 34:10 '. . . there arose not a prophet since in Israel like unto Moses, whom the Lord knew face to face,' and of all the prophets of the Old Testament, Moses was closest in stature to Christ himself. In the New Testament, John records Jesus saying to his persecutors, 'For had ye believed Moses, ye would have believed me, for he wrote of me.'

Baines goes on, 'That the first beginning of Religion was only to keep men in awe.' The history of the Christian Church up to 1593 proves Marlowe right. Its huge power, its vast lands and resources, be they Catholic or Protestant, were kept in part because of men's terror of Hell and the damage done to their souls. The paintings of Hieronymus Bosch from the fifteenth century with their hideous, vicious creatures, and the dreadful description of Purgatory from John Milton in the seventeenth, leave no doubt that to most people, Hell was a real place. It was daubed all over the walls of churches until the Reformation and it featured as a terrible exit on the stage of medieval miracle plays. To avoid that, and to gain the kingdom of

Heaven, a man would go far. He would buy his place on God's right hand with lavish endowments and grants of land to the Church.

It may be hypocritical of Marlowe to bite the hand that fed him – after all, it was the scholarship of Archbishop Parker that had given him the education necessary to make these accusations in the first place. But the Corpus Christi portrait – if it *is* Marlowe – says it all; that which feeds me destroys me. Marlowe's comment is not merely anti-clerical, however. Martin Luther with his famous ninety-five theses nailed to the door of Wittenberg Cathedral in 1517 had launched a far more effective attack; but that was on aspects of Catholic corruption (specifically the sale of indulgences[12]) and not on religion itself.

'That it was an easy matter,' wrote Baines, 'for Moyses being brought up in all the artes of the Egiptains to abuse the Jewes being a rude and grosse people.' The fact that Baines returns to Moses having gone off at other tangents makes it obvious that he is remembering scattered references at random. There is nothing here of an orchestrated whole, of a man skilled in the oral tradition of debate learned at Cambridge. Curtis Breight imagines Baines scribbling down notes as Marlowe talked, but if he did, the end result is a mess. This point, accusing Moses of literally misleading the Jews, should clearly be tacked on to the other jibes against the prophet we have met above. No one in sixteenth-century England would have been offended by reference to Jews as 'rude and gross'; in many parts of the country, especially rural areas (where there were no Jews at all) it was still believed that they ate babies.

'That Christ was a bastard and his mother dishonest' was however among the most offensive things Baines has to report. It is the first of several highly personal attacks on the Son of God by a man who ironically bore his name – Christopher: the carrier of Christ. The discovery of the Dead Sea Scrolls and recent interpretations of the New Testament have led us to re-evaluate who Jesus was. The complexity of Hebrew marriage rites and in particular when children could be conceived and born was unknown to Elizabethan scholars, trained to believe every word of the Bible and not to ask, as the School of Night did, awkward questions. So the Bible's version of Jesus' birth, with the Angel Gabriel visiting Mary to bring her the good news depends on the *two* marriages that

Mary and Joseph underwent as part of their Hebrew tradition. Baines/Marlowe's version reads:

> That the Angell Gabriell was Baud to the holy ghost, because he brought the salutation to Mary.

> That he [Jesus] was the sonne of a Carpenter, and that if the Jewes among whome he was borne did Crucify him theie best knew him and whence he Came,

reads Baines's seventh point and the eighth follows:

> That Christ deserved better to Dy than Barrabas and that the jewes made a good Choise, though Barabbas were both a thief and a murtherer.

Is this why Marlowe used the name Barabas in *The Jew of Malta*? Marlowe is missing the essential point. In God's scheme of things, Barabas *had* to be chosen and Christ *had* to die, otherwise the all-important resurrection could not take place. Eight of Baines's nineteen charges against Marlowe refer to Christ. The eleventh reads:

> That the woman of Samaria and her sister were whores and that Christ knew them dishonestly.

The woman of Samaria was Mary Magdalene, whom many authorities have assumed was a prostitute. Marlowe lumps her sister, Martha, in with her and says Christ had sex with them both. An inference like this would have been shocking in Marlowe's day, but it became appreciably worse with Baines's twelfth charge:

> That St. John the Evangelist was bedfellow to C[hrist] and leaned alwaies on his bosome, that he used him as the sinners of Sodoma.

So, to Marlowe, Christ was bisexual. However liberal we may be today in giving Jesus human frailties, this one is difficult to accept. There was of course not a shred of evidence for it in the Bible itself and no other source for Christ's life had then been found. Was this

Marlowe in his cups? The over-reacher, the maverick who liked to shock? Was he kicking around these outrageous ideas to impress his friends? If they are Marlowe's ideas and if they are puerile, he was only in his twenties and his plays show that he enjoyed putting contentious issues before people to see how they would react, rather as the homosexual playwright Joe Orton would four hundred years later.

Curtis Breight believes that what worried the authorities – and the reason that Baines was given the job of watching and reporting on Marlowe in the first place – is that he had Catholic leanings and may have been a double agent. Baines's ninth charge:

> That if there be any god or any good Religion, then it is in the papistes because the service of god is performed with more Ceremonies, as Elevation of the mass, organs, singing men, Shaven Crownes etc. that all protestants are Hypocriticall asses.

As a playwright and a man well versed in the theatre, not to mention the early experience of performance in the choir at the King's School, Canterbury, the ritualistic panoply would have had an instinctive appeal for Marlowe. The Anglicans by comparison were dowdy and low key, especially the more Puritanical of them, who saw rich vestments as a mark of vanity and therefore a sin. The fascination with ritual is echoed in the sixteenth point of the Baines Note:

> That if Christ would have instituted the sacrament with more Ceremoniall reverence it would have bin had in more admiration that it would have bin better administered in a Tobacco pipe.

Again, the flippancy, again the mention of tobacco with its dissolute associations.

Baines tells us that if Marlowe 'were put to write a new Religion, he would undertake both a more Excellent and Admirable methode and that all the new testament is filthily written.'

It is difficult for us to imagine today the claustrophobic straitjacket of the Bible. It was the only book most families owned and because of superstition was venerated out of all proportion to its actual content. The Old Testament was a garbled and distorted history of the Hebrews, very little of its detail provable historically today. The New Testament, 'filthily written' or not, was essentially a biography of one man. Why this man, translated in all sorts of ways from Galilee to England should have assumed the pre-eminence he has is one of the great mysteries of history. Buddha, Mohammed, Lenin and Che Guevara have all been canonized in the same way. And it was not until the 1960s that the Beatles, famously, could claim to be 'more popular than Jesus'. And the pronouncement could outrage even then.

'These things,' wrote Baines in 1593,

with many other shall by good and honest witness be approved to be his opinions and Common Speeches, and that this Marlowe doth not only hould them himself, but almost into every Company he Cometh he persuades men to Atheism willing them not to be afeard of bugbeares and hobgoblins[13] and utterly scorning both god and his ministers as I, Richard Baines will Justify and approve both by mine oath and the testimony of many honest men, and almost al men with whome he hath Conversed any time will testify the same, and as I think all men in Christianity ought to endeavour that the mouth of so dangerous a member may be stopped, he saith likewise that he hath quoted a number of Contrarieties oute of the Scripture which he hath given to some great men who in Convenient time shall be named. When these thinges shall be Called in question the witness shall be produced.

Who were these men whom Marlowe had convinced with his views on the Scriptures? Ralegh says nothing of Marlowe in this context; neither does Hariot (even when asked directly at Cerne Abbas) or any other member of the School of Night. Perhaps they felt they owed a silence to a fellow seeker after the truth; perhaps they were alienated and afraid of his outspoken stand. There are only three possible names that have survived as Marlowe converts, and one of them is dubious. The first was Thomas Fineaux, of an old Canterbury family, whose gilded arms of the chevron and three eagles displayed still glints in the afternoon sunshine of Christchurch gate into the cathedral cloisters. Marlowe's great-grandfather Richard had leased 20 acres of land from the Fineaux and Thomas was a scholar at the King's School and at Corpus Christi. A legend of the college was that Fineaux was such a fan of the playwright that he 'learned all Marlowe by heart'[14] and actually tried to raise the Devil à la Faustus in his rooms one night.

Fineaux was born in 1574 in Hougham near Dover and went up to Bene't's College as a gentleman pensioner in the Easter term 1587, so that his time with Marlowe still in Cambridge would have been brief. It may be that the two had met before – the Fineaux owned property in Canterbury where Marlowe lived and in Dover where Marlowe's family the Arthurs hailed from. The information about Fineaux comes a little third hand, from Henry Oxinden, of Barham, Kent, who used to chat with Simon Aldrich of Canterbury whose family certainly knew the Marlowes. As with most walks of life in Tudor England, everybody seems to be related to everyone else and the Aldrich family produced a Master of Bene't's in the early 1570s. Oxinden was writing some sixty years after the events he was describing:

> Mr Ald[rich] said that he [Fineaux] was a very good scholar, but would never have above one book at a time and when he was perfect in it, he would sell it away and buy another. He learned all Marlowe by heart and divers other books. Marlowe made him an atheist.

No one records what happened to Fineaux or whether he dared continue to hold these heretical views after Marlowe's death.

The second possible person converted to atheism by Marlowe, although it is extremely unlikely, is Francis Kett. This odd man, who may well have been insane, was a Fellow of Bene't's between 1573 and 1580, so, rather like Fineaux and Marlowe but the other way around, one was coming as the other going and since Marlowe did not reach Cambridge until December 1580, it is unlikely that their paths crossed. It is perhaps no more than a coincidence that Kett was charged with heresy and burnt at Norwich in 1589. An eyewitness who saw him die wrote he went to the fire clothed in sackcloth and went leaping and daucing. Being in the fire, above twenty times together, clapping his hands, he cried nothing but blessed bee God; . . . and so continued untill the fire had consumed all his nether partes and untill he was stifled with the smoke.[15]

The third – and a very important third in the context of Marlowe's death – comes to us from the Baines Note. It is the last charge:

That Ric Cholmley hath confessed that he was persuaded by Marloe's Reasons to become an Atheist.

Richard Cholmeley (the spelling of his surname is as wildly varied as Marlowe's) was a minor landowner from Cheshire. His elder brother Sir Hugh was a local functionary and clearly a keen Protestant. In 1584 he reported on Catholic relics being smuggled into his county in the form of martyrs' bones and locks of hair purported to come from the head of the Virgin Mary. In the year of the Armada, he was busy raising troops in Cheshire along with Ferdinando, Lord Strange, as Lord Lieutenant of the county. Despite their apparent loyalty to the Queen, many of these local families were dyed-in-the-wool Catholics who had never quite shaken off the taint of their failed insurrection during the northern rebellion of 1569.

Cholmeley was in London in 1589, the year in which Kett died; a year in which Marlowe was at the height of his fame as a playwright, and he was involved in riots in the Strand. Most of what we know about Cholmeley comes from another vital document which helps explain Marlowe's death; in 1593 someone wrote *Remembrances against Ric: Cholmeley* which not only gives an idea of his involvement with Marlowe but points directly to Marlowe's murderers too. It is clear from the *Remembrances* that Cholmeley worked for the government as an intelligencer, 'employed by some of her Majesty's Privy Council for the apprehension of papists and other dangerous men'.[16] He also lined his own pockets 'to take money of them and would let them pass in spite of the Council'. On 13 May 1591, a warrant was issued to John Slater, a Messenger of the Queen's Chamber, to arrest Thomas Drury and two companions, one of whom was Cholmeley. As we shall see, this was part of a wide net which ultimately caught Thomas Kyd and Christopher Marlowe – and produced the Baines Note. Drury's lodgings were searched and he was locked in the Marshalsea charged with 'divers fond [sensitive] and great matters', an exactly similar and vague accusation as that which led to Marlowe's arrest two years later. In all this, Cholmeley seems to have been acting as Poley did in the Babington Plot. He was a projecter, an *agent provocateur* dropped into Catholic cells to flush them out. In letters Cholmeley wrote early in 1592 he was actively watching Robert Southwell, the Jesuit poet 'that useth Mr Cotton's in Fleet Street and sometime . . . Dr Smith's'. Cholmeley was proud of his personal acquaintance with Robert Cecil and probably Burghley, and records still survive which show him receiving payment – £6 13s 4d for vague services rendered on or before 21 December 1591.

An anonymous letter written to Mr Justice Young early in 1593 backs up Baines's belief that Marlowe had converted Cholmeley and echoes the Note itself. Cholmeley, says the letter, delighted

> to make a jest of the scripture, with these fearful, horrible and damnabale speeches: that Jesus Christ was a bastard, St Mary a whore and the Angel Gabriel a bawd to the Holy Ghost; and that Christ was justly persecuted by the Jews for his own foolishness; that Moses was a juggler and Aaron a cozener [con-artist] the one for his miracles to Pharaoh to prove there was a God and the other for taking the ear-rings of the Children of Israel to make a golden calf, with many other blasphemous speeches of the divine essence of God, which I fear to rehearse.

Charles Nicholl rejects this letter because it smacks too much of the Baines Note. Yet, if the Baines information *is* actually Marlowe's view and the letter's accusations are correct on Cholmeley's opinion, then the common source could still be Marlowe. In other words, Baines and Cholmeley both heard him say these things at his house in Norton Folgate, in the tap room of the Mermaid, at Durham House, Walter Ralegh's London residence along the Thames, or anywhere else where Christopher Marlowe held court in what Thomas Kyd called his 'table talk'.

The rest of the evidence of Cholmeley's atheism leads us directly to the men who killed Marlowe.

The plague hit London again in 1592. The disease, although there is still some doubt among medical historians today, was almost certainly the bubonic form caused by a virulent bacillus that found a convenient host in the flea *ceratophyllus fasciatus* which in turn lived in the fur of *rattus rattus*, the black rat. A city like London, at once overcrowded, unhygienic and a port, with all its opportunities for the importation of foreign diseases, had all the classic requirements for the disease to flourish.

Its cause was unknown in Marlowe's day, but folk memories of its first deadly appearance in the 1350s still survived. Ashwell church, in Hertfordshire, still carries on its walls the tragic graffiti of that time – 'wild, miserable, violent, the worst people alone survive to bear witness'. Conservative estimates talk of one third of the population dying in three years – that would be a death rate of 20 million today and although there was not to be a similar outbreak until the one that hit London in 1665, the terror and desolation of the plague experience were always in men's minds. There was probably not a year of Marlowe's life when the disease was not prevalent somewhere in England, but 1592 was an explosion year which saw 15,000 deaths in London, out of a population of 120,000. Various writers on Marlowe have made little of this, other than to mention that the theatres were temporarily closed as a result. There were those, of course, who believed that plays themselves were the cause of the disease. Others, especially the more rabid among Puritan and Catholic families, blamed the wrath of God for some sin that mankind had committed. The usual tendency was for Puritan to blame Catholic and vice versa. Allied to this was the notion that a foreign power might be responsible; in the 1590s that meant Spain was the most likely contender.[17]

In 1603 Thomas Dekker described what London was like in the last of the plague's three visitations since 1572. The experience of 1592 would have been exactly similar. The engraving on the cover of his pamphlet shows Death as a skeleton attacking London (St Paul's is depicted accurately with its spire missing after the storm of 1561) while, with true pathetic fallacy, forked lightning bursts from black clouds overhead. Coffins float in the Thames and among the heaps of corpses, armed soldiers are keeping scavenging refugees at bay with their pikes. Using military analogy, Dekker wrote

> The plague took sore pains for a breach, he laid about him cruelly ere he could get it, but at length he and his tyrranous band entered. His purple colours [referring to the painful buboes or swellings which were a symptom of the disease] were presently within the sound of Bow Bells advanced and joined to the Standard of the City. He marched even through Cheapside and the capital streets of Troynovant [New Troy, a poetic term for London]. . . . Men, women and children dropped down before him: houses were rifled, streets ransacked, beautiful maidens thrown on their beds and ravished by sickness, rich men's coffers broken open and shared amongst prodigal heirs and unthrifty servants . . . this intelligence runs current, that every house looked like St Bartholomew's Hospital . . . lazarus lay groaning at every man's door . . . I am amazed to remember what dead marches were made of three thousand trooping together: husbands, wives and children being led as ordinarily to one grave as if they had gone to one bed . . . yet went they (most bitterly) . . . with rue and wormwood stuffed into their ears and nostrils, looking like so many boars' heads stuck with branches of rosemary, to be served for brain at Christmas . . . the price of flowers, herbs and garlands rose wonderfully. . . .

The plague may well have fanned the flames of witch hysteria, since what better example of *maleficium* could there be than the sudden, violent deaths of 15,000 people? Inevitably, with such a death-toll, there were some who profited, literally filling dead men's shoes in the promotion stakes. Sextons' and gravediggers' wages rocketed. Those who could, left, risking the further spread of disease. As Dekker says, 'for all your goldfinches [rich men] were fled to the woods'. One of these was likely to have been Kit Marlowe.

We have no way of knowing whether the plague reached Norton Folgate. It was out of the City and less crowded than the banks of the river. The country is full of 'God's Providence Houses' which marked the end of the plague's run in urban areas. The disease could stop as quickly and randomly as it had started. Even so, the risk anywhere in London or its environs was great and it helps to explain why Marlowe was where he was at Scadbury, the home of his new patron, Thomas Walsingham, in 1593.

We know, however, that he was still in London in May 1592 when the Middlesex Sessions records cite a 'C.Marle, a gentleman of London' as being bound over in the sum of £20 to keep the peace towards Allan Nicholls, Constable of Holywell Street, Shoreditch and Nicholas Helliott, sub-constable of the same. This is presumably our Marlowe. Styled 'yeoman' in 1589 at the time of the Hog Lane fight with Bradley, he is now 'generosi' (gentleman) reflecting the success of his plays and/or continuing employment from Burghley, now in Walsingham's shoes as director of the secret service. No information is given as to the exact nature of Marlowe's offence, but it may have been a drunken fracas involving the two named officers of the law. Neither do we know who stood surety for him this time; perhaps he stumped up the £20 himself. There was no Roger Manwood now to let him go with a stern warning; more seriously, there was no Francis Walsingham watching from the corridors of power.

William Urry, as city archivist, focused on the smaller canvas of Canterbury and discovered that four months later the Plea Rolls of Canterbury Civil Court for 26 September 1592 relate to the fight between William Corkine, tailor and musician, and Christopher Morley, gentleman. The clash took place on the 15th of the month along Mercery Lane, close to the Bull's Inn. It was near the home of George Amcell, a grocer related to the Marlowes by marriage. Both men were arrested when the fight, which possibly involved rapiers and daggers, was broken up by local constables.

Ten days later a 'narrative of plaint' was submitted by Giles Winston, an attorney acting for Corkine who alleged assault by Marlowe. Marlowe countered the next day and the Grand Jury indictment threw the whole thing out. No blood had been shed and the two men were quickly reconciled. Twenty years later, either the same William Corkine or his son, an accomplished lute player, put music to the words of Marlowe's poem *Come, Live With Me*, turning it into a successful 'pop song' of its day.

Marlowe's contention is that Corkine started the whole thing, that he had 'beat, wounded and maltreated him' to his 'grave damage'.

Most commentators mention the Mercery Lane fight as another example of Marlowe's ungovernable temper and his over-ready use of a blade. And there we would leave it too, were it not for the fact that there was possibly a familiar face in the crowd that inevitably gathered to watch the clash. We know he was in Canterbury during that week and we believe he was there that day. His name was Robert Poley – 'sweet Robyn'.

There are only two recorded performances of *Edward II* during Marlowe's lifetime, both in the winter of 1592–3, one given during the traditional Twelfth Night festivities at Court. It was probably performed by Lord Pembroke's Men (Marlowe was assiduously dedicating his poetry to the Countess of Pembroke by this time) and may well have been played in front of Burghley and Cecil, as likely guests of the Queen on this occasion.

In that winter, Elizabeth was sixty years old. There could be no pretence any more that she would beget an heir and talk of marriage had stopped long ago. Some men's eyes looked north to Scotland, where James VI was waiting in the wings. Catholics everywhere were in a state of excited anticipation – the Jezebel of England could not have long to live. The plague still raged, to the extent at least that when the Cambridge don and member of the Aeropagus circle, Gabriel Harvey, heard of Marlowe's death, he assumed he had died from it.[18]

> He and the Plague contended for the game;
> The haughty man extols his hideous thoughts,
> And gloriously insults upon poor souls . . .
> The grand Disease disdain'd his toad conceit.
> And smiling at his Tamburlaine contempt,
> Sternly struck home the peremptory stroke.

The government was under renewed pressure as the Puritan stranglehold on Church and State grew stronger. Problems in Ireland, which had long been a source of threat to Elizabeth's government, were boiling over. In April 1593, only weeks before Marlowe's death, Hugh Roe O'Donnell, Lord of Tyrconnell, sent James O'Hely, the Catholic Archbishop of Tuam, to negotiate with

Philip of Spain. It was a nightmare vision that England had faced before and would again in the centuries ahead; the threat of an invasion from the Irish springboard, a war on two fronts. And in the midst of it all came the Dutch libel.

We have seen how periods of trauma such as the outbreak of an inexplicable and incurable disease led to panic and at best unreasonable behaviour. So in April 1593, there was an outbreak of anti-European feeling aimed specifically at the 'beastly brutes the Belgians', the 'fraudulent Father Frenchmen' and the 'faint-hearted Flemings'. Placards appeared at key places around London shortly before Easter Day, threatening the foreigners with violence from the London apprentices.[19] What had particularly sparked their agitation was a vote in the Commons on 21 March which sought to extend the privileges of foreigners living in England. One of the most outspoken critics of this proposal was Walter Ralegh, who said, 'I see no reason that so much respect should be given unto them'.[20]

On Saturday 5 May another libel appeared, stuck on the wall of the Dutch churchyard in Broad Street. The whole of it is bad verse, fifty-three lines long and elements of it were familiar:

> Your Machiavellian Merchant spoils the state,
> Your usury doth leave us all for dead.
> Your artifex and craftsman makes our fate,
> And like the Jews you eat us up as bread . . .
> Since words nor threats nor any other thing
> Can make you to avoid this certain ill,
> We'll cut your throats, in your temples praying,
> Not Paris massacre so much blood did spill . . .

Any one of these phrases alone would have passed unnoticed, but together they pointed at one man: 'Machiavellian', 'The Jews' who eat up all the bread, 'Paris massacre'. *The Jew of Malta* was performed at The Rose before the theatres closed in 1592; *The Massacre at Paris*, again at The Rose at the end of January 1593. And in case anyone was in any doubt as to the author, the libel was signed *Tamburlaine*.

To imagine that Kit Marlowe put his mind to such rubbish is to forget he was the man he was. If Marlowe was anti-Dutch (and why should he be when he had spent several weeks/months of his life working in Vlissingen?); if he was racist (he, who had probably learned his French from the Huguenots who lived in his native city of Canterbury) he would have written his name on it, or written better poetry, or thought of a better way to conceal his authorship. There is no sign here of 'the mighty line' or the classical allusion or the clever quip. It is heavy-handed propaganda, not *by* Marlowe, but *against* him.

The Privy Council was outraged and alarmed. On Thursday 10 May, they issued a proclamation offering 100 crowns reward for information on the libel's authorship. And the Privy Council meant business – 'you shall by authority hereof put [suspects] to the torture in Bridewell and by the extremity thereof draw them to discover their knowledge.' The next day, among those arrested was Thomas Kyd.

Kyd was probably arrested as a result of his co-authorship of a play called *Sir Thomas More*, which echoed a period of similar anti-foreign feeling in the City sixty years earlier. The Master of the Revels, Sir Edmund Tillney, worked with the Stationers' Company to censor anything potentially seditious. In the margin of a copy of *Sir Thomas More* he wrote 'Leave out ye insurrection wholly and ye cause thereof . . .'[21] thereby castrating the play completely. The offending scene was rewritten, probably in January or February 1593, but someone in authority never forgot Kyd's involvement.

Richard Topcliffe went to work on him and broke him. Perhaps, like the supposedly treasonable Edward Peacham, Rector of Hinton St George in Somerset, he was – 'racked before torture, in torture, between torture and after torture'.[22] The author of *The Spanish Tragedy* was accused of being the author of the Dutch libel. His rooms were searched and a variety of papers discovered – 'Vile hereticall conceipts denying the deity of Jhesus Christ our Saviour, found among the papers of Thos. Kydd, prisoner.' In fact the 'hereticall conceipts', especially when compared with the Baines Note, were fairly mild, but we must remember that the Baines Note had yet to be delivered to the Privy Council. The writing, said Kyd, was Marlowe's, part of a disputation involving Unitarianism, technically a heresy in that Christ was seen as a mere man – in other words asserting that the Resurrection never happened. It did not deny the existence of God, however, or even call into question his divinity. John Assheton, a parish priest, had been forced into print over this theory in 1549 and the official church attitude to it – *The Fall of the Late Arian*[23] by John Proctor – was widely available. It may even be that the idea was considered sufficiently mild to have been read by Marlowe at the King's School, Canterbury.

But Kyd, terrified and in pain, did not leave it there. Although his written confirmation of charges against Marlowe was made after the man's death at Deptford, there can be little doubt that he made it verbally under the pressure of Topcliffe's thumbscrews or his rack. According to Kyd,

> It was [Marlowe's] custom, in table talk or otherwise, to jest at the divine scriptures, jibe at prayers and strive in argument to frustrate and confute what hath been spoke or writ by prophets and such holy men.

In this version, it was St Paul, not Moses, whom Marlowe called a juggler. He added that if Kyd intended to write a poem about Paul's famous conversion on the Damascus Road, he might just as well 'go write a book of fast and loose [cozenage or con-tricks]'.[24]

It was enough for the Privy Council. On Friday 18 May, Henry Maunder, the Queen's Messenger, was given an order:

> to repair to the house of Mr Tho Walsingham in Kent, or to any other place where he shall understand Christopher Marlowe to be remaining, and by virtue hereof to apprehend and bring him to the Court in his company. And in case of need require aid.

By May 1593, Thomas Walsingham was Marlowe's principal patron and the playwright was staying at his country house of Scadbury, in Chislehurst, working on a version of his poem about the classical lovers Hero and Leander. Scadbury has gone now; today part of a National Trust protected park, the estate once boasted a thousand acres and was visited by the Queen four years after Marlowe's death. Walsingham's house was a fourteenth-century fortified manor house with Tudor additions, but it still retained its moat and drawbridge. After the dangerous years of intelligence work and seditious plays and the blasphemous atheism of the School of Night, Marlowe had returned to Greek poetry, the stuff of his Cambridge years.

Maunder shattered the idyll and Marlowe, giving him no trouble, reported to Whitehall where the Privy Council sat:

> This day Christopher Morley of London, being sent for warrant for their L[ordshi]ps, hath entered his appearance accordinglie for his Indemnity therein and is commanded to give him daily attendance on their L[ordshi]ps untill hee shall be lycensed to the Contrary.

There is nothing to tell us that Marlowe failed to keep his daily appointments. We do not know if he returned to Scadbury each day (it was a 24-mile round trip which on horseback would have filled most of the day) or whether he took temporary lodgings nearer to Whitehall.

One thing is certain. On Wednesday 30 May, Christopher Marlowe went to Eleanor Bull's house, on the Strand at Deptford.

TEN

Plot and Counterplot

Plots have I laid; inductions dangerous . . .
> William Shakespeare, *Richard III*

There are several theories which have been put forward to explain Kit Marlowe's death. In the holy trinity of homicide, motive is on a par with method and opportunity. In cases where the murderer is unknown, it becomes essential to establish a reason *why* the victim was killed and the list of possibilities is actually quite small. Criminologist F. Tennyson Jesse established in the 1940s that there are only six categories of motive – elimination, gain, revenge, jealousy, lust and conviction. Depending on the theory put forward to explain the killing at Deptford, any of the six fits the Marlowe case. Various commentators and theorists since Leslie Hotson in the 1920s have put forward their ideas. Before we record our findings of what *really* happened to Kit Marlowe, we must evaluate these.

SIR WILLIAM DANBY'S THEORY

It may seem odd to call the coroner's verdict a 'theory' at all, but J. Leslie Hotson proved as early as 1925 that we cannot take the official version as the truth or even as an approximation of it. Let us look again at Danby's inquest. After listing the sixteen jurymen and giving us the date and place of events, Danby tells us that the body of 'Christopher Morley, there lying dead and slain' was viewed. We do not know exactly where this took place. Was it *in situ*, in the room of Eleanor Bull's house where Marlowe was killed? Was it elsewhere in the house, perhaps in a coffin? Was it in the charnel house which may have stood in St Nicholas' churchyard? Or in a back room of an inn in Butcher's Row nearby? From the time scale, Marlowe had probably been dead for forty-eight hours before this viewing took place. In that time, rigor mortis would have come and gone. The stiffening of a body usually starts within five hours of death, so that by the early hours of Thursday 31 May, Marlowe's muscles would have contracted, beginning with the eyelids and lower jaw. Total rigidity, depending on the temperature in the room where the body was placed, would have been achieved after twelve hours. It would now, assuming the stabbing took place at seven in the evening, be seven o'clock on the Thursday morning. The body would have remained rigid, with signs of lividity in those areas next to a surface (a bed, coffin base or floor) for a further twelve hours. This takes us to mid-evening on the 31st. By the early hours of the next day, the day of the inquest, Friday 1 June, all signs of rigor would have gone.

The purpose of viewing the corpse was twofold: first, to ascertain that a crime had actually been committed; and, second, in the age-old belief that the wounds of a murder victim would bleed anew in the presence of his killer.[1] We cannot assume that any of the three men with Marlowe on the Wednesday – Frizer, Poley or Skeres – was actually there at the inquest; in fact there is good evidence to show that they were not.

Marlowe's wounds were carefully measured – and this is the nearest thing to modern forensic science that the Elizabethans carried out. There was a gash 'over his right eye of the depth of two inches and the width of one inch'. Someone, probably a doctor working for Danby, would have used a probe and the measurements fit exactly the dimensions of the typical Elizabethan dagger, with its one inch wide blade. Some commentators have been puzzled by the inquest's recording of the weapon's worth – 'with the dagger aforesaid of the value of 12*d*' – but this was the *deodand*, the duty of the coroner to ascertain the cash value of all a murderer's belongings. It is this which makes it likely that Frizer at least was not at the inquest, but still in his cell awaiting the outcome. The inquest report goes on, 'but what goods or chattels, lands or tenements the said Ingram had at the time of the slaying aforesaid . . . the said Jurors are totally ignorant'. Had Frizer been there, they could obviously have asked him.

Today, Marlowe's wounds would be crucial in ascertaining the exact manner of his death and expert witnesses would be called to give their words of wisdom. Most writers have assumed that the fatal thrust was into the eye socket, as the path of least resistance. There was even such an attack proscribed in the fencing manuals of the day. A former secretary to the Society of Coroners, Gavin Thurston, went into print in the 1960s with his view that it was impossible to drive a dagger into the higher frontal or superciliary area of the skull, so that the orbit was the only possibility. In this Thurston is demonstrably wrong. He should have consulted the trial records of August Sangret, the Canadian soldier hanged for the so-called 'wigwam murder' of his girlfriend, Joan Wolfe, near Godalming in 1942. In a case that caught the public imagination, even in the middle of a war, Sangret first attacked Joan with an army-issue knife (considerably lighter and shorter than Frizer's dagger) and made several circular holes in the front of her skull.[2] The skull itself was produced at the Old Bailey (the first time such a shocking exhibit was openly displayed in court) and one of the greatest pathologists in history, Keith Simpson, explained to the jury how the wounds had been inflicted.

If a knife as relatively feeble as Sangret's could pierce flesh, bone and brain, then certainly Frizer's could. The outcome, however, would have been the same. The blade's tip would have pierced major blood vessels, the cavernous sinus and the carotid artery. The cause of death would have been haemorrhage or perhaps an embolism caused by a sudden inrush of air with the blade. Either way, unconsciousness would have been instantaneous, death almost so, giving the lie to the rabid Puritans who had Marlowe screaming and spitting oaths and blasphemy in his death agony.

The story of Frizer, Poley and Skeres, according to the inquest, was that after supper, an argument developed between Frizer and Marlowe about the bill, presumably for the day's hospitality to be paid to Eleanor Bull. She had provided them with two meals, and the use of her house and garden and it was settlement time – 'le recknynge'. Marlowe was lying on a bed (implying that the murder room in the Bull house was upstairs) and Frizer was sitting with his back to him, effectively pinned in by Poley on one side and Skeres on the other. Marlowe grabbed the dagger that Frizer carried in the small of his back and gave him two wounds to the head. These wounds were measured, probably when Frizer was in custody. Here the forensics are less sure – 'two wounds on his head of the length of two inches and the depth of a quarter of an inch'. Does this mean that both wounds were identical in size? This strains credulity. Were they delivered in rapid succession or were they the result of a prolonged fight? Some commentators have suggested that the wounds Marlowe inflicted were with the pommel or hilt of the dagger, not the tip of the blade, and this is possible. But if Marlowe intended to *kill* Frizer (as believers in his short temper contend) he would have had ample opportunity to do so, Frizer being temporarily unarmed and with his back to him.

Still unable to move because of Poley and Skeres, Frizer, according to the inquest, struggled with Marlowe 'to get back from him his dagger'. And then 'in defence of his life' (the crucial words that would earn Frizer his pardon, and in record time, from the Queen) Frizer retaliated, giving Marlowe the fatal head wound.

As Hotson realized when he found the records of Danby's inquest in the 1920s, almost nothing about it makes sense. Laying aside for the moment the moral character of Frizer, Poley and Skeres, the only witnesses whose depositions seem to have been taken, nothing adds up. If we accept the Danby account, that Marlowe lost his temper over the payment of a bill, why did he not use his own dagger? Gentlemen carried these habitually in Elizabethan England. Where was Marlowe's? And if he had hung it up somewhere, to sprawl on the bed, as a relaxing gentleman might indoors, why was Frizer still carrying his, equally relaxed during a quiet day among friends?

Even if Marlowe had grabbed the dagger, why did he not kill Frizer when he had the chance or hold the blade at his throat to make further struggling suicidal? We know nothing of the relative strengths and reflexes of the two, but the fact that Marlowe had fought two duels which we know about indicates that he was at least competent, and, as a younger man, should have been faster. Above all, if the Danby version is true, he had the element of surprise on his side.

The oddest aspect, as Hotson pointed out nearly eighty years ago, is that Poley and Skeres seem totally inactive. They did not intervene, they did not try to stop the fight or encourage it. They did not even move to give Frizer a chance.

The problem is that the inquest is far from a verbatim account of testimony. Today, everyone in the house on Deptford Strand would have been interviewed by the police, probably several times, and would probably be called to the inquest as a preliminary to a full blown trial. There is no record of Frizer, Poley or Skeres being questioned directly, still less Eleanor Bull or her servants. We are therefore left with a hopelessly partisan and inadequate account of events. In the absence of real forensic science, perhaps we could not have expected more.

But two things cry out against the version being true. One is the notorious silence of Eleanor Bull.[3] Having spent some time in the writing of this book in a sixteenth-century house complete with timber framing, we *know* how every sound carries. The Tudors built their houses from oak, as the hardest and most durable of English timber. The problem was that if oak was left to season, it became too hard to cut with the saws at the disposal of sixteenth-century carpenters. So they used green wood, which expanded and contracted with the climate, and every sound on hollow floorboards was distinguishable. Eleanor Bull and her servants would have heard the raised voices from the upstairs room, the argument over the reckoning; they would have heard the scuffle as Marlowe and Frizer clashed; they would have heard Marlowe's body thudding to the floor. Why was the widow Bull not called to testify in support of the Frizer/Poley/Skeres story? Was it merely, in the patrist society, that a woman's testimony was considered at best of less worth and at worst irrelevant? We believe there was another answer.

The second area of concern comes from the three wise monkeys whose story was actually so badly constructed: Frizer and Skeres, the coney-catchers, Poley the intelligencer. These were men who lived by their wits; their honesty must be called into question.

What is so infuriating is that most books of a general nature which mention Marlowe still print the nonsense that he died in a tavern brawl. Those offering more detail give the tired motive of the reckoning. The widow Bull would be appalled to see her house described as a tavern. But perhaps Messrs Frizer, Poley and Skeres would take some comfort – their ruse, four centuries later, seems to have worked after all.

THE SWEET ROBYN THEORY

The case of Derek Bentley, hanged in 1953 for a murder he did not commit, has rightly gone down as one of the greatest miscarriages of justice in British legal history. Briefly told, nineteen-year-old Bentley and his sixteen-year-old accomplice, Christopher Craig, were interrupted in the course of attempted burglary and as a result, Craig shot and killed a policeman, Sidney Miles. Even though Bentley was unarmed, offered no violence to the police and was under arrest at the time of the shooting, the law of the land demanded that he should hang under the rule of joint culpability. In 1998 the case of Derek Bentley was overturned by the Appeal Court after years of campaigning by the hanged man's family. The grounds for this were that the trial judge, Lord Goddard, misdirected the jury and that vital evidence on Bentley's intelligence and epilepsy were ruled inadmissible at the time, thus affecting the jury's decision.

What their Lordships of the Appeal Court said they could not do was to try to disentangle the varying accounts of the twenty minute 'gun battle' on the Croydon roof where Sidney Miles was killed. This we find unsatisfactory. Under English law in the twentieth century, a jury can only find a defendant guilty if there is no reasonable doubt about that guilt. The conflicting testimony in the Bentley case meant that there was considerable doubt. If the official response to Miles's death is that we cannot with certainty work out what happened only fifty years ago, what chance do we have with Marlowe four hundred years ago?

In other words, we are at liberty to rewrite the man's death. If we cannot accept the version of Frizer, Poley and Skeres, so readily accepted by Danby and his jurors and the Queen, then we have a blank canvas to work with. We do not even know if it was Frizer who struck the fatal blow. In fact, we believe that the actual killer of Kit Marlowe was Robert Poley.

What no one knows is the precise relationship between the men at the house in Deptford Strand. Because Marlowe and Poley were both agents, working for Walsingham or Burghley as time and conditions dictated, it is highly likely that they already knew each other, although no documentary evidence exists to this effect. Both were Cambridge men, although ten years apart and at different colleges; both came from humble backgrounds. Both, if the veiled references from Poley's letters to the Earl of Leicester are true, entered the secret service in the same year, 1585. Both men, though for different reasons, served time in London prisons. In the early 1590s Poley had become something of an expert on the Low Countries, carrying out 'Her Majesty's special affairs' in Brussels a month after Marlowe's extradition from Vlissingen for coining. The surviving documents in the Public Record Office make it clear that he was an important cog in the secret service wheel by the time he came to Deptford, responsible for a team of agents like Michael Moody in the Low Countries and Robert Rutkin in London, both men posing as merchants. Letters from Moody to Poley survive and add another piece in the Marlowe–Poley jigsaw – the information that they both lived in Shoreditch. The final connection is that, again through intelligence circles, Poley knew Tom Watson, the poet with whom Marlowe shared lodgings and on whose behalf he fought William Bradley in Hog Lane.

Skeres's link with Marlowe is altogether vaguer. Certainly there was a connection via the poet Matthew Roydon, who, while Marlowe was still in Cambridge, co-signed a bond for £40 to a goldsmith with Skeres in January 1582. The fact that Skeres was a 'coney-catcher', fleecing young gentlemen on the London circuit, may not have been known to either Roydon or Marlowe. George Chapman, Marlowe's fellow poet of the School of Night, was also caught up as a 'gull' by the time of Deptford, in debt to Skeres's sometime partner, John Wolfall.

Frizer's connections with Marlowe are the weakest of all, to the extent that they probably revolve around one man – Thomas Walsingham. We know that Marlowe was at Scadbury, Walsingham's home in Chislehurst, when he was summoned to the Council's presence by Henry Maunder on 18 May. By that time, Frizer was working as some sort of property agent for Walsingham, although in what context is unknown. He used the word 'servant' but this was a blanket term in Elizabethan England, surviving for another three centuries in the formal letter ending 'your obedient servant'. It is not likely that Frizer actually lived at Scadbury, but he certainly visited. Whether he did so during Marlowe's stay we cannot know.

The gloss on Marlowe's death given by Francis Meres several years afterwards refers to Frizer as a 'bawdy serving man'. Again, setting aside obsessive Puritan prurience, was there any basis in fact here? Was Frizer a pimp, procuring girls for clients in the stews of Southwark? Or is Meres's mention of 'lewd love' a veiled reference to homosexuality?

It is impossible now to decide whether Marlowe died as a result of the gay connection. As we have seen, there was an ambivalent attitude by the authorities to homosexuality, but the actual law of the land prescribed death and the increasing Puritanism of the 1590s perhaps made this more likely in practice. The need to keep the lid on homosexual affairs was therefore far greater than would be the case today. Is this why Marlowe died?

Let us look again at Poley, in particular his involvement in the Babington Plot. The letter written by Anthony Babington, so trusting and so terrified, has distinct homosexual overtones – 'Sweet Robyn, if, as I take thee, true to me' and 'what my love toward you you yourself can best tell'. In the semantics of Elizabethan speech, this may mean nothing, but we know from the ease with which Poley lured Babington that he had a glib tongue, a way with words. After a stony interview with spymaster Walsingham, one of the most redoubtable and sure-footed of interrogators of the reign, Poley was able to boast, probably truthfully, 'he putt Mr Secretary into that heate that he looked out of his wyndoe and grynned like a dogge.' If Poley ensnared Babington with overt homosexual advances, he would not be the last spy to do so. Let us look again at Poley's background. As a sizar of Clare College, Cambridge, he was forced to act as servant to the richer students, which may have involved all sorts of bed-hopping. The fact that he married and abandoned his wife for the charms of Joan Yeomans in prison makes him bisexual perhaps, but it also proves that he offered his sexual services freely and set little store by them.

Were Marlowe and Poley lovers? Was the killing in Deptford the result of a tiff? Sexual jealousy? This is entirely plausible. It is easy to create a motive like this one because the nature of the case meant a great deal of secrecy. In 1967 the homosexual playwright Joe Orton was bludgeoned to death by his flatmate and lover Kenneth Halliwell, who subsequently killed himself with an overdose of

Nembutal. The motivation in this case lay, according to Halliwell, in Orton's diaries. The playwright was achieving far more fame than his lover, and Halliwell had a history of depression. Like Marlowe, Orton had a desire to shock and subvert, the hallmarks of his plays. In Orton's case, the early forms of this showed themselves in his gleeful defacing of books in Islington Library to offend other borrowers; in Marlowe's perhaps it was 'reading the atheist lecture' and other examples of braggadocio in the School of Night.

In all other respects, however, the Orton–Marlowe parallel cannot be taken further. It was Poley the intelligencer rather than Poley the man, however bisexual he may have been, whom we contend killed Marlowe. He did not run, as Halliwell did, to the medicine cabinet to escape punishment. He did not run because he did not have to.

THE WALTER RALEGH THEORY

Spurred on by Hotson's discovery of Danby's inquest report, Eugenie de Kalbe went into print in the *Times Literary Supplement* in May 1925 with a theory that went beyond Hotson. She suggested, plausibly enough, that Frizer's head wounds might have been self-inflicted to 'prove' the official story that Marlowe had attacked him. This is of course possible, but head wounds are painful and would not be the most likely point of self-mutilation given the scenario that Marlowe had the dagger and a time advantage in which to use it. This took Ms de Kalbe off in a direction that will be examined below, but Dr Stephen Tannenbaum of New York produced *The Assassination of Christopher Marlowe* in 1928 in which he proffered the theory that the 'great Lucifer' Walter Ralegh was behind Frizer's attack.

Tannenbaum too doubted that anyone's Elizabethan dagger could pierce a skull, but in 1927 the 'wigwam murder' of Joan Wolfe had not yet happened and clearly he was unaware of parallel cases. Tannenbaum's more reasonable hypothesis, that death might not occur at all, has led more recent hopefuls like Peter Zenner to conclude that Marlowe did not die at Deptford, but that the wound to his right eye remained visible and obvious for the rest of his life.

Tannenbaum conjectured that Marlowe was invited to Eleanor Bull's house (as at least one Puritan commentator contended), given enough drink to make him comatose, and stabbed to death by Frizer. Interestingly, the chivalric Tannenbaum has Eleanor Bull 'out of the way in another part of the building'.[4] Tannenbaum believed Ralegh to be responsible because of Marlowe's arrest by Maunder and his daily reporting to the Privy Council. What would the man say after hours or days in the company of Richard Topcliffe, the rackmaster? What secrets regarding the School of Night would he give away? Accordingly, in order, as Richard Baines suggested in his Note, that Marlowe's 'mouth may be stopped', Ralegh employed Frizer to kill the whistle-blower with Poley and Skeres as back up.

This theory falls apart very quickly and was demolished by Dr Frederick Boas in his 1940 biography of Marlowe. Apart from the fact that there is no known link between Ralegh and any of the three at Deptford, the whole hypothesis collapses because of the lack of motive. What characterized Walter Ralegh was his fierce courage. Soldier, poet, explorer, romantic, this most universal of men was a soldier first, a man of action. If he had a quarrel with Marlowe and wanted to see him dead, he would have challenged him personally and gone head-to-head with rapiers, not hired some lackey to do the job in an obscure house on Deptford Strand. More crucially, what would be gained by silencing Marlowe? We have already seen that the Jesuit Robert Parsons knew about Ralegh's 'atheist school' and attacked its existence in diatribes from France. Ralegh's cool attitude in defence of his beliefs at Cerne Abbas – indeed, it could be argued, the actions of his entire life – indicates an utter disregard for public opinion.

In other words, too many people already knew about the School of Night and Ralegh did not care whether they knew or not. There is no motive here for killing a man whom Ralegh liked and respected, at least enough to flatter by copying his poetry. 'The great Lucifer' is an angel in the context of the murder of Kit Marlowe.

THE THOMAS AND AUDREY WALSINGHAM THEORY

There were some very odd things happening at Scadbury in 1593, and they led Eugenie de Kalbe to point the finger of suspicion at Marlowe's last patron, the house's owner, Thomas Walsingham. We know there was a link between *this* Walsingham and his much older cousin, Francis, the spymaster, that probably led to Marlowe's seeking out Thomas as his patron in the first place. We know that Marlowe and Thomas Walsingham were friends. It was by no means usual for poets and playwrights to live in with their patrons and in the case of Marlowe, we must always question the gay connection. The publisher Edward Blount, dedicating an edition of poetry to Walsingham, refers to the latter's relationship with Marlowe – 'in his lifetime you bestowed many kind favours, entertaining the parts of reckoning and worth which you found in him'.[5] Peter Zenner openly states that Marlowe was the gay lover of both Walsingham and Henry Wriothesley, the Earl of Southampton. There is not of course a shred of evidence for this, but it is possible to read a great deal into the flowery, fawning poetry and prose of the time. It is possible too that Walsingham may have been a member of Ralegh's School of Night, giving him an altogether more arcane relationship with Marlowe.

What is odd at Scadbury is this. The official version says that Ingram Frizer worked in a property-buying capacity for Walsingham, and was, in that sense, his servant. The very day after Frizer's pardon from the Queen, the man resumed his service with Walsingham, almost as though nothing had happened. In 1603–4 he was involved in law suits and property deals on behalf of Walsingham's wife, Audrey, and was by then living in Eltham, Kent. He was a churchwarden (like Marlowe's father) in 1605, had two daughters and a servant, Margaret. He was buried in the local church on 14 August 1627. Marlowe's friend George Chapman, the poet and member of the School of Night, was also a protégé of Walsingham's and continued to be so for several years. It was he who finished Marlowe's *Hero and Leander* and dedicated it to Audrey Walsingham in 1598. If Walsingham was innocent of Marlowe's death, why did he welcome Frizer back with open arms and why would Chapman not look elsewhere for patronage, if he suspected Walsingham's involvement? According to this theory, the answer lies with the direction in which politics was going in the 1590s, with the king-in-waiting James VI of Scotland and Thomas Walsingham's enigmatic wife, Audrey.

In 1597 the Queen visited Scadbury, on a private visit that was not part of her royal progress. It is very possible that she knighted Walsingham then and also gave him the local manors of Dartford,

Cobham, Combe and Chislehurst on a 21 year lease. There is no date given to Walsingham's marriage to Audrey, but it was probably 1598, the year before she first appeared at Court. Their son, Thomas, was born in 1600 and both Walsinghams continued to patronize the arts as George Chapman's fawning dedication of Marlowe's *Hero and Leander* in 1598 makes clear:

> This poor Dedication, in figure of the other uniting betwixt Sir Thomas and yourself, hath rejoined you with him, my honoured best friend, whose continuance of ancient kindness to my still-obscured estate, though it cannot increase my love to him . . . To My Best Esteemed and Wortheley Honoured Lady, the Lady Walsingham, one of the ladies of her Majesties Bed-Chamber.

Audrey had been born Audrey (Ethelreda) Shelton of an ancient Norfolk family who had long years of royal service. Five years younger than Walsingham, it is likely that a sickly childhood kept her from Court. That she was keen to foster her husband's courtly career is obvious from her first appearance at Harefield, where the Queen was visiting in 1599. Audrey laid on a lavish entertainment called 'The Robe of Rainbowes' and wrote flattering verses which Elizabeth (now sixty-three and looking every minute of it) adored:

> Beauty's rose and Virtue's look
> Angell's mind and Angell's look
> To all Saints and Angells deare,
> Clearest Majestie on Earth,
> Heaven did smile at your faire birth.[6]

De Kalbe's theory was that the rapid rise in favour of the Walsinghams under James I after 1603 is explained by the fact that they were conniving in his accession for years while pretending total loyalty to Elizabeth. The letter, written by Thomas Kyd to Sir John Puckering, by 1594 Principal Secretary, refers to Marlowe's involvement in the same area:

> He [Marlowe] would persuade with men of quality to go unto the King of Scotts whether [where] I heare Royden [the poet] is gon

and where if he had lived he told me when I saw him last he meant to be.

We do not know when Kyd saw Marlowe last and in any case doubt the testimony of either of the man's letters. He had been broken by torture and was being ignored by everyone as a coward, a failure and a traitor to Marlowe.

Certainly, Audrey Walsingham's rise under James was meteoric. She may have become Robert Cecil's mistress (one of his portraits probably hung at Scadbury). She was certainly employed to welcome the new queen, Anne of Denmark, and the Walsinghams were made Keepers of the Queen's Wardrobe. Before blotting her copybook by becoming involved in various scandals including the poisoning of Thomas Overbury, she was James's favourite.

De Kalbe's theory, that Marlowe died as a result of the Scottish succession chicanery, is more complex than Tannenbaum's, but it is still hopelessly vague. There is no evidence at all that Walsingham and Audrey Shelton were even an 'item' as early as the spring of 1593. Other than Kyd's bitter and terrified ramblings, we have no link between Marlowe and Scotland. The Walsinghams certainly benefited from the Stuart accession, but they were already doing very nicely under the Tudor regime. Clearly, Audrey in particular was a vivacious go-getter but *every* courtier had an eye on Scotland in the 1590s; it would be surprising if they did not.

Charles Norman[7] writing in 1948 found the Audrey connection unacceptable – 'it would have been scandalous – even in that cynical era – to accept the honour of a dedication under the circumstances.' Perhaps 1948 was a more naïve year. We believe that Thomas Walsingham was fully aware of what was to happen to Christopher Marlowe at Deptford, but it had nothing to do with his own ambitions.

THE RALEGH–ESSEX THEORY

The only book to date that deals in depth with the murder of Marlowe is Charles Nicholl's *The Reckoning*. It is a masterly piece of research, chronicling as it does the intensely small world of Walsingham's secret service network. Everybody seemed to be linked to everybody else in Elizabethan England, either by marriage, occupation or perhaps even coincidence. Nicholl lovingly unravels these tangles to create his theory and reach his conclusions; then he throws it away.

Nicholl's theory is that Marlowe died as a result of being a pawn in the on-going rivalry between Walter Ralegh and the Earl of Essex, the rising star of the 1590s. Essex, Nicholl contends, saw his chance to discredit the 'great Lucifer' over the business of the Dutch libel. Ralegh certainly did himself no favours when he stood up in the Commons as MP for Devon to attack the foreigners:

> Whereas it is presented, that for strangers it is against Charity, Honour, against profit to expel them; in my opinion it is no matter of Charity to relieve them. For first, such as fly hither have forsaken their own king and religion is no pretext for them, for we have no Dutchmen here, but such as came from those princes where the gospel is preached, and here they live disliking our church.[8]

Ralegh made the valid point that Englishmen were barely tolerated at all in Antwerp or Milan, whereas in England foreigners were given subsidies. We must beware of modern political correctness. It was parliament, not Ralegh, who were out of joint with the times. Giordano Bruno spoke of the rudeness of Londoners, watermen in particular, because he was a foreigner – so did Philip Hentzler. In 1593, Ralegh spoke for England.

Nicholl argues that since Marlowe was well known in Ralegh's circle via the School of Night, the idea came to Essex to link the Dutch church libel with the author of *Tamburlaine*, an appallingly crude piece of anti-Marlovian propaganda. In some obscure way, both Richard Baines and Richard Cholmeley also worked for Essex, providing evidence of Marlowe's atheism and blasphemy which would further blacken Ralegh's reputation. What clinched matters for Nicholl was that by 1593 Robert Poley was working for Essex and therefore was the catalyst that led to Deptford.

The murder itself, Nicholl contends, was not necessarily planned. Marlowe was a maverick; he could not be trusted. The purpose of the day's meeting at Eleanor Bull's house was to find out what Marlowe knew, to discover whether his silence could be bought, to see if he would turn against Ralegh, leaving the field clear for Essex as the Queen's favourite. Nicholl believes that Nicholas Skeres is the true villain of the piece, but only by implication because he believes that both Poley and Frizer were less prone to physical violence.

After over 320 pages building up to his conclusion, a sense of doubt creeps into Nicholl: 'I am not trying to argue that Marlowe's death has to have a meaning'; 'Ingram Frizer may well have struck the fatal blow. It is probable, though not certain, that he did'; 'We will never know for certain exactly what happened in that room in Deptford',[9] etc. He even wonders at one point whether it might not have been a simple fight after all, albeit not over the reckoning.

Nicholl's theory falls down because of the weakness of its motivation on two counts. If Essex wanted to outdo Ralegh as Elizabeth's favourite, doing it indirectly via Marlowe was a pretty long way round. Ralegh was the target, so Marlowe was put in the frame as the author of the Dutch libels. Why, when Ralegh's poetry was already published and available for black propaganda? Ralegh was the target, so Marlowe's reputation was dragged through the mud by Baines and Cholmeley, with only *one* mention of Ralegh – that Thomas Hariot was 'his man'. There is no attempt to smear those even closer to Ralegh, his wife Bess or his brother Carewe. The Cerne Abbas controversy of the following year, while it can be seen in the same anti-Ralegh mould, came about as a result of Ralegh's own recklessness, upsetting rigid and fairly stupid clerics over a supper table. Marlowe was already dead by then. If the idea was to smear Ralegh by smearing Marlowe, then the whole project was appallingly oblique and ineptly handled.

Above all, what would be the point? In 1593, Ralegh was already in disgrace. John Aubrey, writing years later, told the story:

He loved a wench well; and one time getting up one of the Mayds of Honour against a tree in a Wood (twas his first lady) who seemed at first boarding to be something fearfull of her Honour, and modest, she cryed 'Sweet Sir Walter, what do you me ask? Will you undo me? Nay, sweet Sir Walter! Sweet Sir Walter! Sir Walter!' At last, as the danger and the pleasure at the same time grew higher, she cryed in extacey 'Swisser Swatter! Swisser Swatter!' She proved with child.

The wench was Bess Throckmorton, a lady in waiting to the Queen, and although we might doubt Aubrey when he claims she was Ralegh's first conquest, this was the autumn of 1591. By February 1592, court gossips had noticed Bess putting on weight. Her son was born in March and the Queen got to hear of Ralegh's 'brutish offence' in May. Any interference with her ladies was likely to send Elizabeth into one of her famous rages, but that the guilty party was a favourite rankled more than usually. Elizabeth was nearly sixty, with black teeth, thin hair and a scrawny chest, but to all her courtiers she must appear as an object of adoration; indeed, the *only* object of adoration.

> 'S.W.R.,' wrote a courtier, 'will lose, it is thought, all his places and preferments at court, with the Queen's favour; such will be the end of his speedy rising, and now he must fall as low as he was high at which many may rejoice.'[10]

The fact that Ralegh had secretly married Bess Throckmorton and was skirmishing with Spanish warships off Panama at the time made no difference. He was recalled and he and his wife sent to the Tower in June 1592, lodged in separate apartments. Ralegh seems to have been genuinely distraught and even allowing for the sycophancy of the time, his letter to Cecil has the ring of truth:

> I that was wont to behold [the Queen] riding like Alexander, hunting like Diana, walking like Venus, the gentle wind blowing her fair hair about her pure cheeks like a nymph . . . She is gone in whom I trusted and for me has not one thought of mercy. Yours, not worth any name or title, W.R.[11]

He attempted suicide and was only released in August to negotiate with plundering Devon sailors who had helped themselves to loot from the Spanish treasure ship *Nombre de Dios* anchored at Dartmouth. He rescued the Queen's cut, but only by giving her all his own. Even so, she never forgave him for Bess Throckmorton. He was not allowed to return to Court for another five years. He fretted 'like a fish cast on dry land' at Sherborne Castle and fell foul of the local clergy there the following year.

If Nicholl had contended that Bess Throckmorton was a pawn in the game, an alluring *femme fatale* encouraged by Essex to seduce Ralegh, protesting quietly while he took her virginity and lost his place at Court as a result, there might be something in the Ralegh–Essex squabble. But none of this was necessary. Ralegh ruined himself – he would never gain favour at court again – and Essex had no need in 1593 to discredit him further. With respect to Ralegh's interests, therefore, the set-up at Deptford served no purpose at all.

THE SURVIVALIST THEORY

A century ago, an American physicist, Dr Thomas Mendenhall, developed a system for determining disputed authorship based on word length, literally counting the number of two-letter, three-letter, four-letter words per thousand written. He had been commissioned to prove that the plays of William Shakespeare were in fact written by Francis Bacon, the 'golden lad' whose brother Anthony was mixed up in espionage with a homosexual tinge to it.

Mendenhall discovered that Bacon, who wrote a great deal that we *know* to be his, matched poorly with Shakespeare, but Marlowe's match was, in the professor's words 'something akin to a sensation'. The conclusion was, simply, that Marlowe *was* Shakespeare.

Opponents of this theory, for example those who defend the Stratford man, or support Bacon, the Earl of Oxford, the Earl of Derby or a combination of any of the above, pointed out that a mechanical solution like Mendenhall's cannot be applied to a process as complex as literature. The works of Marlowe and Shakespeare (assuming them to be by different hands from each other) have been so copied and edited over the centuries that the analytical process is invalid.

While all this is fair comment (and totally ignores Shakespeare's *real* genius, the art of picking up unconsidered trifles, styles, characters and even whole stories from other people), it did nonetheless create the obvious corollary. If Marlowe was Shakespeare, he either wrote the whole canon (plays and poetry) before 1593 – which is probably physically impossible – or he did not die in 1593.

It is interesting that Marlowe's survival should first appear in the form of a novel, where we believe it should have stayed, when an American lawyer, Wilbur Zeigler, wrote *It was Marlowe: A Story of the Secret of Three Centuries* in 1895. After Hotson's discovery of the Danby inquest and the unlikeliness of that version, some kind of faked death seemed ever more likely. Another American, Calvin Hoffman, went into print thirty years later with *The Murder of the Man Who Was Shakespeare*. He was even allowed to open the vaults of the Walsinghams in Chislehurst church in order to find some clinching evidence. All he found was sand and was not allowed to open the coffins below.

'Clues' that Marlowe survived Deptford, with the connivance clearly of Poley, Frizer and Skeres, and perhaps as the brain child of Thomas Walsingham or even Burghley, abound in the plays of Shakespeare, but particularly in the man's sonnets. This was presented intriguingly by A.D. Wraight in 1994 in *The Story the Sonnets Tell*. Two examples must suffice. In *The Jew of Malta*, not published until the 1630s, some experts believe that the prologue spoken by Machiavelli was inserted later and was autobiographical of Marlowe himself – 'Albeit the world thinks Machevil is dead,/Yet was his soul but flown beyond the Alps . . .'.

And the first letters of the name 'Machiavelli', MACH, are an anagram of 'Ch. Ma', the *nom de plume* used in the publication of *Dr Faustus* in 1604.

Sonnet 74, written, according to conventional scholarship, at some time in 1594–5, reads:

> But be contented: when that fell arrest
> Without all bail shall carry me away
> My life hath in this line some interest,
> Which for memorial still with thee shall stay.
> When thou reviewest this, thou dost review
> The very part was consecrate to thee.
> The earth can have but earth, which is his due,
> My spirit is thine, the better part of me.
> So then thou hast but lost the dregs of life,
> The prey of worms, my body being dead,
> The coward conquest of a wretch's knife,
> Too base of thee to be remembered.
>> The worth of that, is that which it contains,
>> And that is this, and this with thee remains.

Survivalists see in this references to Marlowe and, since the sonnet was written in the first person, proof that he must have been alive after 30 May 1593. 'Fell arrest without all bail' . . . 'the prey of worms, my body being dead', 'the coward conquest of a wretch's knife'; all this, say survivalists, reflects Marlowe. They are guilty, of course, of taking the Sonnet at once too literally and out of context. References to a rival poet (i.e. Marlowe) do not begin until Sonnet 78. Sonnet 74 is part of a series that deals with death. Sonnet 71 begins:

> No longer mourn for me when I am dead,
> Than thou shall hear the surly, sullen bell
> Give warning to the world that I am fled
> From this vile world, with vilest worms to dwell.

Sonnet 74 merely continues this notion. 'Full arrest without all bail' means death with no reprieve and 'The prey of worms' simply reiterates the theme of Sonnet 71. To be as pedantic as the survivalists, Marlowe *was* granted bail of a sort, by being allowed to report each day to the Privy Council shortly before his death.

Survivalists have a clear theory as to why and how Marlowe's death was faked. He was in trouble with the Privy Council and his papers were seized. His friend Kyd was under torture and likely to crack. Whether Marlowe knew it or not, both Baines and Cholmeley were offering devastating evidence against him. If Walsingham was the orchestrator, all he need have done was to get Marlowe away, by ship from Deptford. But if it was a simple dash for the ports, Marlowe could have been intercepted, traced, brought back. Burghley's agents swarmed over Europe. Several of them knew Marlowe; he would not be difficult to find. But if it was believed that he was dead, a hunt would be pointless.

For the subterfuge to work, there had to be a body and survivalists have found one. The fanatical Puritan John Penry, probably responsible for the anti-establishment Marprelate Tracts, was hanged at five o'clock on Tuesday 29 May 1593 at St Thomas-a-Watering, along the old pilgrims' road to Canterbury, some 4 miles from Deptford. Like Marlowe, Penry was a Cambridge man, from Peterhouse, and he was a year older.

The Marprelate Tracts appeared first in the year before the Armada, signed by 'Martin Marprelate', the surname clearly coined because the pamphlets were attacks on the hierarchy of the Anglican Church, the 'bad prelates'; John Bridges, Dean of Salisbury, came in for particular vehemence – 'Master Bridges was a very patch and a dunce while at Cambridge'. An incensed Privy Council persuaded the Queen to use torture to discover the author.

Penry was tried by the Queen's Bench and found guilty on 25 May. After a delay of a few days, his execution was suddenly carried out with no information given to his wife or family. The reason for this was simple, say survivalists; the corpse was necessary to substitute for Marlowe. Additional wounds were made to Penry's head above the right eye and Danby and his jurors fell for the subterfuge wholeheartedly.

After that, Marlowe's life is a blank page for survivalists. Some have invented the pseudonym Louis le Doux (the meek) and have Marlowe going on writing for years. Peter Zenner, in a book littered with mistakes, has Marlowe becoming heterosexual, and committing suicide in May 1622 having been spurned by the love of his life.

The whole idea of survival of our heroes is a deep (and old) psychological one. We find it difficult to accept that someone who has brilliance or goodness beyond the everyday can be taken from us so cruelly. The Welsh believed for centuries that Arthur was not dead, but sleeping under a hillside with his knights until Wales had need of him. The French concocted a story that someone other than Jeanne d'Arc died in the fire at Rouen. Thousands of Russians swore they saw Tsar Nicholas II at large in 1918–19 when in fact his bullet-riddled body was rotting in a makeshift grave in the Koptiaki woods near Ekaterinburg. The Americans could not believe that film star James Dean was dead. We have all seen Elvis!

In other words, Marlowe's survival of Deptford is mere wishful thinking. Some believers contend that such faked deaths were common in espionage circles, but they give no examples of it actually happening. John Penry *could* have been substituted for Marlowe, as neither man's face would be as well known as it would today because of the inevitable media coverage they would have both received. Had Danby's jurors taken even a passing look at the man's neck, of course, they would have seen the tell-tale bruising of the rope. The subterfuge is pure speculation, backed up by cryptic acrostic 'clues' from poetry and prose, that, literature experts notwithstanding, can be made to mean *anything at all*.

Christopher Marlowe died at Deptford. It is time, four hundred years on, that we knew why.

ELEVEN

A Great Reckoning

A great reckoning in a little room.
William Shakespeare, *As You Like It*

Shortly after his release from the Bridewell and the clutches of Richard Topcliffe, Thomas Kyd wrote two letters to Sir John Puckering, Lord Keeper of the Privy Seal and a member of the Privy Council. If the work is in Kyd's own hand, we can be sure that the thumbscrews were not used on him because the writing is immaculate. It is clear from the text that Kyd was asking Puckering to intercede on his behalf with 'my Lorde' who, after Kyd's arrest, has clearly had to let him go. 'Though I think he rest doubtfull of myne innocence, hath yet in his discreeter judgement feared to offend in his retaining me.' Consequently, Kyd wanted a chance to vindicate himself of the charge of atheism – 'a deadlie thing which I was undeserved charged withal.' He wrote

> When I was first suspected for that libel [the Dutch] that concern'd the state, amongst those waste and idle papers (which I cared not for) and was unasked I did deliver up, were found some fragments of a disputation touching that opinion, affirmed by Marlowe to be his, and shuffled with some of myne unknown to me by some occasion of our writing in one chamber two yeares since.

The central portion of the letter went on to vilify Marlowe – 'That I should love or be familiar friend with one so irreligious were very rare . . . besides he was intemperate and of a cruel heart, the very contraries to which my greatest enemies will say of me.' He apologised, almost as a cliché, for speaking ill of the dead. 'Quia mortui non mordent' [because the dead do not bite], but must vindicate himself. Kyd suggested that Puckering talk to Marlowe's friends – 'Hariot, Warner, Roydon and some stationers in Paule's churchyard, whom I in no sort can accuse nor will excuse by reason of his company . . .'.

It is a sad truth that too many biographers have believed every word from Kyd. Marlowe was an atheist, Marlowe was irreligious, Marlowe was intemperate, Marlowe was cruel. How do we know? 'Gentle' Thomas Kyd says so. But 'gentle' Thomas Kyd had faced Topcliffe and he had cracked. Good men, however gentle, however honest, however brave, can break when they are alone and in agony. Which of us would behave differently? Only the fanatics like Edmund Campion and the madmen like Francis Kett.

Kyd was unemployed and friendless by the early June of 1593. He hoped that by ingratiating himself with Puckering, swearing his innocence and distancing himself from Marlowe and his atheism, he would be reinstated by the patron who had fired him. In 1940, Dr Frederick Boas put forward the theory that this lord was Ferdinando Stanley, Lord Strange. He believed that Strange sacked Kyd to avoid any link with Marlowe and the School of Night. We believe that Boas is wrong. It was not Strange who was Kyd's Lord, so that the motive for sacking changes.

The second letter to Puckering was unsigned, but it is clearly in Kyd's handwriting. Now, he is more vitriolic, more desperate. No one in the corridors of power was listening to him.

Pleaseth it your honourable lp [lordship] touching Marlowe's monstrous opinions as I cannot but with an aggrieved conscience think on him or them so can I but particularize few in respect of them that kept his greater company.

First it was his custom when I knew him first and as I hear say he continued it in table talk or otherwise to jest at the divine scriptures, jibe at prayers and strive in argument to frustrate and confute what hath been spake or wryt by prophets and such holie men.

Four specific accusations followed which we have heard before:

He would report St John to be our saviour Christ's Alexis. I cover [report] it with reverence and trembling that in that Christ did love him with an extraordinary love.

That for me to wryte a poem of St Paul's conversion as I was determined he said would be as if I should go wryte a book of fast and loose [con-artistry] esteeming Paul a juggler.

That the prodigall Childe's portion was but four nobles, he held his purse so near the bottom in all pictures and that it either was a jest or else four nobles then was thought a great patrimony not thinking it a parable.

That things esteemed to be done by divine power might as well be done by observation of men all which he would so suddenly take slight occasion to slip out as I and many others in regard of his other rashness in attempting sudden privy injuries to men did overslip though often reproached him for it and for which God is my witness as well by my Lord's commandment as in hatred of his life and thoughts I left and did refrain his company.

The last point refers to Marlowe's going to 'the King of Scots' where the poet Matthew Roydon has already gone.

This second letter smacks of the Baines Note – a list of puerile jibes at the Gospels. And as such some biographers have either disbelieved it, because they disbelieve the Baines Note, or they take the view that Kyd provided Baines with information in the first place. We accept neither version.

Kyd's second letter is markedly different from the first. There is none of the plaintive wheedling and protestations of innocence. It is all Marlowe. This is not a vengeful man nearing the end of his tether, turning on a former friend with whom he once shared lodgings and who may well have worked with him on *The Spanish Tragedy*. Between his first and second letters, we believe that the poet received a visit. Somebody got to Thomas Kyd.

The document which finally explains what happened to Kit Marlowe is among the Harleian manuscripts in the British Museum. It refers to an intelligencer called Richard Cholmeley whom we last saw inciting riots in the Strand in 1592 after the collapse of the Portingale expedition, a failed adventure involving the Earl of Essex. Like Marlowe, Cholmeley too was being watched and for much the same reason. Whoever the agent was who was shadowing him reported to Burghley. Cholmeley was no fool and was beginning to smell a rat, but the agent was able to confirm:

His second course is to make a jest of the scripture with those fearful, horrible and damnable speeches, that Jesus Christ was a bastard, St Mary a whore and the Angel Gabriel a bawde to the holy ghoste and that Christ was justly persecuted by the Jewes for his own foolishness, that Moyses was a Juggler and Aaron a cosoner, the one for his miracles to Pharao to prove there was a god and the other for taking the earings of the children of Israel to make a golden calfe with many other blasphemous speeches of the divine essence of God which I fear to rehearse [repeat]. This cursed Cholmeley hath sixty of his company and he is seldom from his fellows and therefore I beseech your worship have a special care of yourself in apprehending him for they be resolute murdering myndes.

This is the stuff of paranoid conspiracy, but it got better:

. . . their practice is after Her Majesty's decease to make a King among themselves and live according to their own laws and this saith Cholmeley will be done easily because they be and shortly will be by his and his fellows' possessions as many their opinion as of any other religion.

What had happened to Cholmeley? We know that he was a projector posing as a Catholic and a year before Marlowe's death was prominent in bringing to book a man who was probably a genuine double agent, Thomas Drury. Drury did time in the Marshalsea as a result – he may have been the agent shadowing Cholmeley in the spring of 1593 and the author of the *Remembrances* against him. We also know that he was known to various members of the Queen's inner circle. In 1592, Robert Beale, Francis Walsingham's erstwhile secretary, mentioned him in the context of undercover agents in a letter to a possible successor to Walsingham, Sir Edward Wootton – '. . . and first see you have a good warrant to deal in such causes, as Montague and Cholmeley had, saving themselves by special pardons . . .'.[1] Montague was Anthony Browne, 1st Viscount, a well-known recusant, but it is unlikely that such a high profile character would himself be trusted with any espionage.

The rest of what may be Drury's remembrances against Cholmeley was even more bizarre. Much of his work, for Robert Cecil directly, involved the writing of Catholic propaganda – 'That he made certain libellous verses in Commendation of papists and seminary priests very greatly inveighing against the state' and that 'he had a certain book . . . delivered him by Sir Robert Cecil of whom he giveth very scandalous report . . .'. The book was a Jesuit tract 'printed at Paris' and written by Robert Southwell. It was called *An Epistle of Comfort*. He touched on recent events – 'That he saieth that William Parry was hanged, drawn and quartered but injest, that he was a gross ass overreached by cunning and that in truth he now meant to kill the queen more than [Parry] had.' He railed at 'Mr Topcliffe' (hardly surprising; the man was a sadist) but he was also vitriolic against Francis Drake and Justice Young 'whom he saith he will couple up [hang] together because he hateth them alike'. After the Strand riots 'he repented him of nothing more than that he had not killed my lord Treasurer with his own hands, that he could not have done God better service.' He hated the Lord Chamberlain (Hunsdon) 'and had good cause to do so'.

And, in the context of Deptford,

That he saieth and verily believeth that one Marlowe is able to show more sound reasons for Atheism than any divine in England is able to give to prove divinitie and that Marlowe told him that he hath read the Atheist lecture to Sir Walter Raleigh and others.

What we have in Richard Cholmeley is an agent gone berserk. He was a maverick, a loose cannon. His behaviour was irrational, outspoken. Some of it was braggadocio, in that he claimed to be able to treat the Privy Council exactly as he liked and there was nothing they could do about it. Whether the sixty followers of like mind (he cites Henry Young, Jasper Borage and the Tipping brothers as four of them) who had plans to stage a coup on the death of Elizabeth ever really existed or were a figment of a madman's imagination or a clever agent teasing a more gullible one (Drury), we cannot know. Drury himself was to feel Hunsdon's wrath early in August 1593 when the Lord Chamberlain had him arrested, probably because he wanted to know what, if anything, Drury actually *knew*. 'My Lord Chamberlain is too continually set against me,' Drury wrote to Antony Bacon, the 'golden lad' projector now working for Essex, 'His displeasure is everlasting and so is my misery.'[2]

So it is easy to dismiss Cholmeley as a crank and the lines 'that he speaketh in general all evil of the Counsell, saying that they are all Atheists and Machiavellians, especially my Lord Admiral [Howard of Effingham]' likewise. It is when Drury is more specific on that that we should stop and reconsider:

> Mr Cholmeley his manner of proceeding in scoring the Queen's subjects is first to make slanderous reports of most noble peers and honourable counsellors, as the Lord Treasurer [Burghley], the Lord Chamberlain [Hunsdon], the Lord Admirall [Howard], Sir Robert Cecil, these saeith he have profound witness be sound Atheists and their lives and deeds show that they think their souls do end, vanish and perish with their bodies.

Other commentators have ignored Cholmeley as a madman. His sixty rebels did not materialize, so they did not exist. He did not actually attempt to murder Burghley or the Queen, so the threats uttered in the *Remembrances* are just so much hot air. But what if *some* of Cholmeley's ravings were accurate? What if *some* of what Drury was reporting was actually true? The notion that the soul did not survive bodily death was indeed blasphemy and heresy in Elizabeth's England. Walter Ralegh himself was careful to record that he did not accept that – the soul, said Ralegh and the Scriptures with one voice, was immortal. What if some members of the Queen's Privy Council, the highest in the land, at times just feet away from her Majesty in the corridors of Whitehall Palace, *really were* atheists? The 1590s were troubled years. The plague was wreaking havoc in London; there were threats of new rebellion in Ireland; rumours of a Spanish alliance with Scottish Catholics; parliament grew restless; the Queen was old and more difficult to please with each passing week. Burghley too was losing his grasp, falling asleep in crucial meetings, snapping at subordinates and colleagues, desperate to keep the ambitious Essex out and his second son in. The last thing any of the Council wanted was for a whistle-blower to purse his lips.

Such a one was Richard Cholmeley. Another was Kit Marlowe. Cholmeley *knew* and Marlowe *knew*. It has always been assumed that the reference in the Baines Note referred to members of the School of Night – '. . . he [Marlowe] saieth likewise that he hath quoted a number of contrarities out of the scripture which he hath given to some great men who in convenient time shall be named.' In a way, this is correct, because one of these great men was the 'heir of Hunsdon', George Carey, whose father was the Queen's Lord Chamberlain as well as her cousin. But Marlowe, through Baines, was not talking about Ralegh and Percy and Strange as some experts have assumed. He was talking about Burghley and Cecil and Howard and Hunsdon, those four horsemen who would bring about Marlowe's own apocalypse. The fact that none of them was actually a member of the School of Night is irrelevant. Marlowe had evidence against them, of their heretical and blasphemous views, which, being guarded men, they had kept, they thought, to themselves. Exactly how he found out we cannot know, but it is our guess that the weakest link was Carey. Through an over-honest disposition, or careless table-talk in his cups, he may have told Marlowe things he should not. The damage was done and as the winter of 1592–3 turned into spring, Marlowe was becoming ever more outrageous, as, in a different way, was Cholmeley.

Was Marlowe ever a secret Catholic? Had he defected to the enemy? It is unlikely, but he had gone over to an enemy of a different and all the more deadly sort. He had dared God out of his heaven, which today is commonplace. In his own day, it sealed his death warrant.

Edward II was performed in January 1593, but we contend that Marlowe was already being watched before that, as a man with secret knowledge; a man not to be trusted. More pernicious than its overt homosexuality, *Edward II* was a political allegory. Edward of course was Elizabeth and the upstart Gaveston was Burghley and the Cecil clan. Richard Verstigan, an exiled Catholic writing from the safety of Antwerp, wrote in 1591:

Cecill being the causer of the most enormous evils . . . is a traitor himself and the greatest that England ever nourished and far more noisome and pernicious to the realm than ever were the Spensers,

Peter of Gaveston or any other that ever abused either Prince or people.[3]

Verstigan's *Declaration* appeared in England in March 1592, his *Advertisement* five months later. Can his comments merely be dismissed as Catholic propaganda? In Marlowe's play, both the king and Gaveston despise parliament and manipulate it; Elizabeth and Burghley were doing the same thing. Edward makes Gaveston Lord High Chamberlain, Chief Secretary and Earl of Cornwall. Elizabeth had made Burghley her Lord Treasurer and had raised no objections when he blithely took over Walsingham's duties as Principal Secretary in 1590.[4] The Keeper of the Seal may have been John Puckering, but men knew that the Cecils called the shots. Gaveston was given this power in *Edward II*; Burghley already had it. In the play, the nobility of England sit like old wives in agonies of indecision, unwilling to overthrow their king despite his squandering of his birthright. No one dares cross the new power in the land. So it was with the advent of the Cecils. The only man who dared try, the Earl of Essex, went to the block on 25 February 1601.

Gaveston ignores the supplication of the poor. 'And what art thou?' 'A soldier,' comes the reply, 'that hath served against the Scots.' 'Why,' scoffs Gaveston, utterly unmoved by the man's derelict state, 'there are hospitals for such as you. I have no war and therefore, sir, be gone.' Elizabeth herself left her gangrenous sailors to die after they had given her the greatest victory of her reign. Edward fights expensive wars in France and loses Normandy. Elizabeth's war with Spain had no end in sight and in February 1592, that rising star the Earl of Essex was recalled from France where his little army was bolstering the cause of Henri IV against the powers of the Catholic League. While he was distributing knighthoods to twenty-four of his officers (which infuriated Elizabeth, whose right that was) his men were dying of disease around Rouen. And Ireland too was once again ripe for rebellion – in the play, Lancaster warns:

> Thy garrisons are beaten out of France,
> And lame and poor lie groaning at the gates;
> The wild O'Neill, with swarms of Irish kerns
> Lives uncontrolled within the English Pale.

But it was the eventual overthrow of Gaveston and Edward that so worried the controllers of the Elizabethan police state. Curtis Breight describes *Edward II* as 'a subversive fantasy of violence against the established order' and the orchestrator of it was Marlowe. When Burghley reported in January 1593 that he was 'much offended with the libels printed against him',[5] was he referring specifically to *Edward II*? In the play are the lines – 'Libels are cast against thee in the street/Ballads and rymes made of thy overthrow.' But something had gone wrong; the play had slipped through the net of censorship which the Elizabethans had so carefully set up. The Stationers had missed it, even allowing the play into print in July 1593; so had Edmund Tillney, Master of the Revels. What could be done now? There were, Burghley perhaps noticed if he watched the performance of the play at Christmas 1592, three murderers in *Edward II*. . . .

The *Massacre at Paris* had likewise escaped the censor and it may be that its late publication date is a result of official government tinkering. We know that there was an earlier, longer version of which only a fragment remains. We know too that plays like Kyd's *Sir Thomas More* were emasculated; others, like Jonson's *Isle of Dogs* (1597)[6] were destroyed and its author imprisoned. Even in its extant form, *The Massacre* was a golden opportunity for Marlowe to expose audiences to Catholic propaganda, denied them systematically since 1547. The fact that Marlowe refuses to take sides in the play shows his own disregard for denominational religion, but this was probably not how the Privy Council saw it. The play contains an elaborate series of assassinations, exposing for all to see the Machiavellian nature of statecraft. True, Marlowe could hide behind the fact that the events were taking place in a different country (France) and at a different time (the St Bartholomew's Day slaughter) but few would be fooled by that. 'Religion,' scoffs the Duke of Guise, 'O Diabole!' linking the whole religious edifice of the sixteenth century with the theme of Protestants being, at best, in the Baines Note, 'hypocriticall asses'. In *The Massacre* the message is the same as in *Edward II*: the state is evil, corrupt and merciless. It ignores wise counsel and honest men and commits murder on a massive scale to maintain itself in power. Could there be a clearer denunciation of the Machievellians who ran Elizabethan England?

The Privy Council had of course been criticized before, but from the late 1580s something of a pattern was emerging and it was certainly on the increase. The Martin Marprelate tracts had hit out at the hierarchy of the Church in the year of the Armada. Two years later *Certain Discourses Military* by John Smythe, a contact of Burghley's, was suppressed for its seditious content. Smythe himself was imprisoned in Colchester in 1596 for his opposition to the enforced raising of militias to meet another Spanish invasion scare. Even the normally apolitical Edmund Spenser had gone into print in 1591 with *Mother Hubbard's Tale* in which he criticized Burghley:

> So did he good to none, to many ill,
> So did he all the kingdom rob and pill [steal],
> Yet none durst speak, nor none durst of him plaine,
> So great he was in grace, and riche through gaine.[7]

Perhaps because of his courtly connections, Spenser got away with it. Not so lucky Philip Stubbes; when he wrote a seditious article in 1579, his right hand was chopped off.

The dilemma of the Privy Council, spearheaded by the Cecils, was how to deal with Marlowe. In his last two plays, the man was openly taunting them, challenging their authority. What would he do next? Those biographers who have found no conspiracy in Marlowe's death have asked why he was not simply arrested and put on trial for treason. He *was* arrested, by the Queen's Messenger Henry Maunder, on 18 May. The reason that we do not know the exact nature of the charges against him is that the Privy Council dared not frame them. They insisted that Marlowe report to them daily so that they could watch him and gain vital time to decide what to do. Probably early on in this period, a messenger was sent post-haste to the Low Countries, to find Robert Poley, there again on the Queen's business. Had the Privy Council put Marlowe on trial, that would have meant interrogation in the Star Chamber, and the records of that court were public. If Marlowe blew his whistle on the atheism of the 'Council four', then it would have become public knowledge and even the Cecils would have difficulty in preventing that. The Queen herself would find out. And the Puritan Thomas Beard was nearer to the truth than he knew when he wrote

I would to God (and I pray it from my heart) that all Atheists in this realm, and in the world beside, would by the remembrance and consideration of this example, either forsake their horrible impiety, or that they might in like manner come to destruction: and so that abominable sin which so flourisheth amongst men of greatest name, might either be quite extinguished and rooted out, or at least smothered and kept under, that it durst not show its head any more in the world's eye.

Why not, then, simply arrest Marlowe and see that he died quietly in the darkest recesses of some jail? A number of Catholics had met their end this way, as well as more high-profile offenders like Somerville in 1583 and Northumberland in 1585. John Somerville was arrested in October 1583 in Warwickshire for threatening to shoot the Queen. He 'hoped to see her head on a pole, for she was a serpent and a viper'. The story that he hanged himself in his cell in Newgate before he could come to trial fooled no one. We have already discussed the implausibility of the suicide (by pistol) of Henry Percy, Earl of Northumberland, in the Tower.

With Marlowe, it would have to be different. It was right, as Baines said in his Note, that his 'mouth should be stopped' but with careful handling, the man could be a totem, a warning to others like the gibbets that creaked in the wind at lonely crossroads or the bloody heads that rotted on London Bridge. Marlowe, the scourge of God, must die. But those in the know who might be tempted to follow his example must know who had killed him. That alone would prevent them from asking the reason why. Knife the man in some anonymous back alley and once again, the message would not be heard; such a death could be the chance outcome of random street violence. It must be announced, obliquely but clearly, that Marlowe had somehow over-reached himself and suffered the fate of anyone who dared flout the might of the Cecils. That said, there was also a need to cover up the event. Honest souls, worthy men, if they existed in Elizabeth's England, must believe that Marlowe's death was innocent enough – and his own fault.

Armed with this insight, we have to go further than Curtis Breight. He pointed the finger, accurately, at the Cecils in 1996, but does not provide a motive for *murder*. If Marlowe was simply, as

Breight contends, a thorn in the Cecils' side; if he was an increasingly outspoken critic of the system; even if Kyd's ravings were true and Marlowe did indeed intend to follow Matthew Roydon north to Scotland; or go over to the Catholics where perhaps his heart had secretly lain all along; even if all this were so, there were a dozen conventional ways to stop him. It was Marlowe's *knowledge* that made his end special. Because of what he knew about the Council, he had to be silenced in a very particular way. There had to be a reckoning.

With this knowledge, let us plug the gaps that belong to Marlowe's last days. Burghley, Robert Cecil, Howard of Effingham, Hunsdon – who better to coordinate such a plan? A son and his father; a father-in-law and his son-in-law; four of the most powerful and Machiavellian men in the land, with limitless access to the machinery that brought dangerous opponents to their deaths. We cannot know whose idea it was, but we can see all four of them poring over plans in the Council chamber when the others had gone home for the night, the curtains drawn, the candles guttering. It is deliciously tempting to point to the usual number of the Council – thirteen – as the number of the coven, with the horned god Burghley at their head. But there is no evidence for this. Four men had been singled out by Cholmeley; four men made the crucial decisions of May 1593. Burghley knew Marlowe as an agent of Walsingham's. More recently he had employed him himself over the incident of the Dutch coining. He had personally interviewed him on his return from Vlissingen. He or Robert Cecil had sent Richard Baines to watch him and to report back. One of them had sent Robert Poley, too, back in the previous September, to Canterbury. And 'sweet Robyn' was a resourceful man. He understood from Burghley, whose man he was and whose wages he took, that Marlowe was unpredictable, dangerous even; he may have to be silenced. Is it too far-fetched to imagine Poley, with his glib tongue and smooth charm, engaging the tailor William Corkine in conversation and passing the man cash to 'beat and berate' Marlowe, to produce a duel? Poley knew Marlowe already, but he had never seen him in action. He wanted to know what he might be up against and the fight in Mercery Lane perhaps convinced him that Marlowe was too great a risk for him to tackle alone.

Yet Poley was the obvious choice. He was tried and trusted, a man who could think on his feet. But he was abroad. Burghley would have sent word, perhaps, on 20 May, to fetch him home, covering the man's back with the official paperwork that for the whole of May he was in Her Majesty's service and therefore given protection for whatever might happen. It was the same kind of 'special pardon' that Montague and Cholmeley had, according to Robert Beale's advice to Sir Edward Wootton.

Hunsdon may well have known Marlowe best through his son's involvement with the School of Night. Did he suggest smearing the man's reputation in order to arrest him in the first place in a way that would not arouse suspicion? So someone, perhaps Cholmeley, perhaps Drury, but some 'discontented gentleman', was persuaded to write racial taunts in bad verse running to fifty-three lines that he then stuck to the wall of the Dutch church in Broad Street. He larded it with mentions of Marlowe's plays and signed it 'Tamburlaine'. And was it Hunsdon who obtained from his son, George, the papers belonging to Marlowe which were slipped into the papers belonging to Kyd soon after the man's arrest? If Robert Cecil owned underground Catholic propaganda like Robert Southwell's *Epistle to Comfort*, why should Hunsdon not possess something similar? So Kyd was accused of writing the Dutch libel and the Council pretended to panic, sending men everywhere, knocking on shutters, smashing through doors. All the force of the police state was brought to bear.

Kyd was an easy nut to crack. Burghley or Robert Cecil unleashed Topcliffe on him and a torrent of anti-Marlowe information flooded out. Even so, there was nothing to incriminate the Council, so Kyd could live. And Richard Baines was ordered to put in writing everything he had heard Marlowe say in his table talk – all of it, the blacker the better.

By the time Kyd was in prison and the Privy Council had the Baines Note in their hands, the Council four had finalized their plans. It was now about 26 May and a venue had to be found for the killing to take place. Scadbury was out of the question. We believe that Thomas Walsingham knew from 18 May when Henry Maunder came for Marlowe what the score was. It is unlikely that Walsingham was told why; it is unlikely that Maunder knew.

Walsingham was a patriot and an ambitious man. For all Marlowe was his friend and protégé, in an age like Elizabethan England, such men were expendable. He may have agonized over it, but if the Privy Council said there were good reasons, this was probably enough. Even so, he would not countenance the outrage happening at his own door. The Council would have to find somewhere else for their dirty work.

That somewhere else was probably suggested by Burghley, whose cousin, Eleanor Bull, had a house on Deptford Strand, across the green from that of Howard of Effingham, who knew it well. Deptford was ideal on three counts. First, it would provide the fiction that would get Marlowe there in the first place. It was a thriving port, with ships coming and going. From there, Marlowe could sail to the Low Countries, to France, to Scotland, to anywhere in the rapidly expanding world. Second, it was within 3 miles, let alone 12, of the Queen's palace of Placentia; that placed it 'within the verge', in the jurisdiction, not of any old official, but of the Royal Coroner himself. And third, Eleanor Bull was related to Lord Burghley, the Lord Treasurer; to his son, Sir Robert; to John Dee, formerly the Queen's magus. She could be trusted with what she needed to know concerning affairs of state. Her house doubled as an eating-place or Ordinary. She was told to expect certain visitors at the end of May.

Probably on one of his visits to the Privy Council, someone suggested to Marlowe it was safest for him to go, to run, at least until the current mood of unease in the capital died down. The plague still raged; Marlowe was under suspicion; Kyd was in the Bridewell and nothing had been heard of him. Perhaps Marlowe talked the idea over at Scadbury – or perhaps Walsingham was part of the Cecil trap and suggested it himself.

So it was that Marlowe arrived at Eleanor Bull's on Wednesday 30 May. We need not doubt the time mentioned in Danby's inquest – 'about the tenth hour before noon' would have given Marlowe time to report early to the Council, at Whitehall. Deptford was 3 miles away, half an hour's ride. Of course, he may not have visited at all that day, nor would the Council come looking for him, since they knew exactly where he was and why. Alternatively, if the Queen was *actually* at Greenwich that day (and we have no way of proving this after four hundred years) then elements of the Council may have been with her and that made Marlowe's journey between Placentia and Deptford even more straightforward.

Poley was probably waiting for him. We know that he left the Court, in the still peripatetic world of government then at Archbishop Whitgift's house in Croydon, on 8 May. A warrant signed by Sir Thomas Heneage, Treasurer of the Queen's Chamber, and a Cecil man through and through, has survived the ravages of time and is Poley's passport to freedom over the Marlowe killing:

> . . . for carrying of letters in post for Her Majesty's special and secret affairs of great importance, from the Court at Croydon the viiith of May 1593 into the Low Countries to the town of the Hague in Holland, and for returning back again with letters of answer to the Court at Nonesuch the viiith of June 1593, being in Her Majesty's service all the aforesaid time.

In the twenty-six extant records of payment made to Poley for his services to the government, only this one has the last sentence. It serves to exonerate Poley from what was about to happen; the Elizabethan equivalent of Ian Fleming's famous 'licensed to kill'.

Poley was back at least nine days early. Had he transacted his business at the Hague? Had kind winds brought him home quicker across the Channel? Perhaps both, but mostly, Poley was home early because he had a job to do. Perhaps he was told why, but that again is unlikely. What Marlowe knew and what Cholmeley knew about their government masters must remain a secret. Like Thomas Walsingham, like Eleanor Bull, Poley was told that a job had to be done and that there were good reasons for it. But Poley could not work alone. He had already been sent to Canterbury, we believe, to fix a fight to see Marlowe in action. He knew perfectly well that the official line sent out by the Council with the warrants of arrest read 'And in case of need to require aid'. The aid he chose was Nicholas Skeres and Ingram Frizer.

Why these two? Judith Cook in the novel *The Slicing Edge of Death* conjectures that Cecil blackmailed these two into working with Poley. Skeres had already been in trouble for 'coney-catching' and was one of those 'masterless men' whom the Elizabethan police state so feared. It is dangerous to allow fiction to intrude into history, although as we have seen in relation to the death of Marlowe, the Puritans did it happily enough. Marlowe probably knew Skeres anyway on the espionage circuit. There is no record of Frizer being involved in this context, but he did work for Thomas Walsingham and may have known Marlowe on that score. In any case, as is likely from the coney-catching incident on the gull Drew Woodlef a year later, it is reasonable to suppose that Skeres and Frizer were a team by May 1593; hire one and you hire the other.

So the balance between these three now shifts. Rather than Frizer being the central character, attacked by a vicious, short-tempered Marlowe with Skeres and Poley the innocent and no doubt suitably alarmed bystanders, the focus is now Poley. Here was a man who lived by his wits, who mixed with low-life in London prisons and cut-throat agents in France and the Low Countries. We know he brought about the torture and death of Anthony Babington and his friends. All we know of Frizer is that he was a con-man.

Marlowe would not have been alarmed to find Poley there. He was probably told to expect him, again perhaps by Walsingham. What has puzzled a number of commentators is why the four spent (if we accept Danby's times) at least eight hours at Eleanor Bull's house. Nicholl conjectures that Poley's job was to pump Marlowe to find out how much he knew of the Ralegh–Essex rivalry. We believe he was simply waiting for the tide. We also contend that Marlowe was unarmed and do not doubt that it *was* actually Frizer's dagger that killed him. Marlowe's own weapons, his sword and dagger, would have been stored away on the ship waiting for the evening tide. Poley and Marlowe were old hands in the spying game – so, probably, was Skeres. They

> passed the time together and dined and after dinner were in quiet sort together there and walked in the garden belonging to the said house until the sixth hour after noon of the same day and then returned from the said garden to the room aforesaid and there together and in company supped.

So runs Danby's inquest and we have no reason to doubt that either.

But from this point, only seven lines into the actual account of events, fiction takes over, the not altogether convincing collection of lies fabricated by an assassin and his two aides. The exact moves in the 'little room' we shall never know, but we believe it went something like this.

Poley, using his own dagger, sheathed in the small of his back, made the first move. Marlowe perhaps saw it coming and all too aware that he was unarmed, had the quick wits and speed to grab Frizer's dagger and fight Poley off, blade against blade. Skeres was in on the act now, two blades against Marlowe's one. In the scuffle that followed, it was the unarmed Frizer who was hit, Marlowe striking him twice in rapid succession on the head. Bleeding and in pain, Frizer was out of the action for a while, but Marlowe was still outnumbered. Perhaps he disarmed Poley, sending his poignard clattering across the room. Somehow Poley was able to grab Marlowe's weapon, or perhaps Skeres brought his man down and Marlowe dropped the knife.

The fatal wound has long puzzled commentators. For all Nicholl's contention that it was a recognized fencing blow; for all Curtis Breight's belief in symmetrical reversal, that as Marlowe's brain had committed treason against the state, so his brain must be destroyed, neither of these arguments makes much sense. In a knife fight, the biggest target is the torso. Slashing wounds might rip arm muscles to incapacitate a fighter, but the *coup de grâce* is aimed at the heart. The wound to the head, whether it was through the cranium or the eyesocket, was the result of a blow delivered downwards. Marlowe was lying on his back, his arms pinioned by Skeres and probably Frizer, still able to use his weight to hold a man down. Poley threw himself on Marlowe, driving downwards in a desperate stab, before rolling clear of the body.

The deed accomplished, the three had to invent a story that would fit all the facts, and the version they concocted was not perhaps as neat as the Council four would have liked. If the fight happened along the lines above, there would be upset furniture, signs of violence. Frizer was hurt and it was Frizer's dagger that had killed Marlowe. Eleanor Bull and her servants would have heard the scrape of furniture, the clash of steel, whatever shouts and curses may have left the mouths of any of the four men upstairs. The blasphemy which the Puritans attributed to Marlowe probably came from Frizer as Marlowe caught him with his own knife.

Frizer, Skeres, Poley; all were men who, in their various walks of life, worked for money. What more natural then that the story they invented should be to do with money. 'The reckoning' – that would do it. Poley had been briefed that he would be cleared. All he had to do was stand his ground and the authorities would look after him. But it was *Frizer's* head that was cut and *Frizer's* dagger daubed with Marlowe's blood; so they would have to adopt a slightly different plan.

We do not know the mechanics of what happened next. Someone would have contacted the local constable, but the surviving records are silent on this. Frizer was taken into custody since 'he neither fled nor withdrew himself'. He had no need to; Poley would have guaranteed his safety, along with whatever handout Poley gave him for a job done, if not done well. This could mean that Poley visited the coroner himself.

Now, the buck passed to Sir William Danby. We know very little about the man, except the vital fact that he was a personal friend of Burghley from the old days in the Inns of Court, but we do understand his office. The coroner or 'crowner' was a royal appointment (literally a substitute for the king and a reminder of the days when the monarch was not only the highest court in the realm, but physically sat as a judge) and was created in the twelfth century to collect and guard royal revenue. The *deodand*, the value of the object which led to a death (Frizer's infamous 12d dagger) was technically forfeit to the king as was the entire estate of a felon guilty of murder. Originally, the coroner's role was to catch criminals, extract confessions and confiscate goods. He also investigated all incidences of violent death.

On 1 June, Danby's jury met to decide the events of two days earlier – exactly where this meeting took place, we do not know. What we do know is that Danby was extremely keen to exert his royal authority over the case. He uses the phrase 'within the verge' three times, underlining the fact that this was no ordinary squabble over a bill. When Thomas Watson killed William Bradley in Hog Lane, that was also 'within the verge' (a radius of 12 miles from the person of the monarch) but the coroner in that case was the Middlesex county official, not Danby. Danby was necessary because Danby had to control events at the inquest itself. He too would have been briefed, possibly by his old friend Burghley, and told to find Frizer innocent; that he had acted in self-defence.

Before the First World War, the coroner's jury were to be 'not less than twelve, nor more than twenty-three good and lawful men'. Their task was to identify the body (which actually none of them could do without the help of Poley, Skeres and Frizer) and to decide 'how, when and where and by what means the deceased came by his death'. The normal procedure today is that all relevant witnesses would be called – Poley, Skeres, Frizer, Eleanor Bull, any servants in the house at the time. The coroner's duty is to examine their evidence and write it down in the form of a deposition checked by the witnesses. The jury then decides their verdict, in this case 'in the defence and saving of his own life'. As we have seen, the facts as presented by Poley, Skeres and Frizer make little sense, but then, in the *Regnum Cecilianum*, they did not have to.

We have no record of questions put to any witnesses, no cross-examination. And what of the jury? We know their names. Nicholas Draper was a gentleman, perhaps from Leigh, near Tonbridge; Wolstan Randall was of the same social class, from Deptford; William Curry lived in tenements in Deptford with a wharf and yard; George Halfepenny was a baker from Limehouse with tenements in Deptford; Henry Dobyns fits the same description; Henry Awger was a tenant in the local manor house of Sayes Court; James Batte was a husbandman from Lewisham; Giles ffeld was a grocer; John Baldwyn was a yeoman from Greenwich across the Raven's Bourne. Of Adrian Walker, John Barber, Robert Baldwyn, Henry Bendin, Thomas Batte, Alexander Burrage and Edmund Goodcheape we know nothing. It is a sad indictment of his abilities that a researcher as diligent as Canterbury archivist William Urry could write in 1964:

> There is everything to show, in the identification of these men, that the jurors were good, solid, middle-class Englishmen, a group utterly unlike any kind of jury which might be suborned into giving a false verdict.

This is to misunderstand the nature of the Elizabethan hierarchy and the extraordinary power of the Privy Council. As recently as 1921,

Dr W. Aitchison Robertson in his scholarly *Manual of Medical Jurisprudence* wrote

> It is notorious that great discredit is sometimes thrown on the findings of the Coroner's Court. This is due to the fact that the verdict is given by a body of men who are often in rural districts drawn from the illiterate classes.

Danby's jury comprised worthy small businessmen with some local status, but throw into the equation two factors and their integrity becomes irrelevant. First, William Danby had orders to find Frizer guilty only of a killing in self-defence and second, the second-named juror, Wolston Randall, held his houses and stables in Deptford on a lease from the Lord Admiral, Howard of Effingham. Both men were leaned on. Danby was a knight, and a servant of the Crown; Randall was the tenant of a local member of the Privy Council who also happened to be, after the Armada, a national hero. Could there really have been any other verdict?

The rest of it was a formality. Whatever happened to Marlowe's belongings, his clothes, his books, his weapons, we do not know. They were probably hocked to the sailors of Deptford, who were now told that Mr Marlowe would not be taking any tide. His unfinished poem, *Hero and Leander*, which he may not have had room for or asked Walsingham to send on, lay where Marlowe had left it, at Scadbury, to be finished by his friend George Chapman.

Marlowe himself was carried to the churchyard of St Nicholas in Deptford and buried on 1 June in an unmarked grave. The priest, Thomas Macander, wrote in the parish register

Christopher Marlowe slaine by ffrancis ffrizer.

He got it wrong.

We do not know who, if anyone, attended the burial. It is highly unlikely that his family in Canterbury was informed and, even if his friends were, it is likely they stayed away. The news of Kyd's arrest and Marlowe's murder, albeit in a quarrel over 'le recknynge', caused the wiser ones to put two and two together. Only slowly did those friends on the literary scene drop veiled references to his passing – Shakespeare's comments on 'dead shepherd' and 'a great reckoning in a little room'; a little known poet called Thomas Edwards wrote

> Amyntas [Thomas Watson] and Leander's gone.
> Oh, dear sons of stately kings.
> Blessed be your nimble throats
> That so amorously could sing.

In 1598, dedicating *Hero and Leander* to Thomas Walsingham, Marlowe's friend the stationer Edward Blount wrote

We think not ourselves discharged of the duty we owe to our friend when we have brought the breathless body to the earth. For albeit the eye there taketh his ever-farewell of that beloved object, yet the impression of the man that hath been dear unto us, living an afterlife in our memory, there putteth us in mind of further obsequies due to the deceased.[8]

Perhaps this means that literally, Blount and Walsingham saw Marlowe buried and took part in any service the Reverend Macander cared to say over Christopher, the carrier of Christ, the scourge of God. Bearing in mind Walsingham's part in all this, it could be construed as hypocrisy – 'all Protestants are hypocritical asses' – or it could be the last honour he did his protégé and friend.

And Thomas Nashe may have come closer to the truth than he knew when he wrote of Marlowe in *The Unfortunate Traveller*, 'His tongue and his invention were foreborn; what they thought they would confidently utter. Princes he spared not, that in the least point transgressed.' Within what may be a record time, the Queen gave her pardon to Ingram Frizer. She had by this time been sent the Baines Note – 'Copye of Marloes blasphemyes As sent to her H' – together with various annotations by Burghley to make sure that she got the point; there must be no doubt about Marlowe's guilt. If Frizer had killed a godly man, even in self-defence, he may have suffered for it; but to kill a self-confessed atheist could barely be called a crime at all.

We therefore moved by piety have pardoned the same Ingram ffrizar the breach of our peace which pertains to us against the said Ingram for the death above mentioned and grant to him our firm peace. . . . In testimony and witness the Queen at Kewe on the 28th day of June.

Poley's accomplice was a free man.

'The cursed Cholmeley', the only other man who knew the real views of the Council four, was arrested on the same day that Frizer received his pardon. With heavy irony, he came before Justice Richard Young, whom he had already libelled, and Young passed him 'upstairs' to Sir John Puckering, every inch a Cecil man. Cholmeley was imprisoned while the Council searched for the 'sixty' who were supposedly his team of rebels bent on the overthrow of the state.

'I do know the law,' Cholmeley told his interrogators, 'and when it comes to pass I can shift well enough.'

Despite odd attempts by followers of the Earl of Essex (never associated with atheism, but certainly by 1601, deeply seditious) to intercede on Cholmeley's behalf, Cholmeley himself vanishes from history at the end of June 1593. How well he 'shifted' we cannot say, but it is our contention that he was too dangerous to be kept alive. He did not have the brilliance or the power to move men like Christopher Marlowe, but he knew too much. Mr Topcliffe's services were probably sought, because in the text of the Baines Note that was passed to the Queen, were the ominous words, probably in Burghley's own handwriting 'He is laid for'.

The Privy Council let Thomas Kyd go, realizing that he knew nothing that could hurt them. In pain, traumatized and deserted, he wrote his pleading first letter to Puckering, who would have shown it to Burghley or Cecil. And here was a final twist of the knife. Between his first and second letters, we believe that the Privy Council sent for Kyd. The second letter does not read like the first. Its content is different and it is unsigned. We believe that Kyd was forced to write this second version. There is nothing here of the man who also wrote *The Spanish Tragedy*. It backs up the Baines Note, it invents Marlowe's treachery in defection to the king of Scots and above all, it makes Marlowe's lightning attack on Frizer all the more probable – 'he would suddenly take slight occasion to slyp out as I and many others in regard of his other rashness in attempting sudden pryvie injuries to men.' It really is too pat. And their lordships of the Council filed it away, just in case anyone came along asking awkward questions about the death of Christopher Marlowe.

And we believe that in Kyd's first letter, when he was complaining to Puckering about the loss of his Lord, that he was not referring to Lord Strange. Whatever Strange's precise position ideologically, he was a member of the School of Night, a pseudo-scientist and free-thinking intellectual who must already have been familiar with Marlowe's views. He would not have been so horrified by Kyd's supposed atheism as to disown him. But a man who would was Charles, Lord Howard of Effingham, patron of the actors' company called The Lord Admiral's Men. In the plague year of 1593–4 Ned Alleyn took the Admiral's Men and Strange's Men on the road as a combined troupe. If this troupe performed *The Spanish Tragedy*, then there is every likelihood that Kyd regarded *him* as his 'Lord'. And Howard of Effingham, given the situation, would have been very anxious to ditch Kyd as soon as possible and distance himself from any taint of the atheism of which he himself was guilty. According to Jeffrey M. Bale, writing in the context of the death of Princess Diana,

> Very few notions generate as much intellectual resistance, hostility and derision within academic circles as a belief in the historical importance or efficacy of political conspiracies. Even when this belief is expressed in a very cautious manner, limited to specific and restricted contexts, supported by reliable evidence and hedged about with all sorts of qualifications, it still manages to transcend the boundaries of acceptable discourse and violate unspoken academic taboos.
>
> The idea that particular groups of people meet together secretly or in private to plan various courses of action, and that some of these plans actually exert a significant influence on particular historical developments, is typically rejected out of hand and assumed to be the figment of a paranoid imagination.
>
> The mere mention of the word 'conspiracy' seems to set off an internal alarm bell which causes scholars to close their minds. . . .[9]

That Christopher Marlowe did not die in a futile squabble over a bill was demonstrated by J. Leslie Hotson nearly eighty years ago. That the myth still persists is testimony to the efficacy of Bale's argument above. Yet who was better placed to engineer such a conspiracy? And how easy must it have been? Marlowe was a maverick, a rebel, a whistle-blower. He was a dangerous man 'whose mouth must be stopped'. And in the corridors of power, men like Burghley and Cecil, Effingham and Hunsdon had all the apparatus of government to do just that. Key documents were carefully fabricated and preserved; witnesses were told what they saw; juries were nobbled. In the paranoia of the Elizabethan police state, great men bent the law to their own ends. There were many people who suffered as a result; Christopher Marlowe was only the most famous of them.

Three murderers killed Edward II. Three devils carried off the screaming Faustus. Three magi formed the scientific core of the School of Night – Hariot, Warner and Hues; 'the infamous triplicity that denies the Trinity'. Of the three killers of Christopher Marlowe, Ingram Frizer became a tax assessor for his parish of Eltham, Kent, in 1611. He was married with two daughters, who were probably at the graveside when he was buried on 14 August 1627. Nicholas Skeres is last heard of being transferred under a Privy Council warrant to the Bridewell on 31 July 1601, his offence and his end unknown. Robert Poley, 'sweet Robyn', appears in government records for the last time in the same year, with a recommendation that he be made a Yeoman of the Tower. Two successes out of three.

And what of the Council four, those men who had so much to lose if Christopher Marlowe talked? Lord Burghley, with all the hypocrisy in his nature, yelled at Essex in 1596, 'Men of blood shall not live out half their days.' He was quoting from the prayer book the old humbug carried in his pocket. In the event, he did live out all his days and only at the end, terrified, like Robert Greene, of coming death, did he gasp the words, 'Come, Lord Jesus, one drop of death.' It was 4 August 1598. His son, Robert, made similar noises on his death-bed, in Marlborough on 24 May 1612. His enemies – and they were many – chanted a rhyme when the news reached London:

> Here lies, thrown for the worms to eat,
> Little bossive Robin that was so great.
> Not Robin Goodfellow or Robin Hood,
> But Robin th'encloser of Hatfield Wood,
> Who seemed as sent from Ugly Fate
> To spoil the Prince and rot the State,
> Owning a mind of dismal ends
> As trap for foes and tricks for friends.

Howard of Effingham, heroic as ever, sacked Cadiz with the Earl of Essex in 1596 and was created Earl of Nottingham. Given total command of all land and sea forces, he died at Croydon on 14 December 1624, his memory untarnished, his secret with him in the grave. The last of them, Henry Carey, Baron Hunsdon, the Lord Chamberlain, died in July 1596. Today, most collections of potted biographies ignore him entirely.

And Kit Marlowe? Today, he is once again 'all fire and air', 'that pure elemental wit' of the 'mighty line', the 'dead shepherd', 'the Muses' darling'. His ghost can be found, not just in the 'churchyard of Paules', but in cobbled Canterbury, scholastic Cambridge, roaring London or anywhere where men's hearts and souls are free.

Notes

Introduction

1. J.B. Black, *The Reign of Elizabeth* (Oxford, Clarendon Press, 1959).
2. S.T. Bindoff, *Tudor England* (Harmondsworth, Penguin, 1950).

Chapter One

1. Sir Frank Benson (1858–1939) was one of the greatest of the Shakespearean actor-managers, producing Marlowe's plays in the period of revival of interest in him.
2. This was the central action of the Peasants' Revolt in 1381.
3. Although the version written in 1898 by W.G. Zeigler takes some beating. In this, it is Marlowe who killed his assailant Frizer and wrote Shakespeare's works under Frizer's name until he was killed by fellow poet and duellist Ben Jonson in 1598! (Quoted in J. Leslie Hotson, *The Death of Christopher Marlowe* (London, Nonesuch, 1925).) In the summary of accounts presented here, we have not included *actual* fiction. Ironically, Anthony Burgess's overrated novel *A Dead Man in Deptford* closely follows the known facts.
4. Tax return documents.
5. Le Gay Brereton quoted in Hotson, *The Death of Christopher Marlowe*, p. 19.
6. Property documents.
7. The Queen's Bench (originally King's Bench) was a court of record and the supreme court of common law. It followed the peripatetic kings of England throughout the Middle Ages and had come to rest by Elizabeth's reign in the Strand.
8. The Assize was the local court at the heart of a judge's circuit, where cases were heard two, three or four times a year.
9. Patent Rolls were the records of privileges granted by the monarch.
10. *A certiorari* was in effect an edict from the superior court (in this case the Queen as the highest court in the land) to an inferior one (in this case the office of coroner). All translations are by J. Leslie Hotson.
11. Presumably a clerk of the court.
12. The French article has confused a number of commentators, but seems to be nothing more than a legalistic survival of Norman jargon. For example in 1672, John Cutbert died and was admitted to a messuage next to 'le howse called the Holy Lambe' in the parish of Ely.

Chapter Two

1. William Lambarde's *Perambulation of Kent* published in 1576 described the garden of England: 'The soil is for the most part bountiful . . . as for orchards of apples and gardens of cherries and those of the most exquisite and delicious kinds, no part of the realm has them, either in such quantity or number or with such art and industry set and planted.'
2. Quoted in Charles Norman, *The Muse's Darling* (London, Falcon Press, 1947), p. 9.
3. The 1560s saw an upsurge in witchcraft activity.
4. We do know that John could sign his name, but this in itself does not prove literacy.
5. Edward of Woodstock, Prince of Wales, who had perhaps died of the plague in 1376 and whose magnificent latten tomb in Canterbury Cathedral Marlowe would have known well.
6. Extracts from D.L. Edwards, *A History of the King's School, Canterbury* (1957) quoted in A.D. Wraight and Virginia Stern, *In Search of Christopher Marlowe* (Chichester, Adam Hart, 1993), p. 40.
7. We are not counting the hapless Jane Grey, the sixteen-year-old pawn in the succession game who reigned for nine days before her execution on Tower Green on 12 February 1554.
8. Quoted in Alison Weir, *Elizabeth the Queen* (London, Pimlico, 1999), p. 60.
9. Letter from le Simier to Alencon, 12 April 1579; quoted in Black *Reign of Elizabeth*, p. 349.
10. Quoted in Weir, *Elizabeth the Queen*, p. 211.
11. Black, *Reign of Elizabeth*, p. 195.
12. Knox (*c.* 1513–72) was a Catholic converted to Lutheranism and hugely influenced by Calvin during a stay in Geneva. He opposed Mary with dogmatic fervour as much because she was female as Catholic. Modern writers have tried to play down his fanaticism, but bigotry like his led to open warfare and backstairs murder.
13. A particularly sadistic torture instrument in which a suspected heretic was made to ride a triangular 'horse' at the apex of which was a dull blade. Ever greater weights were added to the victim's stirrups to increase the agony.
14. Julius II (1443–1513), for instance, was not only the patron of the arts who engaged the services of Michelangelo for the Sistine Chapel, but he commanded troops in the field and may have personally killed men in battle.

Chapter Three

1. Report to Parliament, quoted in Norman, *The Muse's Darling*, p. 15.
2. The late sixteenth century was appreciably colder than today, leading to what some historians have called a 'mini Ice Age' in the seventeenth century.

3. H.P. Stokes, *Corpus Christi* (1898) (University of Cambridge History series); quoted in Wraight and Stern, *In Search of Christopher Marlowe*.

4. Norwich scholars (also endowed by Parker) were provided with 'two mattresses, two bolsters of feathers, two coverlets of tapestry, two chairs of three feet, a table and three trestles, two forms to the same' (quoted in Wraight and Stern, *In Search of Christopher Marlowe*). We have no way of knowing whether this comparative largesse extended to King's Scholars too.

5. Report to Parliament, quoted in Norman, *The Muse's Darling*, p. 15.

6. Quoted in Michael Davis, *The Landscape of William Shakespeare*.

7. Ibid.

8. The game was prohibited by Elizabeth because it took too many young men away from the altogether more acceptable (and militarily useful) practice of archery.

9. Robert Greene, *A Groatsworth of Wit*; quoted in Wraight and Stern, *In Search of Christopher Marlowe*, pp. 83–4.

10. Thomas Nashe, *Have With You to Saffron Waldron*; quoted in Charles Nicholl, *The Reckoning* (London, Jonathan Cape, 1992), p. 183.

11. Aristotle (384–322 BC) was one of the most influential figures in the history of Western philosophy. The less prestigious Ramus was Pierre de la Ramée (1515–72), who outraged Aristotelians by rewriting the science of logic. His *Dialectic* was suppressed by the academic hierarchy at the Sorbonne, and, turning Protestant, he was killed in the massacre of St Bartholomew's Day.

12. Ovid was Publius Ovidius Naso (43 BC–AD 17), a lawyer from a patrician family who was the most prolific of the Roman poets. The Amores on which Marlowe worked at Cambridge was a series of short poems about his mistress, Corinna. Lucan was Marcus Annaeus Lucanus (39–65), an altogether darker character and perhaps more Marlovian than the playwright knew. A philosopher specializing in rhetoric, he became a favourite of Nero before the Emperor, perhaps jealous of the poet's superior ability, banned him from writing further. Lucan joined a conspiracy, one of many, against Nero and he was forced to commit suicide. The only writing of his that has survived is *Pharsalia*, three books that outline, in epic poetry, the civil war between Caesar and Pompey.

13. Even though this, one of the many nicknames for the Devil, predates Machiavelli by at least two centuries.

14. *Eyewitness to Oxford* debates; quoted in Nicholl, *The Reckoning*, p. 206.

15. Quoted in Roy Porter, *London: A Social History* (London, Penguin, 1996).

16. Quoted in Nicholl, *The Reckoning*, p. 135.

17. Wolsey was Henry's Chancellor. His ambition and ability, not to mention his position as the Pope's envoy (*legate a latere*) in England, were thought to make him the perfect choice for negotiations for the king's divorce from Catherine of Aragon. He failed, however, and the less talented Bonner was dragooned in to replace him.

18. Quoted in Nicholl, *The Reckoning*, p. 135.

19. There was no attempt in the sixteenth century to segregate male and female prisoners. It was this potential for promiscuity that John Howard and Elizabeth Fry, the later reformers, found most shocking about prison conditions.
20. Often spelt 'Persons', undoubtedly a result of the complexity of deciphering Elizabethan handwriting.
21. Quoted in Black, *Reign of Elizabeth*, p. 182.
22. A Milanese source quoted in Weir, *Elizabeth the Queen*, p. 339.
23. A mark was worth 13s 4d (about 67p).
24. Black, *Reign of Elizabeth*.
25. Quoted in Weir, *Elizabeth the Queen*, p. 175.
26. Quoted in Norman, *The Muse's Darling*, p. 20.

Chapter Four

1. G. Mattingly, *The Defeat of the Spanish Armada* (London, Pelican, 1962), pp. 26–7 (first published 1959).
2. As Edward was only ten on the death of his father, the Earl of Somerset ruled as Protector on the boy's behalf, considerably hastening the country's move towards Protestantism.
3. At the height of his fame, Marlowe wrote *The Massacre at Paris* based on this bloodbath.
4. Report of Juan de Olaegui, 1572; quoted in P. Erlanger *St Bartholomew's Night* (London, Weidenfeld & Nicolson, 1962), pp. 96–7.
5. Quoted in Nicholl, *The Reckoning*, p. 107.
6. In Alan Haynes, *The Elizabethan Secret Services* (Sutton, Stroud, 1992).
7. Many agents used by Walsingham (Poley among them) were Catholics originally. It was that which gave their various 'fronts' an air of respectability in Catholic circles.
8. And Canterbury, of course, was also a staging post on the road to Dover, from where a ship could have taken Marlowe to France or the Low Countries.
9. Quoted in Black, *Reign of Elizabeth*, p. 171.
10. Bene't's College's old rival Caius produced the most.
11. Walter Walsh, *The Jesuits in Great Britain* (London, Routledge Trench Trübner, 1904), p. 27.
12. Letter from Parsons to Acquaviva, September 1581; quoted in Nicholl, *The Reckoning*, p. 96.
13. An epistle from English priests to Pope Clement VIII 1601; quoted in Nicholl, *The Reckoning*, p. 122.
14. D. Morris, *Manwatching: a Field Guide to Human Behaviour* (London, Jonathan Cape, 1977).
15. Details here are taken from Lailan Young, *Secrets of the Face* (London, Coronet, 1983).
16. The evidence of Marlowe's new found wealth in 1585 comes from the Buttery accounts of Corpus Christi. As well as proving his irregular attendance in this

period, itself a marked change from earlier, he was now spending up to 21*d*, almost twice the allowance of 12*d* he had previously chalked up. We know of no other source to explain this. In the will of Katherine Benchkyn of Canterbury he is merely a witness and received nothing. His father, whose will has also survived, lived for a further eleven years after Deptford. It is *possible*, given the infuriating problem with first editions, that he had already gone into print with poetry or a play, although there is no evidence for this and in any case, the pay was meagre. Actors like Ned Alleyn, the superstars of their day, made money; so did theatrical impresarios like Philip Henslowe. Writers like Marlowe (and, at first, Shakespeare) did not. Marlowe *may* have found a rich patron who subsidized his Buttery expenses and furnished him with the funds to buy the expensive velvet doublet of the Corpus Christi portrait and indeed to have it painted. Most likely, however, is that the financial fortunes came directly from the purse of Francis Walsingham, the Queen's spymaster, in return for Marlowe's 'faithful dealing'.

17. Letter from Cobham to Francis Walsingham, 12 November 1581; quoted in Nicholl, *The Reckoning*, p. 116.
18. Ballard's exorcisms in this period speak volumes for the hysteria of the age.
19. Letter from Babington to Claude de Nau, Mary's Secretary, July 1586; quoted in Nicholl, *The Reckoning*, p. 116.
20. Ibid.
21. Cuisses were thigh defences. Many of the nobility were painted in full suits of armour, but increasingly in the field, such lavishness was ignored. No armour then made could withstand round-shot or even a pistol-ball at close range, so it was discarded.

Chapter Five

1. Porter, *London, A Social History*.
2. John Stowe, *A Survey of London* (1598); quoted in Porter, *London, A Social History*, p. 43.
3. Ibid.
4. Ibid.
5. In all probability hiring an animal from the carrier Thomas Hobson, from whom the phrase 'Hobson's choice' entered the language. The carrier would only allow the freshest horse to be hired.
6. John Earle, *Micro-cosmographie* (1628); quoted in J. Dover Wilson, *Life in Shakespeare's England* (London, Penguin, 1911), p. 144.
7. Philip Stubbes, *The Anatomie of Abuses*; quoted in Wilson, *Life in Shakespeare's England*, p. 145.
8. The character of Evil in the medieval mystery plays.
9. Derek Traversi – an essay on *Literature and Drama* (The Cambridge Cultural History of Britain, Vol. 3).
10. Black, *Reign of Elizabeth*, p. 297.

11. Norman, *The Muses' Darling*, p. 60.
12. Letter from William Cornwallis to Sir Thomas Heneage, March 1594; quoted in Nicholl, *The Reckoning*, p. 189.
13. Trismegistus was the great magus of folklore; Pythagoras the more prosaic Greek geometrician.
14. Anthony à Wood, *Athenae Oxoniensis* (1691); quoted in Wraight and Stern, *In Search of Christopher Marlowe*, p. 161.
15. 'Eastward Ho' and 'Westward Ho' were the cries of the Thames watermen to let travellers know the direction they were rowing.
16. Letter from Burghley to Edward Kelly, May 1591; quoted in Nicholl, *The Reckoning*, p. 259.
17. Richard Tarleton was the best known clown, along with Will Kempe, of Elizabeth's time.
18. Con-artistry.
19. Cheating (especially at dice or cards) and picking pockets.
20. Garry O'Conner, *William Shakespeare, a Popular Life* (London, Applause, 2000).

Chapter Six

1. Sodom was, with Gomorrah, one of the cities of the plain in the Dead Sea area of Palestine. Synonymous with wickedness, and especially homosexual acts involving anal intercourse, Sodom was destroyed by God, according to Genesis 19, with fire and brimstone – 'because the cry of Sodom and Gomorrah is great and because their sin is very grievous' translated the compilers of the King James Bible, eighteen years after Marlowe's death.
2. Quoted in Robert Lacey, *Sir Walter Ralegh* (London, Cardinal, 1975), p. 102.
3. Robert Greene, *A Quip for an Upstart Courtier* (1592); quoted in Wilson, *Life in Shakespeare's England*, p. 151.
4. George Whetstone, *A Touchstone for the Time*; quoted in Wilson, *Life in Shakespeare's England*, p. 153.
5. *A Disputation between a he-cony catcher and a she-cony catcher* (1592; quoted in Gamini Salgado, *The Elizabethan Underworld* (London, BCA, 1977), p. 53).
6. Ibid.
7. Quoted in G. Rattray Taylor, *Sex in History* (London, Thames & Hudson, 1968), p. 150.
8. Quoted in Alan Bray, *Homosexuality in Renaissance England* (Brighton, Gay Men's Press, 1982), p. 78.
9. The phrase is coined by G. Rattray Taylor in contrast to the more usual 'patriarchal' which he believes has the wrong connotation. Patrism specifically refers to church, as opposed to purely male, authority.
10. In 1580, sword blades were by law reduced to 3 feet; daggers to 12 inches, from pommel to blade-tip.
11. Quoted in Bray, *Homosexuality in Renaissance England*, p. 81.

12. Edward Coke (1552–1634) with his Cambridge background became Recorder for Coventry and rose to become chief justice of the King's Bench and a Privy Councillor by 1613. An outspoken critic of James I and Charles I, he wrote what became enormously influential textbooks on English common law.

13. In the days of the 'blackmailers' charter' it was a particularly useful tool to trap vulnerable men who could not afford, because of social ostracism, to be outed. In 1962, William Vassal, an Admiralty clerk, was blackmailed by the Russians into betraying secrets, after attending a homosexual party where compromising photographs were taken.

14. Marston (1576–1634) was an Oxford educated dramatist who wrote plays before taking holy orders in 1616. His first work was condemned by Archbishop Whitgift as obscene – *The Metamorphosis of Pygmalion's Image*.

15. Drayton (1563–1631), like Shakespeare, came from Warwickshire and is buried in Westminster Abbey as poet laureate. His first work, *The Harmony of the Church* in 1591 offended the authorities and was destroyed. His poem on the homosexual favourite of Edward II, Piers Gaveston, appeared in the year of Marlowe's death.

16. Jonson (1572–1637) was one of the greatest playwrights of his age, second only to Shakespeare. Hot-headed, impatient and a convert to Catholicism in a dangerous age, he killed a fellow actor in a duel, which led to the later mistaken belief that he had stabbed Marlowe.

17. Guilpin (fl. 1598–1601; dates of birth and death unknown) wrote *Skialetheia or a Shadow of Truth*, another of those works destroyed at Stationers' Hall in June 1599.

18. Brathwaite (1588–1673) intended to practise law after Oxford, but settled for poetry and drama instead. He wrote a great deal about tobacco and drinking and various satires including *A strappado for the devil*.

19. Middleton (1570–1627) was a dramatist who specialized in writing about London. *Father Hubbard's Tale* and *The Black Book*, published in 1604, exposed the city's underworld. His *Micro-Cynicon* was burned by the Bishop of London.

20. Donne (1572–1631) is famous today as the best known of the Metaphysical Poets. A Catholic convert to Protestantism, he eventually became Dean of St Paul's, after a lifetime's writing of satirical and erotic poetry.

21. All the extracts here are quoted in Bray, *Homosexuality in Renaissance England*.

22. Quoted in ibid.

23. Ibid.

24. Ibid.

25. Preface to Henry Chettle, *Kind-Harts Dreame* (1592); quoted in Norman, *The Muses' Darling*.

26. Quoted in Mattingly, *The Defeat of the Spanish Armada*, p. 20.

27. Quoted in Weir, *Elizabeth the Queen*.

28. Ibid.
29. A forthcoming book by A.D. Wraight, *Christopher Marlowe and the Armada*, is based on a newly discovered report written for Lord Admiral Howard and supposedly in Marlowe's handwriting, indicating that he had an important role to play. The whole basis of this rests on the existence of a text of *The Massacre at Paris* in the Folger Library, Washington D.C. The authenticity of this must lie in a comparison with the only example of Marlowe's writing, his signature on the will of Katheryn Benchkyn. Here he spells his name 'Marley', so that in the full name, only nine different letters appear. We are no graphologists, but would prefer to keep an open mind as to the authenticity of the Folger play. If that is not authentic, then clearly the Armada link falls apart.
30. Ibid.
31. Morrison Fynes, *Itinerary* (1617); quoted in Wilson, *Life in Shakespeare's England*, p. 130.
32. *A Dialogue against the Pestilence*; quoted in Wilson *Life in Shakespeare's England*.
33. Bertram Osborne, *Justices of the Peace* (1960); quoted in T.A. Critchley, *A History of Police in England and Wales* (London, Constable, 1967), p. 11.
34. In an age when glass was still expensive, horn was used to shield the candle flame and still allow light to filter through.

Chapter Seven

1. Greene, *A Groatsworth of Wit*; quoted in Wraight and Stern, *In Search of Christopher Marlowe*, p. 188.
2. For all that Heywood attacked Machiavelli ferociously, he was no stock Puritan, being a playwright himself and reviving *The Jew of Malta* in 1633 in the dedicatory epistle to which, he writes, 'This play, composed by so worthy an author as Mr Marlowe . . .'.
3. Puritans would have found this notion, laughing in the face of death, appalling and a fitting example of God's judgement (see Chapter 9).
4. Julian 'the Apostate' (Heretic) was Roman Emperor between 361 and 366. He was a brilliant and popular general, and there are elements of him in Marlowe's Tamburlaine. Julian became a pagan about 360 when as Emperor he stripped the Church of much of its property and power. He died in battle against the Persians, betrayed by a trusted friend.
5. Henri, Duc de Guise, known as 'Le Balafré' (the scarred) was one of the instigators of the Massacre of St Bartholomew's Day and headed the Catholic League against the Bourbons. He was assassinated at Blois on 23 December 1588.
6. A copy of Certain Notes written by Mr Parmont, sent by Richard Verstigan to Parsons; quoted in A.G.R. Smith, *The Government of Elizabethan England* (London, Edward Arnold, 1967), p. 12.

7. Thumbscrews perhaps speak for themselves; they were crushing devices large enough to take the fingers as well as the thumbs of a man's hand. For someone like Thomas Kyd, who made his living as a playwright, torture of this kind, assuming he survived the shock, would mean the end of his career.

   The iron maiden was a metal sarcophagus with a hinged lid. As the lid was closed the spikes on the inside sank into the flesh of the victim.

   Strappado was the Spanish word for the machinery (rope or leather straps) that hauled a man to the ceiling of a cell by his thumbs or toes.

   Skeffington's Gyves or the Scavenger's Daughter worked in the opposite way to the rack. It was a huge iron hoop that could be tightened to squeeze a crouching body inside it.

8. Ibid. There is a similar piece of unbridled nonsense in the account of one of the Bolshevik guards responsible for the Romanov family of Nicholas II in 1918. He claimed to have participated in an orgy of rape carried out on the Tsaritsa and the four princesses and boasted that he could now die happy 'because he had had the Empress'.

9. Quoted in David Cecil, *The Cecils of Hatfield House* (London, Cardinal, 1973), p. 65.

10. Ibid., p. 71.

11. Ibid., p. 57.

12. Ibid., p. 77.

13. Letter from Robert Southwell to Richard Verstigan, December 1591; Quoted in Nicholl, *The Reckoning*, pp. 220–1.

14. Quoted in Peter Brimacombe, *All the Queen's Men* (Stroud, Sutton, 2000).

15. Some of this debt, it must be said, was due to the chronic overspending of Walsingham's son-in-law, Philip Sidney. Walsingham picked up the man's arrears after his death at Zutphen.

16. David Starkey, *Elizabeth* (London, Chatto & Windus, 2000).

17. Quoted in the *Dictionary of National Biography*.

18. A bellwether was a castrated ram and 'pecora campi' refers to any grazing animal. Perhaps Elizabeth knew something about Hatton that we don't!

19. The original Anabaptists were a German sect led by Thomas Münzer in 1521. Rejecting infant baptism and believing that all existing order should be destroyed, their notions of equality and nihilism terrified most Europeans and all landowners. The sect itself, practising polygamy by the 1530s, was wiped out, but the term survived to describe any extreme Protestant.

20. Quoted in the *Dictionary of National Biography*.

21. Quoted in ibid.

22. Alison Plowden, *Elizabeth Regina* (Stroud, Sutton, 2000), p. 67.

23. Quoted in Cecil, *The Cecils of Hatfield House*. Curtis Breight's theory that it may have been Cecil himself who recruited Marlowe to Walsingham's secret service is rather tenuous, implying an extraordinary degree of forward planning in a young man of twenty-two who, as yet, had no actual role in central government at all.

Chapter Eight

1. Despite the hypocrisy of James's advice to his son – that homosexuality was a 'horrible crime' that a king was 'bound in conscience never to forgive' – there can be little doubt that he was homosexual and that everyone at Court knew it.

2. Quoted in Jeffrey B. Russell, *A History of Witchcraft* (London, Thames & Hudson, 1980).

3. Trentino in northern Italy.

4. Assizes. Most of the men afflicted had visited the court house in Oxford during the summer months of 1577.

5. The classic study of English witchcraft by Alan McFarlane cites nineteen trials held in Essex between 1564 and 1569. There is another concentration – twenty-nine cases – between 1590 and 1599. So, curiously, the decades of both Marlowe's birth and death coincide with an outbreak of witch-fever.

6. Even in a much later and more secular age, men of realpolitik like Napoleon and Hitler consulted astrologers and tarot experts when planning the timing of their foreign policies.

7. Definitions are confused in the sixteenth century. The *Concise Oxford Dictionary* defines alchemy as 'chemistry of the Middle Ages; especially pursuit of the transmutation of baser metals into gold', but an alchemist in Dee's time followed many aspects of science. Likewise astrology and astronomy, though separate disciplines today (one a science, the other 'nonsense') were indistinguishable in Elizabethan England.

8. We cannot help wondering whether similar advice given about the total eclipse of the sun in 1999 had more to do with this sort of folk-memory than any actual risk to eyesight.

9. Older books on England before 1751 give two dates. The Russians did not adopt the 'new' date structure until the early twentieth century, so that the diaries of Nicholas II and his wife read 'OS' and 'NS' – 'old style' and 'new style'. When the Whig government of Henry Pelham introduced the new style in 1751, there were riots in London and the Pelhams were accused of shortening men's lives by 11 days!

10. Ben Jonson, *The Alchemist* (1610). Equally, Jonson could have been talking in terms of intellectual disagreement, about history, archaeology or any branch of science!

11. He was accused of supplying the poison with which Lady Frances Howard killed Sir Thomas Overbury in 1601.

12. A heraldic term meaning a bar down the centre of a shield and applied to the strip of 'civilized' English society around Dublin. The native Irish outside it, wild, lawless, unintelligible in their Gaelic, were 'beyond the Pale'.

13. Fuller, *The Worthies of England* (London, 1662).

14. Sir Robert Naunton, *Fragmenta Regalia*; quoted in Brimacombe, *All the Queen's Men*, p. 22.

15. Ralegh's poetry, his dazzlingly handsome face and his exotic dress sense appealed to Elizabeth. When he took Hugh Piere to court for theft in April 1583, he listed

the stolen goods as 'a jewel worth 80 pounds, a hat band of pearls worth 30 pounds and five yards of damask silk worth three pounds'. As Captain of the Queen's Guard he had a suit of silver-embossed armour made for himself.

16. Roanoke (from the native American word meaning shell-money) was the name of Humphrey Gilbert's colony of Virginia Island. When Ralegh visited it in August 1590, 'we let fall our grapnel [anchor] near the shore and sounded with a trumpet and call and afterwards many familiar English tunes of songs . . . but we had no answer.' All Ralegh found was dead trees and grasses and a single word carved onto a post – 'Croatoan', an island 30 miles away. There was no one there either. A hundred people seemed to have vanished. Ralegh contined to conduct searches for the next twelve years.

17. *The Anatomie of Abuses* (1583).

18. Wood, *Athenae Oxoniensis* (1691); quoted in Wraight and Stern, *In Search of Christopher Marlowe*, p. 141.

19. Harleian MS 6349; quoted in Muriel Ruckeyser, *The Traces of Thomas Hariot* (London, Gollancz, 1972), p. 135.

20. Quoted in Wraight and Stern, *In Search of Christopher Marlowe*, p. 137.

21. The dag could only fire one shot at a time. After each, a cumbersome operation was necessary to reload.

22. In *Historical Trials* (Oxford, Clarendon Press, 1927), p. 67.

23. Ibid.

24. Review by Damian Thompson in the *Mail on Sunday*, 20 August 2000.

Chapter Nine

1. John Poole was a Cheshire gentleman imprisoned in Newgate in 1587 for coining. Since Marlowe did time there two years later over the Hog Lane fight, it is likely that he met Poole then.

2. Letter from Robert Sidney to Burghley in State Papers (Holland) SP84, Public Record Office; quoted in Nicholl, *The Reckoning*, p. 235.

3. P. le Franc's observation, that Ralegh believed 'we die like beasts and when we are gone there is no more remembrance of us', refers to the decay of the body and the short memories of the living, not of the soul.

4. Pride, Avarice, Lust, Anger, Sloth, Gluttony and Envy.

5. Some accounts give Trinity College.

6. From the Ashmolean Collection in the Bodleian Library, Oxford; quoted in Keith Thomas, *Religion and the Decline of Magic* (London, Weidenfeld & Nicolson, 1971).

7. All the examples that follow are quoted from Thomas, *Religion and the Decline of Magic*.

8. L. Stone in *English Historical Review* (1962); quoted in Thomas, *Religion and the Decline of Magic*.

9. C. Geertz, *Anthropological Approaches to the Study of Religion*, ed. Banton (1966); quoted in Thomas, *Religion and the Decline of Magic*, p. 172.

10. We do not know exactly which version of the Bible Marlowe was using. The quotations in this chapter are from the King James edition of 1611 because that, until our own time, was the universal version used. A Vulgate was available in English in the late fourteenth century, but it was William Tyndale who produced the first English work from the original. Between 1525 and 1535 he translated the New Testament, the Pentateuch and Jonah. In 1535, Miles Coverdale published the first full English version, using Tyndale, the Vulgate and Martin Luther's German translation. Matthew's Bible, published by John Rogers, appeared two years later and the Tavener edition in 1539. The Greek Bible appeared in the same year, but the Geneva edition of 1560 became the obligatory version for Calvinists and many other Protestant groups. The Bishops' Bible produced when Marlowe was four was an antidote to this and in 1582 a Catholic New Testament translation was published at the English college in Rheims. Marlowe of course could read Latin and perhaps Greek, so he may have had access to other editions.

11. From K.M. Briggs, *Pale Hecate's Team* (1962); quoted in Thomas, *Religion and the Decline of Magic*.

12. Indulgences included any dispensation provided by the Catholic Church for cash payments, including pardons for sins not yet committed, glimpses of holy relics, etc.

13. Baines should have read Reginald Scot's *The Discovery of Witchcraft* (1584), in which he, like Marlowe, pours scorn on the superstitious nonsense of their age:

They have so frayed us with bull-beggars, spirits, witches, urchins, hags, elves, fairies, satyrs, pans, fauns, sylens, kit-with-the canstick, centaurs, dwarfs, giants, imps, calears, conjurers, nymphs, changelings, Incubus, Robin Goodfellow, the spoorn, the mare, the man in the Oak, the hell-wain, the firedrake, the puckle, Tom Thumb, Hob Goblin, Tom Tumbler, Boneless and other such Bugs, that we are afraid of out own shadows.

14. Quoted in Wraight and Stern, *In Search of Christopher Marlowe*, p. 59.

15. Burton, *David's Evidence* (1596); quoted in ibid., p. 59.

16. All the quotations regarding Cholmeley are from Nicholl, *The Reckoning*.

17. In 1666 when the heat of the Great Fire caused the stones of St Paul's Cathedral to explode, people swore they saw Dutch/Spanish/French warships in the Thames pounding the city into submission.

18. Charles Nicholl contends that as Harvey spent most of each year in London and his brother Richard was rector of a London parish, he ought to have known the actual cause of Marlowe's death. Was there, Nicholl wonders, deliberate disinformation on that score and did Harvey fall for it? On the other hand, the analogy of the last line – striking home a strike – is very like the thrust of a knife.

19. These lads were a particular problem. Although waged, their behaviour was rather like that of the 'sturdy beggars' of whom polite society and the

government alike were also afraid. At the slightest provocation, they would shout 'clubs' and this was a signal for a mob of them to form, armed with cudgels and join in whatever mayhem was going on. They were the original 'roundheads' of the opening of the Civil War in 1642.

20. Sir Simmonds d'Ewes, *Journal of the House of Commons* (1963); quoted in Nicholl, *The Reckoning*, pp. 290–1.
21. Quoted in Wraight and Stern, *In Search of Christopher Marlowe*, p. 236.
22. Quoted in Geoffrey Abbott, *Rack, Rope and Red-Hot Pincers* (London, Brockhampton Press, 1993), p. 41.
23. This refers to Arius, a Libyan theologian who lived between 250 and 336. In 319 he argued that Christ was 'only the first and highest of all future beings'. This idea attracted quite a following but he was excommunicated in 321 by a synod of bishops at Alexandria. The controversy raged for centuries after Arius' death (either by poison or the hand of God).
24. All these statements from Kyd are quoted in Nicholl, *The Reckoning*.

Chapter Ten

1. In Shakespeare's *Richard III*, for instance, a distraught Anne Neville, mourning her dead father-in-law, cries out at the arrival of his murderer, Richard of Gloucester – 'Oh, gentlemen, see, see! Dead Henry's wounds/Open their congeal'd mouths and bleed afresh!'
2. Circular because of the peculiar notch in the blade tip – 'like a parrot's beak' as it was described in court – and requiring a twist to pull it out.
3. In the absence of any word from her, Norman in *The Muses' Darling* resorted to melodrama – 'Perhaps Misstress Bull burst into the room, saw the body, the poet's head streaked with clotted red, and then, with a cry of horror, turned and rushed out'.
4. S.A. Tannenbaum, *The Assassination of Christopher Marlowe* (New York, 1928).
5. The use of the word 'reckoning' by Blount is interesting. Is this coincidence or a veiled reference to what happened at Deptford?
6. From Nicholl, *Progress of Elizabeth*; quoted in Wraight and Stern, *In Search of Christopher Marlowe*.
7. Norman, *The Muses' Darling*, p. 234.
8. Quoted in ibid., p. 179.
9. Nicholl, *The Reckoning*.
10. Quoted in Weir, *Elizabeth the Queen*.
11. Ibid., pp. 412–13.

Chapter Eleven

1. Robert Beale, *Instructions for a Principal Secretary* (1592); quoted in Nicholl, *The Reckoning*, p. 273.

2. Letter from Drury to Anthony Bacon, August 1593; in ibid., p. 316.

3. Quoted in Curtis Breight, *Surveillance, Militarism and Drama in the Elizabethan Era* (New York, St. Martin's, 1996).

4. Technically there was no Principal Secretary until 1596 (when Robert Cecil was given the post) but Burghley held the post in all but name.

5. Quoted in Breight, *Surveillance, Militarism and Drama in the Elizabethan Era.*

6. No copy of this anti-establishment play has survived.

7. Quoted in Breight, *Surveillance, Militarism and Drama in the Elizabethan Era.*

8. Blount's dedication to *Hero and Leander* (1598); quoted in Nicholl, *The Reckoning,* p. 19.

9. Quoted in Peter Hounam and Derek McAdam, *Who Killed Diana?* (London, Vision Paperbacks, 1998), pp. 4–5.

Select Bibliography

Abbott, Geoffrey. *Rack, Rope and Red-Hot Pincers*, London, Brockhampton Press, 1993

Adair, John. *Puritans*, Stroud, Sutton, 1998

Ahmed, Rollo. *The Black Art*, London, Arrow Books, 1971

Anon. *The Truth About Christopher Marlowe*, The Marlowe Society, Canterbury, n.d.

Bakeless, J. *The Tragicall History of Christopher Marlowe*, Cambridge, Mass., Harvard University Press, 1943

Breight, Curtis. *Surveillance, Militarism and Drama in the Elizabethan Era*, New York, St. Martin's, 1996

Bindoff, S.T. *Tudor England*, Harmondsworth, Penguin, 1950

Black, J.B. *The Reign of Elizabeth*, Oxford, Clarendon Press, 1959

Bray, Alan. *Homosexuality in Renaissance England*, Brighton, Gay Men's Press, 1982

Brimacombe, Peter. *All the Queen's Men*, Stroud, Sutton, 2000

Cecil, David. *The Cecils of Hatfield House*, London, Cardinal, 1973

Cooke, Judith. *The Golden Age of the English Theatre*, New York, Simon & Schuster, 1995

Critchley, T.A. *A History of Police in England and Wales*, London, Constable, 1967

Cunningham, Lt. Col. Francis. *The Works of Marlowe*, London, Chatto & Windus, 1889

Dodd, A.H. *Elizabethan England*, London, BCA, 1973

Duncan-Jones, Katherine. *Sir Philip Sidney, Courtier Poet*, New Haven and London, Yale University Press, 1991

Elliott, J.H. *Europe Divided*, London, Collins, 1972

Elton, G.R. (ed.). *The Tudor Constitution*, Cambridge, Cambridge University Press, 1960

Gardner, Laurence. *Bloodline of the Holy Grail*, Element, 1996

Gray, Henry F.R.S. *Gray's Anatomy*, London, Robinson, 1994

Halliday, F.E. *Shakespeare*, London, Thames & Hudson, 1961

Haynes, Alan. *The Elizabethan Secret Services*, Stroud, Sutton, 1992

Hotson, J. Leslie. *The Death of Christopher Marlowe*, London, Nonesuch, 1925

Hussey, Maurice. *The World of Shakespeare and His Contemporaries*, London, Heinemann, 1978

Ingram, J.H. *Marlowe and his Associates*, London, 1904

Irwin, Margaret. *That Great Lucifer*, London, Allison & Busby, 1998

Kocher, Paul. *Christopher Marlowe*, Chapel Hill, N.C., University of North Carolina Press, 1947

Kramer, H. and Sprenger, J. *Malleus Maleficarum*, tr. Montague Summers, London, Arrow, 1971

Lacey, Robert. *Sir Walter Ralegh*, London, Cardinal, 1975

Leach, Katherine. *Sixteenth-Century Europe*, London, Macmillan, 1980

Levi, Peter. *The Life and Times of William Shakespeare*, London, Macmillan, 1988

Levin, Henry. *Christopher Marlowe, the Over-reacher*, London, Faber, 1973

MacDonell, Sir John. *Historical Trials*, Oxford, Clarendon Press, 1927

Macfarlane, Alan. *Witchcraft in Tudor and Stuart England*, London, Routledge and Kegan Paul, 1970

Michell, John. *Who Wrote Shakespeare?*, London, Thames & Hudson, 1999

Morris, Christopher. *The Tudors*, London, Collins, 1968

Nicholl, Charles. *The Reckoning*, London, Jonathan Cape, 1992

Norman, Charles. *The Muses' Darling*, London, Falcon Press, 1947

O'Connor, Evangeline M. *Who's Who and What's What in Shakespeare*, Gramercy, 1978

Plowden, Alison. *Elizabeth Regina*, Stroud, Sutton, 2000

Porter, Roy. *London: A Social History*, London, Penguin, 1996

Quennell, M. and C.H.B. *A History of Everyday Things in England*, London, Batsford, 1968

Radford, Ken. *Fire Burn*, London, Guild Publishing, 1989

Rattray Taylor, G. *Sex in History*, London, Thames & Hudson, 1968

Rowse, A.L. *William Shakespeare*, London, Macmillan, 1963

Rukesyer, Muriel. *The Traces of Thomas Hariot*, London, Gollancz, 1972

Russell, Jeffrey B. *A History of Witchcraft*, London, Thames & Hudson, 1980

Saint, Andrew and Darby, Gillian. *The Chronicles of London*, London, Weidenfeld & Nicolson, 1994

Salgado, Gamini. *The Elizabethan Underworld*, London, BCA, 1977

Seligman, Kurt. *The History of Magic*, New York, Quality Paperbacks, 1997

Smith, A.G.R. *The Government of Elizabethan England*, London, Edward Arnold, 1967

Starkey, David. *Elizabeth*, London, Chatto & Windus, 2000

Thomas, Keith. *Religion and the Decline of Magic*, London, Weidenfeld & Nicolson, 1971

Tourneur, Cyril. *The Atheist's Tragedy*, ed. Brian Morris and Rona Gill, London, A & C Black, 1989

Turner, E.S. *May It Please Your Lordship*, London, Michael Joseph, 1971

Walker, D.P. *Spiritual and Demonic Magic*, Stroud, Sutton, 2000

Walsh, Walter. *The Jesuits in Great Britain*, London, Routledge, 1904

Weir, Alison. *Elizabeth the Queen*, London, Pimlico, 1999

Wheatley, Dennis. *The Devil and All His Works*, London, BCA, 1977

Wilson, Jean. *The Shakespeare Legacy*, Stroud, Sutton, 1995

Wilson, John Dover. *Life in Shakespeare's England*, London, Penguin, 1911

Wraight, A.D., and Stern, Virginia, *In Search of Christopher Marlowe*, Chichester, Adam Hart, 1993

Zenner, Peter. *The Shakespeare Invention*, Bakewell, Country Books, 1999

Index